A Penguin Special
Thalidomide and the Power of the Drug Companies

Robert Nilsson was born in 1940 in Stockholm and graduated
from university in 1963. His research in the fields of
radiobiology and biochemistry has centred around the
participation of oxygen in physiological, photochemical
and radiochemical processes; his findings have been
extensively published in scientific journals. During 1965,
together with his colleagues, Dr Nilsson played an important
part in preventing the use of mercury-containing pesticides
in Sweden. He also participated as main scientific adviser
and technical coordinator of the thalidomide trials in
Scandinavia on behalf of the plaintiffs (1965–9), as well as
technical adviser for the prosecution in Aachen, Germany.

Henning Sjöström was born in 1922 in the north of Sweden.
His father was a farmer with a very large family, and Mr
Sjöström worked to begin with as a miner, farmhand and in
forestry, at the same time studying for his examinations. He
passed his matriculation in 1943 and became a lawyer in
1953. He has dealt with many thalidomide cases and also with
those injured or damaged by medical preparations. He is at
present concerned with the implications of oral contraceptives.
He has published several books, mainly dealing with court
cases. In 1968 he married another lawyer, Kerstin Sandels.

Thalidomide and the Power of the Drug Companies

Henning Sjöström and Robert Nilsson

Penguin Books

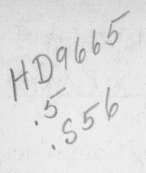

Penguin Books Ltd, Harmondsworth,
Middlesex, England
Penguin Books Inc., 7110 Ambassador Road,
Baltimore, Maryland 21207, U.S.A.
Penguin Books Australia Ltd, Ringwood,
Victoria, Australia

First published 1972

Copyright © Henning Sjöström and Robert Nilsson, 1972

Made and printed in Great Britain by
Hazell Watson & Viney Ltd,
Aylesbury, Bucks
Set in Linotype Juliana

Contents

06801

I

Introduction: General Background

On 16 July 1945, 9,140 metres from a steel tower in a desolate part of New Mexico, a select group of scientists and military personnel watched with horror and fascination as the whole landscape was lit up by a burning light several times the intensity of the desert sun. Thirty seconds later the explosion wave deafened the onlookers. As the mushroom-shaped cloud towered up in the sky one of the scientists, the physicist Robert Oppenheimer, reflected upon a sentence from the *Bhagavad Gita* about the deity Krishna: 'I am death who takes everything away, the destroyer of worlds.' The destructive power of nuclear energy was revealed to man from the very beginning, long before it had been put to peaceful uses.

During the same era the world also saw modern chemotherapeutics being introduced for the benefit of mankind by a peaceful and active biological and chemical science. First came the introduction of the sulphonamides, following the startling discovery by Domagk in 1932 that a dye, patented by I. G. Farbenindustrie by the name of Prontosil, was effective in experimental streptococcal and staphylococcal infections in test animals. In 1935 Trefouels and Fourneau showed that a split product formed from Prontosil in the organism, sulphanilamide, was as effective in curing infections as the original dye stuff. In the five years following this discovery more than one thousand sulpha drugs were synthesized, although only a few proved really promising. The sulphonamides worked wonders with infectious diseases like meningitis, certain types of pneumonia, gonorrhoea, etc. However, the widespread use of sulphonamides, even in cases where chemotherapeutic treatment was not indicated, quickly produced resistance in the micro-organisms against which the drug was being used. Today a large number of sulphonamide-resistant strains of the bacteria causing gonorrhoea and other infections are found all over the world. A new breakthrough, however, came when penicillin was made available on a large scale, primarily due to the work of scientists in a laboratory affiliated to the US Department of Agriculture in Illinois.

In 1944 Shatz, Waksman and Bugies, of Rutgers University discovered streptomycin. In 1947 Burkholder at Yale, with a grant from Parke & Davis, discovered chloramphenicol (Chloromycetin). In 1948 scientists at Lederle isolated and described chlortetracyline (Aureomycin) and in 1949 Chaz Pfizer & Co. introduced oxytetracycline (Terramycin). The discovery of these antibiotics really meant a revolution for medicine and the pharmaceutical industry expanded explosively. Along with these important drugs, successful against many severe infectious diseases, came pharmaceutical preparations aimed to cure less severe ailments. Stressed post-war man needed an efficient hypnotic to cure his insomnia at night; he might need a tranquillizer to calm his nervous tensions during the day. The pharmacological armament of the practising physician grew rapidly each year.

The extraordinary acceleration in the discovery and development of chemicals used in the diagnosis, prevention and treatment of human disease has changed modern medicine and improved public health. This has influenced the entire social structure. The 'pharmaceutical revolution' has been primarily based on our expanding knowledge of the nature of disease – the causes as well as the details of the physiological, psychological or biochemical disorders that underlie disease. This knowledge has enabled pharmaceutical science to treat disease at various levels, from the underlying cause to the purely symptomatic level.

An important requisite for this vast development has been investigation of the manner in which drugs interact with the living organism – the science of drug action. This research has been directed towards the study of both desirable and undesirable effects. Since, for technical and ethical reasons, it is not always possible to investigate the action of a pharmacologically active compound on man himself in an accurate and detailed way, the use of experimental animals has become more and more important. Drugs produce different reactions in different animal species, and it has become necessary to investigate the causes of these variations. Moreover, it has been necessary to observe the influence of the drug on specific organs, and on the cellular and subcellular processes, as well as on the organism as a whole. Nor must we forget the important achievement of solving the many technical difficulties involved in large-scale production of pharmaceuticals, so as to ensure purity and consistent quality. We need hardly be surprised that the industry has taken over and developed the subtle and extravagant techniques of promotion and distribution characteristics of other branches of the modern company in the market society of the Western world.

Development of modern pharmacological science has not occurred solely within the privately owned industrial sector. Decisive contributions have been made by governmental and academic institutions throughout the world. Of the antibiotics, chloramphenicol was discovered at Yale University, streptomycin and neomycin at Rutgers University, thyrothricin at the Rockefeller Institute, and bacitracin at the Columbia

University Hospital. Among other pharmaceuticals the Salk polio vaccine was developed at the University of Pittsburgh and the local anaesthetic Xylocain, used by dentists all over the world, was discovered at the Royal University of Stockholm. The discovery of the utility of para-aminosalicylic acid (PAS) for treatment of tuberculosis was made by a Swedish scientist, Jörgen Lehman, at the Sahlgrenska hospital in Gothenburg.

In many cases the research programmes in universities, which have resulted in the development of important new drugs, were supported by grants from the pharmaceutical industry, but many major discoveries have also been made possible by governmental funds. The value of governmental support and planning as a competitive alternative is amply demonstrated by the development of penicillin production on a large scale. Already in 1941 the US Office of Scientific Research and Development initiated research on the industrial production of penicillin. Several drug companies were enlisted in this programme and received aid from the state, but for several years little progress was made. Finally a team of scientists managed to develop a successful method for large-scale production of the antibiotic at the Northern Regional Laboratory of the Department of Agriculture at Peoria, Illinois. The department obtained a patent for the process which was made available to any producer without charge. In this way penicillin rapidly became available on the market for the benefit of all mankind. The free availability of the patent ensured sound competition between various producers from the start, and prevented the excessive prices often encountered for drugs produced in a monopoly situation.

Because of the complexity of modern pharmaceutical research, major advances in the field are no longer possible without close cooperation between scientists with non-medical as well as purely medical backgrounds. This has been realized by the more important companies who nowadays employ a horde of organic chemists, biochemists, physiologists, physicians, biologists, engineers and, more recently, geneticists. The fantastic drop in the price of penicillin, which occurred after the war, was mainly made possible by the use of methods taken from radiobiology. By treatment of the antibiotic-producing fungi (*pencillium*) with X-rays and mutagenic chemicals, fungi strains with changed hereditary characteristics (mutations) were obtained. Among these new variants, mutated types giving increased yields of antibiotic could be selected. By means of such 'mutation-breeding', strains were isolated with a productivity exceeding that of the original strains by a factor of 25 to 30. In 1945 the price of penicillin was about $20 per 100,000 units. In 1952 the price had dropped to less than 2 cents per 100,000 units.

The development of modern biology has made the demarcation lines indistinct between medicine and subjects like biochemistry and molecular biology. In the USA and Great Britain this type of joint research beyond the borders of the different disciplines has become increasingly important. It is no wonder that during the last decade the Nobel Prize in medicine has been given mainly to biochemists and molecular biologists active outside the borders of classical medicine and working, for example, with fundamental biological problems in simple organisms like viruses and bacteria.

While constituting a major advance in the rational treatment of many diseases, this quick development of new pharmaceuticals has also generated its share of problems. Dr Louis Lasagna, a member of staff of the Johns Hopkins University School of Medicine, Baltimore, wrote in *Science*, a journal with a world-wide circulation (5 December 1969):

Paradoxically, medical care has in some ways been impaired by the availability of new medicaments, in terms both of overtreatment of patients and of confusion regarding the diagnosis of disease because of the temptation to treat symptoms without having determined their cause. The manufacture, legal and illicit, of powerful psychotropic drugs has led to drug abuse and addiction. Advances in drug development have generated the false hope that most of our disease problems can be handled by drugs, and that applied research in pharmacology is all that is required to meet these needs, whereas in fact a fully effective attack on the major health problems facing the public requires not only new basic information concerning such diseases as artherosclerosis, cancer, arthritis, and schizophrenia but preventive measures as well as, or instead of, therapeutic manoeuvers . . . The burgeoning research on drugs has led to impingements on clinical investigation, as the public's anxieties have been kindled by the revelation of unethical behaviour on the part of clinical investigators in the search for new drugs.

In 1963 Dr E. M. Schimmel in the *Journal of Chronic Diseases* analysed the problems of major toxic reactions and accidents in a university hospital in the USA. He found that approximately one patient in ten suffered from some kind of drug-induced disease. The well-known medical journal *Clinical Pharmacology and Therapeutics* runs a section in each issue ironically called 'Diseases of Medical Progress'. Despite the fairly high frequency of reported troubles from drugs, the published cases, as has already been pointed out, constitute merely the floating tip of an iceberg. A large part of the true extent of damage remains hidden.

In a lecture delivered in October 1963 in San Francisco Lasagna gave an example from the Johns Hopkins School of Medicine of a random survey of one hundred hospital charts of patients signed out by the house staff as free from untoward effects from drugs, which revealed that 7 per cent of the patients could be unequivocally classified as having suffered from drug reactions. He remarked, 'In addition, however, my opinion is strongly affected by the abundant historical evidence to the effect that a varying length of time is required before the medical profession becomes fully aware of the trouble that a drug can cause, and that this interval can be quite long at times.'

Through neglect of the basic principles of safety, much unnecessary and severe damage has no doubt been inflicted by the introduction of poorly tested pharmaceutical preparations. There are horrifying examples of avoidable, severe damage caused by the medicaments Peteosthor and Spirocid in West Germany. Peteosthor was a preparation containing the element thorium X, a natural radioactive radium isotope formed by the decay of thorium 232. Before the First World War this radio-isotope was being used in clinical therapy but it was soon abandoned as it was found to have a deleterious effect on the blood-producing tissues. In 1942 P. Troch reintroduced thorium X for the treatment of tuberculosis and other diseases. Peteosthor was used clinically for treatment of at least 900 patients until approximately 1952.

From the very early days of the discovery of radium and other radioactive isotopes, there has been a persistent and dogged belief in their beneficial effects, a tragic belief which has resulted in a great deal of radiation damage. There are also well-known cases of radiation-induced cancer found among workers employed in painting watch-dials with phosphorescent paints containing radium and mesothorium. The radioactive substances were ingested due to the workers' habit of moistening with their tongues the tips of the brushes bearing the paint. In public health surveys of such radium-dial plants made around 1930 a high incidence was found of bone tumours, bone changes in the jaw and abnormal blood pictures. These effects could easily have been demonstrated by chronic toxicity tests in laboratory animals. In 1933 Thomas and Bruner demonstrated various types of bone changes including decalcification and thinning of the compact bone, general interference of skeletal growth, anaemia and a high incidence of bone tumours in rats given radium chloride. Similar findings from animal experiments were confirmed in various other laboratories.

The isotopes of radium as well as those of strontium belong to the same main group of the Periodic Table (II A) as does calcium and consequently they have similar chemical properties. In the organism these elements behave in most respects like calcium and are incorporated and accumulated in the skeleton. Thus thorium X, similarly to other radium isotopes, are 'bone-seeking' radioactive elements, capable of being incorporated in the bones and producing a strong, local alpha-irradiation of these structures.

The first case of cancer in man as a result of exposure to ionizing radiations was described by Frieben in 1902 and it would have required but a little basic knowledge of elementary chemistry and of medical radiology to foresee the delayed effects of the Peteosthor treatment carried out in West Germany. However, Troch believed that he had noted a beneficial effect of this radioactive poison on tuberculosis, an effect which has never since been conclusively verified by medical science. When a check-up was made in 1955 of fifty-three patients treated with Peteosthor in childhood, malignant bone tumours were found in nine cases. In 1962, after ten to fourteen years of treatment, nineteen of the fifty-three patients had died of cancer.

The second example mentioned was the organic arsenical, Spirocid, a more modern variant of Salvarsan, sold by Farbwerke Hoechst AG, Frankfurt, mainly for the treatment of congenital syphilis. In the USA and in many other countries, treatment of this disease by arsenic-containing drugs has been abolished in favour of the less toxic, and more efficient penicillin. From 1947 to 1951, seventy-nine children in the

University Paediatric Clinic of Hamburg were treated with Spirocid. As a result twelve developed a severe encephalitis resulting in permanent damage of the nervous system. The intoxication symptoms were very similar to those previously described for Salvarsan (Salvarsan encephalitis) and other organic arsenic compounds. The affected children exhibited spastic pareses and atrophy of muscles and became mentally underdeveloped with signs of brain atrophy. Eyesight also became impaired due to atrophy of the optic nerve. Kidney damage, agranulocytosis and other syndromes typical of chronic arsenic poisoning were also frequently observed. The compound evidently also produced cumulative effects when taken in repeated smaller doses. In a detailed article which appeared in 1955 in *Archive für Kinderheilkunde* Dr J. R. Bierich from the University Paediatric Clinic of Hamburg concluded : 'As penicillin therapy produces good results the further use of Spirocid is not advisable.' Eight years after this report was published, Hoechst not only continued to sell Spirocid for treatment of diseases such as syphilis, amoebic dysentery and stomatitis, but recommended the use of this extremely dangerous drug as 'an easily taken tonic', 'two tablets daily as a tonic ...'

Beyond doubt, the USA has been the leading nation when it comes to control and legislation of the manufacture of drugs, and it seems therefore in order to say something about the developments in the USA in this field. As is well described in *The Real Voice* by Richard Harris, the initial impetus which led to the hearings of the Senate Committee on Antitrust and Monopoly in the USA, under the chairmanship of Senator Estes Keafauver, was the discovery of the strange system which seemed to govern the prices of drugs. Some pharmaceuticals made in the USA could be obtained at much lower prices abroad; the price difference between one and the same drug could vary by a factor of

50, depending on the manufacturer. On the open market price-fixing seemed to be widespread. When offers were made under competitive conditions to large buyers like the US Army, the prices could be forced down to a fraction of the current market price. The profits of the pharmaceutical industry were much higher than other types of chemical industry. A disproportionally large amount of money seemed to be spent on sales promotion, etc. A number of these curious facts were revealed by the Senate hearings. It was found, for instance, that Schering bought a corticosteroid used in menopausal disorders from the French firm Roussel at a price of $3.50 per gram and marketed it at about $116, corresponding to a mark-up of 7,000 per cent. We cannot generalize from such an example but, taken as a whole, the pharmaceutical industry had sufficiently high profits to spend some 25 per cent of the difference between gross income and production costs on advertising and promotion, and still have a profit rate double that of US industry in general. The answer given by representatives from the drug companies was essentially that given by Francis G. Brown, president of the Schering Corporation, before the Subcommittee on Antitrust and Monopoly. 'For every good compound that is found, there are many failures.' 'Some failures come after years of effort and hundreds of thousands of dollars in expense.' To this Dr A. Ball Console, previous medical director of Squibb, remarked: 'This is true, since it is the very essence of research. The problem arises out of the fact that they market so many of their failures . . . but I should point out,' Dr Console told · Senator Keafauver, 'that with many of these products it is clear while they are on the drawing board that they promise no utility. They promise sales.'

Unfortunately, the industry has often not been very helpful in dispelling doubts about the proportions of income used respectively for research and for advertisements. It is also not clear what kind of expenses are included in the research expenditure.

A questionnaire was sent to five large pharmaceutical industries in Sweden to gather information about the allegedly high cost of sales promotion and to ask these companies what percentage of their production costs was represented by advertising. The following answers were obtained:

(1) 1·6 per cent of the sales income.

(2) 1·5 per cent.

(3) As our costs of production are confidential this question can hardly be answered. Further costs for advertisement as well as for production may be calculated according to such different principles that a percentage will tell hardly anything without a very detailed specification.

(4) 25 per cent in the initial phase.

(5) As the company has entered a phase of intensive expansion a percentage will not give a just figure.

The investigation on this issue made by the official drug investigation committee gives a completely distorted figure for total advertising costs, since the expense of printing catalogues and of employing visiting salesmen were not considered as sales promotion, which hardly seems justified. The latter expenditure is at least as high as that for all other types of sales promotion for pharmaceuticals in Sweden.

Dr Austin Smith, president of the US Pharmaceutical Manufacturers' Association, testified in February 1960, before the Senate subcommittee: 'The US Department of Labor Statistics show that the wholesale price of drugs increased only 3 per cent between 1948 and 1958, while the wholesale price index for all industrial products has in the same period risen 22 per cent.' To this Keafauver remarked that if a drug manufacturer could stay in business under such conditions his prices must have been so high to begin with that he did not have to raise them. Similarly, in an investigation of the price development of eighteen drugs in Sweden between 1957 and 1965, eight drugs did not change in price at all, while seven increased and three decreased. Using 1957 as a base the price indexes for 1965 varied between 97 and 102. During this period the consumers' price index in general increased by some 30 per cent.

Certainly, expenditure on research in many large pharmaceutical companies is large. Not only are large sums of money spent for this purpose inside the enterprises, but generous grants are often given for sound research within universities and hospitals. The CIBA foundation further sponsors international symposia which are well recognized over the whole world for their high scientific standard. The absolute sums spent on research are, however, of not much significance until related to the other expenditure of such firms.

The strange marketing situation within this sector became very well documented during the Senate hearings. The basic problem is that the patient, the consumer, has no influence on the choice of drugs. 'The one who orders does not buy, and he who buys does not order,' Keafauver remarked. In the USA it is the patient who must bear the majority of the costs of most drugs. In Sweden the majority of costs for drugs are paid by social welfare. This naturally makes Swedish doctors even less concerned about drug prices. During the period 1967 to 1969 the sales of prescription drugs, as returned by the total turnover value of drugs sold by Swedish pharmacies, increased by almost 50 per cent. It is quite safe to assume that this marked increase in drug consumption was not due to a greater need for drugs based on a corresponding deterioration in the general health of the Swedish people during these three years.

The great difficulties facing smaller drug companies who try to get into the market both in the USA and in Sweden are well known. Blackman, one of the witnesses brought before the Senate subcommittee, represented a small company called Premo. Premo had tried, with little success, to introduce penicillin at a price of $3.75 for 100 tablets. Squibb, at the same time, were selling the same preparation very nicely at $14.85 a hundred. Blackman told the Senate subcommittee : 'The only real competition that we have in our field is the tremendous competition for the eye and ear of the physician – how many pages of advertisement we can put out, how many samples we can distribute, how many detailmen we can put in the field. These, and these alone, govern the ultimate acceptance of the product.'

The general picture of a few large firms dominating the market also holds true for many European countries. In Sweden out of about forty producers of pharmaceuticals, five companies (Astra, Pharmacia, Kabi, Bofors, ACO) were responsible for around 80 per cent of all drugs sold in 1956. This situation is surely the main reason for the pharmaceutical industry's bitter opposition to the sale of drugs by so-called generic names instead of by trade names. (The generic name is a generalized name for the active constituent of the drug, which is the same, irrespective of producer.) The main purpose of the massive propaganda campaigns sponsored by big enterprises is to plant the trade name of each specific product firmly in the minds of physicians.

One reason for the difficulties in introducing generic names is that probably many physicians are afraid they will receive drugs of inferior quality. When choosing between equivalent preparations from different firms the physician tends to select a brand produced by a large, well-known company even if this is more expensive. The name of the company represents some sort of guarantee of the quality of the product. There are, of course, historical reasons for this attitude.

The assessment of quality and purity of drug preparations

has a long history. Around the fourth century BC Theophrastus, in his *Enquiry Into Plants*, was expressing concern about adulteration of medicines. In his *Materia Medica* the first century Greek physician Dioscorides mentioned forty examples of fraud among some 1,000 drug entries. When the *Nuovo Receptario* (its full title being *New Formulary Compiled by the most Renowned College of the Distinguished Doctors of the Arts and Medicine of the Magnificent City of Florence*) was published in 1498 in Italy, its purpose was to codify standard concepts and to provide uniformity as an aid to pharmacists. It was based entirely on classical Greek and Arabic drug therapy.

In the eighteenth century, Van den Sande, the master apothecary of Brussels, advocated some sort of governmental control, with compulsory qualifications and examination of pharmacists, regular inspection by experienced agents, price schedules, standard weights and measures and the supervision of pharmaceutical education.

However, it was not until the development of analytical chemistry and biological assays made possible more rigorous testing of drugs, hand in hand with increasing possibilities of analysing the composition of drugs, that a more objective method of testing drugs clinically came about. The results of clinical trials began to be analysed with the aid of statistics. It was quite some time, however, before legislation provided some control of the field. The Pure Food and Drugs Act was only finally accepted in the USA in 1906, as a result of the zealous activities of certain journalists. The more antiquated formulations of unicorn horn, pepper, and asafoetida began to disappear. The industry predicted a poor future for drug manufacturers as a result of this legislation.

The 1906 law prohibited false or misleading labels on pharmaceuticals but, by a decision of the Supreme Court in 1911, these statements were only to be related to the identity of the product and not to its curative properties. The Sherley Amendment passed in 1912 did not make things any better. The 1906 law was re-phrased to say that false *and* fraudulent therapeutic claims were prohibited. Since it was almost impossible to prove such claims to be both false *and* fraudulent (fraud involves intent to deceive), for most purposes the legislation was ineffective in practice.

In 1937 the Samuel E. Massengill Co., Bristol, Tennessee, marketed an 'elixir of Sulfanilamide', in which the solvent was diethylene glycol. No clinical tests were made with this 'elixir' prior to marketing and at least ninety-three persons died as a result, including the chemist who had developed the product. (The chemist in fact committed suicide.) According to Commissioner George P. Larrick of the FDA a simple experiment on animals would have revealed the toxic properties of this 'elixir'. As the drug was called 'elixir', implying that the preparation contained alcohol, the FDA was able to make seizure of the product on the basis of misbranding. This event resulted in new legislation in the USA : the Federal Food, Drug and Cosmetic Act of 1938. One of the important provisions contained in the act was that the manufacturer of any new drug had to present evidence of safety to the FDA. The FDA was also given authority to remove a drug from the market if it could be shown to be unsafe. The producers were not, however, required to present evidence that the product was effective and this led to the marketing of a number of medically useless compounds. In such a situation the name of the company was naturally very important to the prescribing physician. Companies such as Eli Lilly, Merck, Squibb, CIBA and Hoffman La Roche were reputed to maintain a very high standard in their products, and no doubt such firms have made an important contribution to the advancement of modern pharmacology.

There are many examples of errors in manufacturing practice made by both small and large companies. A thyroid extract marketed by the Swedish Astra Co., called Thyreototal, was withdrawn when it was found that the preparation was contaminated by *salmonella* bacteria. According to Professor Lasagna in his 1969 article in *Science*, a large and reputable firm in the USA was found to have been using an enteric coating that produced capricious absorption of drugs; another large firm sold a tetracycline that decomposed to a toxic product when stored; and an epidemic of precocious puberty was traced to contamination of isoniazid with estrogen in an improperly cleaned tablet-making machine in the plant of a small manufacturer.

In 1968 nine brands of chloramphenicol were withdrawn from the market when on testing in healthy volunteers they were found to be both inferior and less predictable than the original product marketed by Parke, Davis & Co.

Pharmaceutical chemists in many countries have developed laboratory standards for quality control compiled in official compendiums such as the United States Pharmacopoeia (USP), the National Formulary (NF), the British Pharmacopoeia (BP), etc. According to A. E. Slessor of the Smith, Kline and French Laboratories, the main fault lies not in the inadequacy of these standards, but in the failure to adhere to the USP and NF criteria. There is no reason to assume that pharmaceutical trade based on generic names should endanger the safety of patients provided that the drugs meet the standards set out in the USP and NF. It also seems unreasonable to suppose that the first drug version put on the market will be the best. In point of fact, the Military Medical Supply Agency, the largest buyer of pharmaceuticals in the USA, and many large hospitals have for a long time purchased drugs on the basis of generic name. A similar situation also exists in Sweden. It is obviously in the public interest that this system becomes established, in combination with competitive bidding, to ensure major savings for social welfare services, hospitals, and for the individual consumers.

When Senator Keafauver submitted his original version of the bill for improved drug control on 12 April 1961, (designated S 1552), he included the following main provisions:

(1) The FDA should have control over production, distribution and advertising of prescription drugs, including quality control and periodic inspection of factories.

(2) The Secretary of Health, Education and Welfare was to have authority to decide upon the use of generic names on the basis of simplicity and usefulness. Generic name and trade name should both be included in all sales promotion material as well as on labels.

(3) Advertisements should not omit to mention side-effects, and statements of efficacy should be included.

(4) The Secretary of Health, Education and Welfare should publish a list of potentially harmful drugs every year.

(5) Package inserts should be sent directly to doctors and not to pharmacists.

(6) No antibiotics should be marketed unless adequate control of quality, purity and potency had been certified by the FDA.

(7) The previous time limit of sixty days included in the 1938 law, after which a new drug would automatically be registered by the FDA, unless the agency found justification to refuse approval, should be abolished.

(8) The manufacturer had to prove that the pharmaceuticals he sold would not only be safe but would also be effective.

In the patents section of the bill, Keafauver suggested that no modified or combined drug should be patentable unless it was proved to be a 'significant improvement' in comparison with previous drugs.

The background of this provision is well illustrated by the testimony of the former chief medical director of E. R. Squibb and Sons, Dr Console, before Keafauver's subcommittee on 1 November 1961 :

Stated very simply, one of the problems to which the proposed bill is directed is this :

A company develops a new drug for which it receives a patent and which turns out to be highly profitable. Immediately, its competitors put their research staffs to work on devising their own versions of the drug.

This may or may not result in improvement but, in any case, a point is soon reached where the successive modifications represent no further improvement in utility. Yet, part of the industry's limited supply of skilled researchers continues to be directed to the development of further minor variants, instead of being allowed to pursue more significant lines of inquiry...

A patent-evading facsimile of a drug may be the original goal of some drug companies when molecule-manipulation starts. But in many instances this is not the case. The search may, and frequently does, start out as a sincere attempt to create a significant drug. Since molecule manipulation cannot be rationalized, chance plays an important role in success . . . If one is unlucky, and this is usually the case in this empirical approach, the best compound created may still be no better than, or even inferior to, the parent compound.

In most other research disciplines this is considered failure, since the purpose of research is not to confirm the obvious. When the motivation of the researcher is not influenced by easily obtained patents, when advertising and promotion cannot be used to mask the deficiencies of poor or inadequate research, the researcher is motivated to continue to strive for research success. He may continue the search or abandon it, to turn his effort to a more fruitful line.

In drug research as practised by the industry, commercial success is the primary goal. If research success and commercial success were identical, there would be no problem. Unfortunately, in this industry research failure can be turned into commercial success.

Since to continue the search for a worthwhile drug or to abandon the research underway costs dollars, these decisions do not come easily to the businessman. Commercial success can be achieved in other ways which are quicker, easier, and less risky. One of the compounds is selected, and the rest of the research effort invested in it is directed towards converting it into a commercial success. The decision may be based on the simple fact that the chemical compound is patentable as a compound or that medical magic can make it patentable as a drug.

But the process does not stop here. At this stage it is still a compound, not a drug, and it still requires further research effort to convert it into a safe drug. Depending on the reliability of the screen, detailed animal pharmacology, chronic toxicity studies, studies in human pharmacology, and clinical evaluation in selected patients may be among the steps which must still be carried out. This may take one or two years, or more, requiring many man-hours of time contributed by experts in various disciplines. Most, if not all, of this research is wasted as is the time of scientists who might be better engaged in producing something worthwhile.

All along the line of this misdirected effort the pressure is on to make the compound appear better than it is. This is not conducive to integrity in research. The distortion reaches its peak on the phase of clinical evaluation. Here the criteria are least rigid and there is wide latitude for poor research . . .

Since they are deficient, it is safer to subject them to superficial studies rather than critical examination. Claims rather than scientific evidence are the primary objective. And, so, poor research breeds more poor research. In a recent speech FDA Commissioner Larrick commented on the increasing awareness of 'rigged research – the study that was set up – to support a claim rather than to seek for truth'.

This leads into so-called promotional studies and testimonials and research blends into advertising and promotion.

In the drug industry promotion is used as a logical extension of research. Poor research breeds not only poor research but also excessive advertising and promotion. The fact that it costs several times more than research is an indication of its importance in this chain of events.

Keafauver recommended a system similar to that already in use in Great Britain, Canada, Australia and India, called compulsory licensing, according to which the governmental control agency could force a manufacturer to give production rights to other firms on a royalty basis, if prices were considered too high.

The patent section was bitterly opposed by the Pharmaceutical Manufacturers' Association through its chairman, Eugene N. Beesley, president of Lilly. He was, however, favourably inclined to other parts of the bill. The principles outlined in the bill concerning safety and efficacy had already been observed for some time by many of the reputable pharmaceutical houses. One would think that safe and effective drugs were in the interest of every practising physician, but for extremely obscure reasons representatives of the American Medical Association would not accept any of the new suggestions included in the bill.

Keafauver remained optimistic. In 1962 President Kennedy stated in his State of the Union Message: 'To protect our consumers from the careless and the unscrupulous I shall recommend improvements in the food and drug laws.' After making a few minor alterations, Keafauver submitted his bill again on 4 March 1962. The patent section proved to be too controversial and the Senate Judiciary Committee decided to refer S 1552 to the Subcommittee on Patents and Trademarks. This subcommittee sent the bill back without the essential parts of the patent section. What was more, on 23 April, the Kennedy administration presented a bill of its own, the Harris bill, which in general was much weaker than the original S 1552. The obscure manoeuvrings and amazing intrigues which followed have been described fully by Harris in *The Real Voice*. The industry represented above all by Senators Dirksen from Illinois and Hruska of Nebraska made every effort to dilute each part of the original Keafauver bill. The prospect seemed dark of getting any kind of improvement in the 1938 law.

On 15 July, Morton Minz released the story of the FDA's fight against thalidomide under the headline 'Heroine Of FDA Keeps Bad Drug Off Market' and next day Keafauver released the material compiled on thalidomide to the press. Keafauver pointed out that his bill, which had now been stopped, included safeguards to protect the American people against just such disasters. The press began to react and shortly afterwards a new story hit the headlines about a Mrs Finkbine, who had taken thalidomide, bought in England during early pregnancy, and had announced her intention of trying to obtain a legal abortion, which she ultimately obtained in Sweden. The foetus was deformed. United Press International further released the news that part of the thalidomide sent by the Merrell Company to more than 1,200 doctors for testing had not been recovered. When the Associated Press revealed that clinical testing of new drugs could be carried out with almost no governmental supervision of the conditions under which it was done, or of the qualifications of the physicians concerned, or, indeed, without even the patient's knowledge, public pressure for some new legislation began to build up.

When Senator Hubert H. Humphrey began his hearings before his Subcommittee on Reorganization and International Organization to study 'inter-agency co-ordination in drug research information', the press was already on the warpath. Keafauver had managed to link thalidomide with his bill. On 20 August, the Judiciary Committee approved the fourth version of S 1552.

When the Senate took up S 1552 on 23 August, Keafauver and Humphrey suggested an additional amendment that all prescription drugs should be tested on experimental animals before being used clinically. This was unanimously accepted. The amendment was rejected that a doctor should get the permission of the patient before using drugs at an experimental stage. After some minor adjustments the S 1552 was approved by the Senate. In Congress, however, progress came to a standstill and a hard fight broke out again about many control questions taken up by Keafauver. Although the final, so-called Keafauver-Harris amendments to the Federal Food, Drug and Cosmetics Act of 1938, signed by President Kennedy on 10 October 1962, was stripped of its patent part, as well as the provision that package inserts should be sent to the doctors, most of the main provisions relating to safety and efficacy were included: the requirement of adequate controls in manufacture; the obligatory presentation of evidence for effectiveness and safety of new drugs; the provision requiring manufacturers to keep proper records of the development of new drugs (test reports from animal experiments, etc.); a new drug clearance procedure; certification of all antibiotics; federal authority to standardize names; the inclusion of generic names in all sorts of labelling and advertisement; prescription drug advertisements to include information on side-effects, contra-indications and effectiveness; the authorization of FDA officials to inspect laboratories and factories.

Similar developments have occurred in many other countries in the West, although the changes in legislation have not resulted in such an efficiently controlled pharmaceutical industry as is the case in the USA.

After the Keafauver drug bill had been unanimously accepted by the American Senate on 23 August 1962, Senator Paul H. Douglas of Illinois rose and stated: 'Mr

President, the vote by which the Keafauver drug bill was passed just now – seventy-eight to zero – is quite a commentary on how time and history frequently bear out the views of some unpopular people and how what may seem to be a majority opinion at one moment in time is later proved not to be the case.

'The Senator from Tennessee [Mr Keafauver] has waged a long and lonely fight for an adequate bill. He has been attacked by the powerful drug industry, and in the press he has been derided as one of the despised band of liberals. He has not received a great deal of cooperation from some of his colleagues, although I think to their dying day, the Senator from Michigan [Mr Hart], the Senator from Connecticut [Mr Dodd], the Senator from Colorado [Mr Carroll], and the Senator from Missouri [Mr Long], can take pride in the aid they gave the Senator from Tennessee at a time when, with his back to the wall, he waged his apparently hopeless battle against these powerful interests.

'But now, Mr President, because of the many terrible tragedies which have occurred in European countries from the use of the drug thalidomide and the cases which have occurred in this country, it has been proved that the Senator from Tennessee was right all the time, and that the scoffers, scorners, and bitter opponents were wrong.

'Now, by its unanimous vote, the Senate has placed its generous seal of approval on what the Senator from Tennessee and his colleagues have long fought for. Men who had openly and secretly fought him now flock to get on the bandwagon, and pretend that they were always his supporters.

'As a humble American citizen, I wish to commend the Senator from Tennessee, and all those who helped him, for fighting for all these months and years for this great reform.

Certainly the American people will eternally be grateful to him.

'Mr President, can we learn from this lesson, or can mankind educate itself only by disaster and tragedy?'

In this book we shall present the story of thalidomide, the unfortunate drug whose impact had such far-reaching effects over the entire pharmacological sector. Fortunately it is not representative of the drug industry as a whole, but it has revealed many deficiencies both in development and control of drugs.

The background to the disaster is the Federal Republic of West Germany. By tradition, Germany had a good pre-war foundation to build on in the form of chemical, pharmacological and technical know-how. As its battered industries were rebuilt, pharmacological products found a good market, with few restrictions imposed by the controlling authorities. During the hectic years of the West German 'economic miracle' the brash new generation of the German Federal Republic, with its overweening belief in the divine right of commercial success, guaranteed a dynamic development in this sector.

In an article by Dr G. Schreiber of Munich, published on 25 November 1965 in *Pharmazeutische Zeitung*, it is stated that there are more than 2,000 manufacturers of pharmaceutical products in West Germany. The number of registered pharmaceutical products exceeds 60,000. This figure may be contrasted with countries like the USA and Sweden where, at about the same time, 6,000 and 3,000 drugs respectively were registered with the authorities and available on the market. Of the 2,000 German producers, Dr Schreiber stated, not even 2 per cent have satisfactory modern pharmacological and experimental departments. More than 98 per cent of the West German pharmaceutical firms invest less than 10 to 15 per cent of their income in scientific research.

The reason for this state of affairs may surely be traced to a lack of proper control of pharmaceutical products exerted by the authorities. Registration of a new drug was merely a formality. The Drug bill of November 1958 reads: 'The law does not require that specialized drugs which have to be submitted for registration shall be tested for their therapeutic effectiveness.' Until 1961 no guidelines for testing drugs existed at all. The 1961 law seems designed to protect the pharmaceutical industry rather than the health of the consumers. On the third reading of this bill in the Parliament of the Federal Republic, Dr Stefan Dittrich, the attorney, pointed out: 'In particular, it has become almost vital for the pharmaceutical industry, with an eye to its exports, to be able to rely on domestic [German] legal standards in order not to be placed at a disadvantage with regard to other drug-producing countries.'

West Germany was the country most heavily stricken by the thalidomide disaster, but it has not acted on this experience. Every painted line on the excellent autobahns is vigorously controlled by regulations but no proper guidelines exist to ensure safe and efficient protection of the millions of German drug consumers. Pre-clinical animal tests are recommended only indirectly, and although test reports should exist for new drugs, the 1961 law relies mainly upon the manufacturer's written declaration that the drug in question has been carefully tested in the light of current scientific knowledge. In addition to the 1961 law the German Pharmacological Association issued in 1963 some 'Guidelines for the Entry of New Drugs' which no one, however, is obliged to follow. Before the thalidomide trial in Alsdorf the professor of internal medicine, Hans von Kress, declared that 'the clinical testing of drugs constitutes the dark side of medicine in our country'. 'In most other civilized countries,' he continued, 'there have been regulations for a long time. Only with us has it not been possible to achieve this.'

No reliable figures of the total number of affected children are available. In the German Federal Republic, according to Professor Lenz, between 5,400 and 6,700 cases of phocomelia have occurred. In Great Britain about 400 cases have been listed by the Ministry of Health. In Sweden there are around 100 cases. In Japan about 700 phocomelia cases have been reported but this figure is unreliable for two reasons: non-thalidomide malformations are included and the reports are incomplete. In view of the wide distribution of these drugs in Japan the real figure is estimated to be more than 1,000.

Because of the poor reporting methods and the uncontrolled sale of thalidomide under many different names, the real number of cases is certainly much higher than those reported from countries like Italy, Brazil, Portugal, Spain and some countries in Asia. According to Lenz the total number of cases throughout the world is somewhere between 8,000 and 10,000, which reveals the full extent of the catastrophe.

Since the mortality rate of thalidomide children is around 40 per cent, the original number has been considerably reduced. The life-expectation of the severe cases still alive is expected to be low, one factor being the extreme sensitivity to high temperature, due to the absence of extremities playing their important role in the regulation of the body temperature.

Naturally the rehabilitation of these children in society presents a serious social problem and few can realize the economic and above all the psychological handicap of these poor children and the suffering of their parents.

2

Chemie Grünenthal and the
Development of Thalidomide

Although expanding rapidly, Chemie Grünenthal does not belong to the well-established group of West German pharmaceutical companies. It has a comparatively short history. In 1946 a large company employing 1,500 workers, Dalli-Werke, Mäurer & Wirtz, producing soaps, detergents and cosmetics, formed a subsidiary company in Stolberg, Chemie Grünenthal, which started its own production in an abandoned copper foundry. Hermann Wirtz, one of the partners in Dalli-Werke, Mäurer & Wirtz, became director in the new firm, and the financial director of Dalli-Werke, Jacob Chauvistré, was made deputy-manager.

In post-war Germany health conditions were such that the authorities feared an outbreak of epidemics, and the newly founded factory started by producing antibiotics. In 1954 Chemie Grünenthal had 420 employees, in 1959, 900 and in 1961, 1,300. By 1959 Chemie Grünenthal was in a position to obtain a share in Knoll AG of Ludwigshafen, a firm with 1,500 employees in 1961 and with an annual turnover of more than DM 60 million. When on 15 July 1960, Chemie Grünenthal helped raise the capital stock of Knoll AG from DM 7 to 9·8 million, Hermann Wirtz joined the board of Knoll AG, Ludwigshafen. During the fifties Chemie Grünenthal produced several types of antibiotic, a few of which were marketed under the company name, while

33

large quantities were sold as bulk material to other industries. For example, Grünenthal produced Aureomycin for the American company Lederle. Besides producing the more conventional type of antibiotics, the firm ventured to market new and modified types at the beginning of the fifties. One of these was named Pulmo 500, a dyhydroiodide of a penicillin G ester. This esterpenicillin, originally discovered in 1950 at the Institute of Pathology of the University of Copenhagen, was claimed to have superior qualities in the treatment of certain types of meningitis and pneumonia. Reports of severe adverse reactions to this drug, including several fatal cases, soon appeared in the medical literature. The Council on Pharmacy and Chemistry of the American Medical Association published a short report in 1953 which appeared in the *Journal of the American Medical Association*, based on information voluntarily submitted to the council by the American manufacturers, Smith, Kline & French. In a letter to Dr Nilsson, the director of the Clinical Services of Smith, Kline & French Laboratories declared frankly about their experience with this type of penicillin (given the name Neo-Penil in the USA):

We discontinued 'Neo-Penil' on 30 April 1954. After a period of general clinical use it appeared that the toxicity of the drug (and also, possibly, its allergy-provoking properties) was greater than that of procaine penicillin. Reports of serious reactions appeared, including some fatalities, and we did not feel that the superiority of Neo-Penil over large doses of other related penicillins was sufficient to outweigh its potential risks.

Chemie Grünenthal, on the other hand, seemed to pay no attention to the serious risks connected with the use of this preparation, which gave rise to side effects with an incidence about 130 times that of procaine penicillin. In 1956 three West-German scientists, Wichmann, Koch and

Heiss published a very critical article in *Zeitschrift für Klinische Medizin*. The authors reviewed current experience with the drug and published a toxicological study of their own. They particularly pointed out that 'the penicillin ester was used in man before thorough experiments on animals had been published'. Although testing on animals at that time was certainly done on a more modest scale than now, clinical use in man before exhaustive tests had been conducted on animals was certainly against the ethics of the more reputable firms. Animal experiments performed by Wichmann, Koch and Heiss revealed a strikingly higher level of toxicity in this drug by comparison with conventional penicillin, such as penicillin G. They found no evidence to support any therapeutic superiority in the Grünenthal preparation.

Another serious pharmacological failure from Chemie Grünenthal was a drug called Paratebin. On 29 August 1952 it was announced by the Broadcasting Station of Hessen (Hessischer Rundfunk) that Dr Mückter, director of the scientific department of Chemie Grünenthal, had developed a new drug called Paratebin, for the treatment of tuberculosis. The company's publicity claimed that this drug was 'the first highly effective penicillin against tuberculosis bacteria'. Chemie Grünenthal's claims met with violent indignation from some investigators. The weak tuberculostatic action of the drug found in preliminary investigations with tuberculosis bacteria in culture could be ascribed entirely to the PAS (para-aminosalicylic acid) present in this compound (oxy-procainpenicillin). PAS was at that time a well-known tuberculostatic drug. In the doses prescribed for clinical use the amount of PAS administered would only be one one-hundred-and-fiftieth of the amount of PAS which had proved effective in the treatment of tuberculosis, in other words the patient would receive only homoeopathic doses of the active component. Controlled tests proved the drug to have no therapeutic value whatsoever. Again, Chemie Grünenthal had marketed a drug without publishing evidence of the necessary pre-clinical trials and without that evidence appearing elsewhere. The therapeutic value was based mainly on vague theoretical considerations. In the treatment of such a serious disease as tuberculosis, the use of an ineffective drug like Paratebin might be very hazardous to patients since it could postpone a course of rational and effective treatment.

The company's marketing policy may also be illustrated by the manner in which other antibiotics were advertised. Streptomycin and dihydrostreptomycin are very efficient antibiotics, but they may have the disadvantage of damaging the hearing when administered for prolonged periods. Scientists at Chemie Grünenthal advertised a new streptomycin combination called Surpacillin-Forte in which panthothenic acid (a B vitamin) was included. The presence of this vitamin was claimed to prevent the development of damage to hearing. Several investigators, both inside and outside West Germany, have been unable to find any such effect to support the company's claims.

The examples cited also demonstrate a dangerous line of approach which has unfortunately been all too common among certain drug manufacturers. Dr Ralph G. Smith, Director of the Division of New Drugs of the Food and Drugs Administration, took up this problem in the July 1962 issue of the *American Journal of Nursing*.

To compete in the marketing of drugs, the pharmaceutical firm must maintain interest in its products. To maintain interest in its products it helps to have something new to promote, a new story to tell. Most of these 'new' products represent different dosage forms of new drugs, repetition of the same type of products by various firms and new combinations of existing agents.

While from 300 to 400 new products may be introduced in a year, only from 10 to 20 per cent of these are new chemical substances. Even these may include drugs with minor variations in chemical structure, or different salts of an original new drug of varying degrees of significance.

Thalidomide was a genuinely new drug, however, and with thalidomide Chemie Grünenthal entered a quite new sector of pharmaceutical preparations. From being concerned mainly with antibiotics, they moved into the profitable field of sedatives and hypnotics.

The release of thalidomide scheduled for July 1956 was postponed as a consideration to Lederle of America (with whom Grünenthal had commercial associations), which at about this time introduced the sedative Miltown (Meprobamate) with an area of indication similar to thalidomide. Before thalidomide, under the name of Contergan, was introduced as a sedative on the West German market on 1 October 1957, it had already been marketed on a trial basis in the Hamburg area at the beginning of November 1956, not on that occasion as a sedative, but as a drug supposed to be active in the treatment of respiratory infections! This drug combination was named Grippex and was introduced solely on the basis of sales propaganda directed to the layman.

During the last part of 1957, however, Grünenthal informed physicians about its new sedative, Contergan, on a more modest basis.

In 1958 Grünenthal's publicity campaign for Contergan was massive. Fifty advertisements were placed in medical journals, 200,000 letters were distributed to medical doctors, and 'therapeutic circulars' were sent to more than 50,000 doctors and pharmacists. Soon a launching for the international market was started and eventually thalidomide was sold by licensees in eleven European, seven African, seventeen Asiatic and eleven countries in the western hemisphere.

During 1961 Chemie Grünenthal marketed thalidomide for a total sales value of DM 12·4 million. To this should be added exports which amounted to at least 25 per cent of the quantity sold in West Germany.

Grünenthal combined thalidomide with other pharmaceuticals like aspirin, phenacetine, quinine, aminopyrine, bacitracine, dihydrostreptomcyin, and secobarbital, and Germans took these compounded drugs (Algosediv, Enterosediv, Grippex, Prednisediv, Noctosediv, Poly-Gripan and Peracon-Expectorans) for conditions such as colds, coughs, flu, nervousness, neuralgia, migraine, other headaches, and asthma. A liquid form made especially for children became West Germany's baby-sitter. Hospitals employed it to quieten children for electroencephalographic studies and, of course, Contergan gave many a pregnant woman a good night's sleep.

Pharmaceutical companies in other countries began to make or market thalidomide under licence from Grünenthal. Distillers (Biochemicals) Ltd sold it as Distaval in the British Isles, Australia and New Zealand. Combinations received the trade names of Valgis, Tensival (a tranquillizer), Valgraine and Asmaval. An advertisement in Great Britain emphasized the safety of the drug with a picture of a small child taking a bottle from a medicine shelf. In Finland, as well as some other countries, thalidomide was distributed under the name of Softenon. In Canada Frank W. Horner Ltd of Montreal marketed it as Talimol and the Canadian branch of the Wm. S. Merrell Company of Cincinnati marketed it as Kevadon. In September 1960 Merrell applied to the Food and Drug Administration for clearance to sell Kevadon in the USA. In Scandinavia a licence agreement was signed on the 12 March 1957 between Astra Co. and Chemie Grünenthal. Astra Co., the largest pharmaceutical industry in Scandinavia, was to have sole sales rights for this area. The drug was introduced in Sweden under the name of Neurosedyn in February 1959.

The following is a list of trade names and manufacturers of thalidomide-containing drugs, prepared by the American Pharmaceutical Association and taken up by Senator Humphrey in his hearings before the Subcommittee on Reorganization and International Organizations:

Algosediv – 50 mg. combination with acetylsalicylic acid in tabs.; also 12·5 mg. combination with APC in suppositories. (Chemie Grünenthal, West Germany)

Asmaval – 12·5 mg. combination with ephedrin HCl in tab. (The Distillers Co. Ltd, Great Britain)

Contergan – 25 mg. tabs.; syrup containing 50 mg./teaspoon; 100 mg. suppositories. (Chemie Grünenthal, West Germany)

Contergan Forte – 100 mg. tabs. (Chemie Grünenthal, West Germany)

Distaval – 25 mg. tabs. (The Distillers Co. Ltd, Great Britain)

Distaval Forte – 100 mg. tabs. (The Distillers Co. Ltd, Great Britain)

Grippex – 12·5 mg. combination with quinine, ascorbic acid, phenacetin and Salicylamide capsules. (Chemie Grünenthal, West Germany)

Kevadon – 100 mg. tabs. (William S. Merrell Co. Ltd, Canada)

Neurosedyn – 25 mg. and 100 mg. tabs. (Astra, Sweden)

Peracon-Expectorans – 40 mg. combination with ipecac dragees; also liquid. (Kali-Chemie AG, West Germany)

Softenon – 25 mg. tabs. (Chemie Grünenthal, West Germany)

Softenon Forte – 100 mg. tabs. (Chemie Grünenthal, West Germany)

Talimol – 100 mg. tabs. (Frank W. Horner Co. Ltd, Canada)

Tensival – 12·5 mg. combination with hydrachlorothiazide tabs. (The Distillers Co. Ltd, Great Britain)

Valgis – 50 mg. combination with acetylsalicylic acid and phenacetin tabs. (The Distillers Co. Ltd, Great Britain)

Valgraine – 12·5 mg. combination with ergotamine tartrate tabs. (The Distillers Co. Ltd, Great Britain)

Calmorex – 25 mg. tabs. (Laboratorio FRC, Italy)

Enterosediv – 10 mg. tabs. combination with bacitracin, dihydrostreptomycin pantothenate and diiodohydroxyquinoline (Chemie Grünenthal, Switzerland)

Gastrimide – 50 mg. tabs. combination with triethyl (4-stilbenehydroxyethyl) ammonium chloride (LIVSA, Milan, Italy)

Imida-Lab – 50 mg. tabs. (Laboratorios Lab, Lisbon, Portugal)

Imidan – 50 mg. tabs. (Lab. Peyta, Spain)

Imidene – 50 mg. tabs. (Smit, Torino, Italy)

Imidene Ipnotico – 50 mg. tabs. combination with allylmethylbutyl barbiturate (Smit, Torino, Italy)

Lulamin – name given by Nordiske Pharmakope; no manufacturer given

Noctosediv – 25 mg. tabs. combination with secobarbital (Chemie Grünenthal, Switzerland)

Noxodyn – 40 mg. tabs. and suppositories, combination with pentobarbital (Astra, Sweden)

Pantosediv – (Chemie Grünenthal, West Germany)

Prednisediv – 5 mg. capsules, combination with prednisolone, salicylamide, aminopyrine, ascorbic acid and aluminium hydroxide (Chemie Grünenthal, West Germany)

Profarmil – 25 mg. regular tabs. 50 mg. strong tabs. and 10 mg. pediatric tabs. (Profarmi, Milan, Italy)

Quetimid – 50 mg. tabs. (Biocorfa, Milan, Italy)

Quietoplex – 50 mg. tabs. (LIVSA, Milan, Italy)

Sedalis – name given by Arzneimittel-Forsch., no manufacturer given

Sedi-Lab – 50 mg. tabs. (Laboratorios Lab, Lisbon, Portugal)

Sedimide – 50 mg. tabs. and 150 mg. suppositories (Mugolio Soc. Acc., Italy)

Sedoval K-17 – 50 mg. tabs. (Italfarma, Torino, Italy)

Theophyl-choline – 20 mg. tabs. combination with theophylline and choline (Perkins Chemical Co., Italy)

Ulcerfen – 20 mg. tabs. combination with hydroxyphenyl-cyclamine chloride (Biocorfa, Milan, Italy)

The policy for the sales promotion of all thalidomide-containing drugs in countries outside West Germany was worked out in general by Chemie Grünenthal. Between the licence department, led by Dr von Schrader-Beielstein, and the licensees, an extensive exchange of propaganda material occurred, and the information and sales promotion material for the export countries was mainly printed in Stolberg. One of thalidomide's main competitors both inside and outside Germany was CIBA's Doriden. Outside Germany meprobamate, marketed by Lederle under the name of Miltown, was also an important sedative, with approximately the same area of indication as thalidomide. As is seen from an internal CIBA report, the producers of Doriden were quite distressed by this development, since in a short time thalidomide had taken over most of the market. The turnover quotient in Germany for Doriden/Contergan in 1960–61 was 1 : 5 while for Doriden/Distaval in Great Britain and the Commonwealth it was 1 : 3. When promoting the introduction of thalidomide in some foreign countries it was important to engage local physicians who could clinically test the drug.

In a report to Chemie Grünenthal from Spain we find the remark that a Dr Lorenzo Frutes Carabias, who had long had connections with Grünenthal's representative Mr Garcia, 'had declared that he was prepared to write a short report on Noctosediv [trade name of thalidomide in Spain] whereby he would leave it to us to revise the final draft'. This matter is discussed in a letter from Chemie Grünenthal of 27 July 1960 : 'on which we have agreed that it need not be a highly qualified scientific work, but primarily printed case reports with a suitable summary which we invariably need for the registration in various countries'.

Similar considerations were presented in connection with another drug sold by Chemie Grünenthal, called Prevethenat, in a letter of 14 April 1960 to the representative in Portugal, Parcelsia :

Scientifically well-supported works are certainly very valuable, but in this case they are not the most important. To be quite frank, quick publication (perhaps in three months), with the case history of fifteen or twenty successfully treated cases which tolerated the drug well, is more important than a large work with a broad basis which will appear first in eight to twelve months. From these considerations it should also be quite clear what kind of investigators we have in mind.

The 'kind of investigators' which Grünenthal had in mind is quite evident in a letter of 25 July to the Portuguese company :

Because of the aforementioned regulation that no preparations are acceptable unless they are accompanied by published articles, there is a likelihood that material will appear, written solely for the money, and adding merely to the excessive amount of material on medical matters, without, in fact, contributing anything worthwhile to scientific knowledge. Nonetheless, one must run with the pack as we all know, and for this reason we would ask you to find a suitable researcher for Ultra-Grunovit as well, who would produce a favourable report on this preparation. There will, of course, be suitable remuneration (we should like you to suggest terms).

The Portuguese representative evidently had difficulty in finding a suitable researcher :

... you must understand that we were forced to make contact with a different kind of researcher, that is, with unknown, younger doctors who were prepared to do this work for financial reasons, but on the condition that the work should not be published in Portugal.

... However, we feel that there must be plenty of such researchers in Germany, and would therefore prefer not to comply with your request, as it is personally distasteful to us and we would only do it with extreme unwillingness.

The thalidomide-containing drugs were sold in Germany without prescription. This made the intermediate hand of a doctor unnecessary and further contributed to the uncontrolled use of the drug. A considerable proportion of sales were of this type. In many other countries this was not permitted, and in England as well as in Sweden, thalidomide could only be obtained on prescription.

In the publicity for thalidomide special stress was placed on the 'complete atoxicity' of the drug. This claim was mainly based on the fact that it had been practically impossible to kill experimental animals by injecting any amount of the drug in a *single* dose. This lack of *acute* toxicity was considered a great clinical advantage because it would make suicide impossible by using thalidomide. It would also be valuable when considering the number of accidental poisonings of children by sedatives and hypnotics which regularly occur. However, it has long been recognized by pharmacologists that a low acute toxicity does not guarantee that a drug will be harmless when taken repeatedly in low doses over a prolonged period of time, i.e. a low *acute* toxicity by no means offers a guarantee of a low *chronic* toxicity. Before thalidomide, a long series of drugs including such compounds as urethane, originally used as a sedative, phenacetin, a widespread analgesic (pain reliever), and chloramphenicol (Chloromycetin), an effective antibiotic, were known to cause serious toxic effects when used for a long period of time which were not evident when taken in very high doses on a single occasion. Thus, urethane was found to be a potent cancer-inducing compound which also could damage the foetus. Phenacetin was shown to cause blood changes as well as mental disturbances. Chloramphenicol caused fatal, aplastic anaemia, etc. From a scientific standpoint there is not, and has never been, such a thing as a 'completely harmless' or 'atoxic' drug.

At the end of 1957 the propaganda for thalidomide became intense. A massive and concentrated campaign began for the use of the drug in paediatrics and geriatrics. The use of thalidomide for diabetics and in cases of liver damage was also repeatedly recommended. Grünenthal's promotion resulted in an increase in thalidomide in every possible category and age group. Thalidomide was represented as 'completely innocuous', 'completely atoxic', etc. This policy was due to Dr Mückter, but worried some of his employees. Dr Werner recommended modifying these formulations and wrote in a memorandum of 3 March 1958 : 'Theoretically it is possible ... that the substance might in some manner be made more chemically soluble and the result could be that a lethal dose could be demonstrated experimentally (in animals).' In practice the company paid little attention to such considerations and a circular to salesmen and scientific workers on 28 May 1958 recommended that the 'atoxicity' should be underlined and that 'continuous control of consumption' of patients by doctors in the hospitals 'would be superfluous'. This would naturally have the effect that possible risks in the use of a new drug like this would tend to increase, and make the discovery of possible side-effects more difficult by the absence of satisfactory medical check-ups.

'The substance N-phtalylglutamic acidimide (thalidomide) is so atoxic that it can be administrated even to newborn and infants,' said Grünenthal in a letter to all pharmacists in the Federal Republic. In a circular (of 161,916 copies) to all physicians in free practice sent during the spring of 1959 can be found: 'Also with overdosage and prolonged medication the drug's effectiveness is not impaired by unwanted side effects.'

On 1 August 1958 a summary of work by Dr Blasiu was sent to 40,245 physicians in general practice. In the covering letter, signed by Dr Werner, Contergan is described as the best drug to be administered to pregnant and nursing mothers 'which does not damage either mother or child'. So far as the assertion applied to pregnant women, this was supported neither by Blasiu's work nor by any other investigation carried out to this day. As will be seen in the sequel (pp. 194–5) Blasiu strongly denied that his experiments could bear this meaning.

Nevertheless, the first somewhat disturbing accounts of other thalidomide effects were beginning to reach Grünenthal – effects which were to end, some ten years later, in the Alsdorf trial.

3

The First Reports of Toxic Effects and the Firm's Reactions

Since we shall be referring to documentation from the files of Chemie Grünenthal and other firms, it will be as well first to say something of how this was obtained, and also list the principal managerial staff of the company.

On 12 April 1967 Josef Havertz, the prosecutor of the city court of Aachen, handed over his 972 pages of *Anklageschrift* (indictment) to the responsible employees of Chemie Grünenthal. The act was based on approximately 70,000 pages of written material. From the end of 1961 Prosecutor Havertz had worked alone for two years on this gigantic undertaking, but he was later assisted by two assistant prosecutors and seven detectives. For five years about 1,200 witnesses were questioned in the longest court procedure in Europe since the Nuremberg trials.

A large part of the prosecutor's material is based on detailed records of the accused company itself. When the criminal law suit was instituted, the Chemie Grünenthal files were seized. After all the material had been gathered by the police and taken to the city court of Aachen, Dr Havertz received an anonymous telephone call which told him that a great deal more thalidomide material existed at the Stolberg offices. Havertz was given hints as to where the police should search. A second raid was made with good results. In a second anonymous telephone call the same person told Havertz where still more documents could be found; the 'bunker' should be searched. The police authorities had no idea of the existence of any 'bunker' within the factory area of the firm, but the officers took a chance and asked one of the senior members of the Grünenthal staff for the key to the 'bunker'. Taken by surprise the company representative handed over the key and took the prosecutor and the police to a huge factory chimney beneath which a well-disguised bunker lay concealed. The bunker had been transformed into an archive where numerous documents were neatly piled. In spite of the successful search of the archives of Chemie Grünenthal, not all the original documents were made available to the city court of Aachen. A comparison with the correspondence (obtained by other means) between the German factory and its licensees shows that an essential part of the original documentation is missing.

The people principally connected with the thalidomide case in Chemie Grünenthal – those put on trial in 1967 – were as follows:

Hermann Wirtz, the owner, entered the firm Dalli-Werke, Maurer & Wirtz in 1921. He had been managing director of the Dalli-Werke since 1930 and managing director of Chemie Grünenthal GmbH since 1946; he was also responsible for the general management of the latter firm.

The director of the scientific department, *Dr Heinrich Mückter*. Admitted before the court of Aachen that he was responsible for the development of thalidomide until it was put on the market. It is quite clear that even after this stage, Dr Mückter was responsible for the main directives for sales promotion and information to physicians. Dr Mückter was also the scientist kept regularly informed about the side-effects reported from various sources. He is the man who on 14 July 1961 was supposed to have declared at an internal meeting with the Staff of Chemie Grünenthal: 'If I were a

47

physician, I would now not prescribe Contergan. Gentlemen, I warn you – I do not want to repeat an earlier judgement – I see great dangers.'

Dr Mückter passed his medical degree in 1940. From December 1940 to August 1945 he was a soldier and rose to the position of *Stabsarzt* and director for the Institut für Fleckfieber und Virusforschung des Oberkommondos des Heeres in Krakau.

Jacob Chauvistré, 'procurist' of the Dalli-Werke 1924 and later deputy manager of Chemie Grünenthal. *Hermann Leufgens* and *Klaus Winandi* were also closely attached to Dalli-Werke before they were given prominent positions on the board of Grünenthal during the fifties.

Dr *Gotthold Erich Werner*, employed by Chemie Grünenthal as scientific assistant in the company's public relations department in 1952. In 1953 he was given responsibility for building up a scientific department for foreign affairs. From 1957 he was director of the medical-scientific department of the firm. He left Chemie Grünenthal in 1962.

Dr *Günther Sievers*. He originally made visits to doctors, hospitals and pharmacies. In 1958 he became responsible for technical correspondence inside the Federal Republic, and was in special charge of thalidomide within the medical-scientific department. Since the trials against Chemie Grünenthal were instituted, Dr Sievers has been engaged extensively as the principal adviser on medical questions for the defence.

Dr *Heinz Wolfgang Kelling*, made director of the public relations section of the scientific department, left the company in 1962.

Dr *Hans Werner von Schrader-Beielstein*, entered Chemie Grünenthal in 1957 and was engaged in supporting the scientific department managers. From July 1961 he was given increasing responsibilities in problems relevant to thalidomide, especially as medical adviser to the syndicate handling compensation claims.

What kind of physicians were employed to test the safety and efficiency of thalidomide? We have been informed from the material collected by the prosecutor in Aachen that most of the doctors carrying out clinical testing for Chemie Grünenthal lacked special training for that purpose. Their reports were in general overwhelmingly enthusiastic but lacking in precision and detail. In a report to the management of 9 June 1959 Dr Mückter himself points out that from June 1957 to February 1960 the pharmacological department was 'without a qualified leader'. He stressed that other enterprises of a similar size employed three to five times as many pharmacologists. It took the Grünenthal company much longer 'to test a substance even superficially'.

Dr Keller, who was responsible for pharmacological testing in experimental animals, was described by Dr Mückter as a man who 'was not particularly well known in pharmacological circles'. This remark of Dr Mückter's may be somewhat unjustified, since Dr Keller was a very young man at the time and could not be expected to be very well known.

Dr G. Resemann, who wrote one of the basic articles in the field of paediatrics for Chemie Grünenthal (which was published in *Die Medezinische* 1959 under the title 'Therapy of Behavioural Disturbances in Child Age') had previously been working mainly on the testing of antibiotics on amoebae and bacteria. Chemie Grünenthal used another clinical work, published by a Dr Jung in 1956 in the journal *Arzneimittel Forschung*, despite the fact that the company itself expressed reservations about this article.

We can now turn to the development of events in West Germany from 1959 onwards.

When Professor Schmaltz in Frankfurt-am-Main reported to Chemie Grünenthal that he had observed 'disturbances of balance' and light 'giddiness' in an elderly patient, which he ascribed to the use of Contergan, Dr Sievers answered that this was the first time the company had heard of such side-effects. In fact Professor Kloos had made reports of 'giddiness' during the clinical testing of thalidomide. Similar observations were also made during 1955 and 1957 by the clinical investigators, Dr Jung, Dr Baumann, Dr Schildwäcter and Dr Hug, as well as from Smith, Kline & French of the USA.

As the sales of Contergan increased explosively during 1959, the number of critical reports also tended to increase. Doctors and pharmacists made reports of severe constipation, dizziness, hangover, loss of memory, decrease in blood pressure and other paradoxical symptoms. These side-effects were minimized by the company and ascribed to overdosage and prolonged usage.

Meanwhile, some members of the staff of Chemie Grünenthal found the situation unsatisfactory. Dr Günther Michael, who had taken over the section for clinical testing, criticized the absence of any investigations relating to the important question of the effect of thalidomide on the liver function (although for a long time Grünenthal had recommended the use of thalidomide for patients suffering from liver damage). He also criticized the fact that practically nothing was known about the metabolism and destruction of the drug in the human body, that thalidomide, even clinically, 'was still an open issue', and that Contergan was used in combination with a number of other drugs without sufficient information about the substance itself.

In the *Basisprospekt* (preliminary advertising material) for Contergan printed in August 1959 some 'occasional side-effects' are mentioned, including 'drowsiness next day' and a 'moderate tendency to constipation' although 'these applied exclusively when the individually required dose was exceeded'. It further mentioned, 'Paradoxical reactions such as restlessness and trembling of the extremities are exceedingly rare'. 'Allergic reactions ... cannot be excluded, although they have very seldom been observed.'

In September 1959 the use of Contergan in the district hospital of Hellersen was stopped in view of severe allergic reactions in the form of severe cases of purpura (local haemorrhages of the skin). The information that these side-effects were possibly to be discussed in an article written by the physicians of this hospital caused great alarm at Chemie Grünenthal, and a report of 12 October 1959 reads: 'In accordance with our agreement Dr Michael will appear on Thursday 13 October to clarify the situation and so to stop eventual publication.'

Pharmakolor A G, the Grünenthal partner in Basel, gave the following report on the situation in Switzerland on 27 August 1959:

Twenty well-known physicians have now informed our PR men that they themselves, or their patients, have still had severe side-effects the morning after taking one whole tablet of Softenon Forte, in the form of extreme tiredness, tremor (shaking) of the hands, etc. Professor Ludwig, head doctor of the Second Medical Section of Bürgerspital, Basel, added: 'Once and never again. This is a horrible drug.'

However, as these side-effects were reversible and as the majority of reports were still very positive, no special attention was paid to them in Stolberg.

The situation became far more serious for the company when on 3 October 1959, a written report was received from the neurologist Dr Ralf Voss of Dusseldorf. This physician had observed a case of polyneuritis which could possibly be due to Contergan. He wanted to be informed 'if anything was known about whether Contergan could cause damage to

51

the peripheral nervous system'. Dr Werner and Dr Sievers replied that such effects had never been observed before. We now know that this information given to Dr Voss was false. During the clinical trials of thalidomide back in 1956 Dr Piacenza had described a case of polyneuritis, an effect which he had traced to the drug. Other reports relating to the same side-effect were as follows :

On 26 August 1958 Dr Kreideweiss reported that Contergan could cause disturbances of the gait after prolonged use. On 14 July 1959, the Grünenthal salesman, Johannes Zila, from Dusseldorf, came in contact with a pharmacist who told him about a customer who was convinced that he had developed paraesthesia because of Contergan.

During August 1959 Dr Consten from Schwelm reported several cases of polyneuritic syndromes after the administration of Contergan.

On 15 October 1959 Margot Vogel, a Grünenthal representative, wrote that Dr Angermann in Iserlohn 'had observed disturbances of sensibility in the toes and the fingers after monthly use of Contergan Forte ... completely independently, his sister-in-law, who had taken Contergan at the same time, had complained about similar effects'. To Dr Angermann, Dr Sievers and Dr Werner wrote similarly that they were not aware of such symptoms. On 27 November 1959 new reports of similar effects were obtained from a Dr Sartorius in Dusseldorf.

A few words of description would be appropriate to clarify this type of affliction, the so-called polyneuritis, described by Dr Voss and by others.

Nerve damage caused by thalidomide is classified as a toxic polyneuritis, and, because of its characteristic symptoms, may be distinguished from polyneuritis caused by other factors, such as abuse of alcohol, etc. After continuous use of thalidomide over a shorter or longer period (two weeks and up to three years) a prickling feeling of the extremities appears followed by a sensation of numbness (paraesthesia) and coldness. The numbness usually begins in the toes and is not initially noticed by the patient. The numbness then spreads to the ball of the foot, then to the ankles, and finally to the calves, but not further up than to the knee. Many months later, hardly ever at the same time, numbness begins in the tips of the fingers. After some time the complete picture of a toxic polyneuritis develops, including severe muscular pains and cramps in the extremities, weakness of the limbs, disturbances of the reflexes and coordination of the limbs (ataxia). The patient is unable to judge the position of his legs by feeling; consequently his gait becomes unbalanced and uncoordinated. In its fully developed form partial paralysis may occur and in the majority of cases even unexacting forms of manual work become impossible. The victim becomes permanently disabled. In severe cases the clinical picture may resemble that of funicular myelosis, a severe degeneration of parts of the nervous system. In the internal report made by the Swiss pharmaceutical company, CIBA, the effects of thalidomide are compared with that of 'thallium (rat poison) diphtheria, and even tri-orthocresylphosphate'.*

Apart from the polyneuritis, severe symptoms of effects on the central nervous system often appeared. Involuntary twitchings of the facial muscles occurred, trembling of the muscles of the entire body, abnormal bodily sensations and severe disturbances of the ability to concentrate, together with speech difficulties, double vision and in some cases even epileptic seizures. In contrast to the peripheral neuritis type of damage, these effects on the central nervous system disappeared when the medication was stopped. In cases of

---

*This is an organic phosphate used as an ingredient in certain lubricants. It caused the intoxication of thousands of people in Morocco when mineral oil was used in the adulteration of olive oil.

peripheral neuritis the damage caused by thalidomide is permanent in the majority of cases, and although some improvement may be noted, most of the symptoms remain. The frequency of such effects is not clear but in cases of prolonged administration such high figures as an incidence of between 5 and 20 per cent have been reported in the literature on the subject. Apart from the medical staff employed by the pharmaceutical companies engaged in the marketing of thalidomide and a few physicians closely affiliated with them, there is now a universal medical agreement on the etiology of severe nervous damage caused by thalidomide.

In December 1960 Dr Voss, who was seriously concerned about the nerve damage, initiated a systematic survey of similar cases. On 1 May, during a postgraduate course in neurology, he had already pointed out to a wider circle of physicians that thalidomide was capable of damaging the nervous system.

During 1960 thalidomide sales continued to rise, and in May it represented 46 per cent of the total turnover of Chemie Grünenthal. However, many physicians thought that the use of the drug should be more rigorously controlled. On 14 April Dr Mückter outlined some principles for the future:

Unfortunately, we are now receiving in increasing numbers reports on the side-effects of this drug, as well as letters from doctors and pharmacists who want to put Contergan on prescription. From our side, everything must be done to avoid prescription enforcement, since already a substantial amount of our turnover comes from over-the-counter sales.

Such counter measures were to be 'argument about the lack of toxicity ... and a careful approach to the responsible authorities'.

The number of reports of various side-effects, including

polyneuritis, went on increasing rapidly, but Grünenthal continued to minimize them or even to deny any previous knowledge, as in the case of polyneuritis. On 8 March a physician at St Franziskus Hospital in Colonge-Ehrenfeld wrote inquiring about the possible neurological effects of Contergan since he had himself suffered from such symptoms after using the drug for seven months. He received the following reply : 'We should like to inform you that up to now no such reports have reached us, in spite of the fact that for several years Contergan has been used to an ever-increasing extent.'

During the spring of 1960 a wave of polyneuritis reports reached the company from every corner of the Federal Republic. From Dr Ervenich in Duisburg, from Professor Laubenthal in Essen, from Dr Wiesfeld in Katzenellenbogen, from Dr Konz in Neheim-Hüsten, and from several other members of the medical profession came alarming and detailed descriptions of severe polyneuritis.

To counteract the negative impression caused by these reports, which sooner or later would become generally known, Grünenthal made great efforts to secure favourable publications. An Austrian physician, Dr Schrober, presented such a work in *Wiener Medizinische Wochenschrift*. On 8 January 1960 Dr Werner commented on this article : 'Dr Schrober's work is very uncritical.'

The sales promotion campaign was further stepped up, and from January to April 1960 a quarter of a million leaflets were distributed. These brochures stressed over and over again 'non-toxic', 'completely harmless even for infants', 'harmless even over a long period of use', 'misuse and damage practically excluded'.

During January to March 1960 Grünenthal representatives visited 19,186 physicians.

In an internal memorandum for salesmen and scientific

associates on 17 May 1960, it was admitted that the frequency and severity of the side-effects of Contergan showed a tendency to increase, and that the polyneuritis 'which had been confirmed by several sources' was in fact severe disturbances of health. By the end of 1960 Chemie Grünenthal had received 1,600 reports of various side-effects which had been connected with thalidomide, among which were over 100 cases of the severe polyneuritis. On 8 November the sales office in Frankfurt had to inform the company in Stolberg that the University clinic would not use thalidomide because of the risk of polyneuritis. During the autumn Grünenthal learned that Distillers, the licensee in England, had received seven reports of effects on the nervous system ascribed to thalidomide. Mention of these side-effects was made in the Distillers' commercial literature. In August and December a circular letter was sent to over 20,000 doctors, which included a warning of the risk of peripheral neuritis. Chemie Grünenthal continued to ignore all such information directed to the medical profession inside Germany, as well as to the licensees of other countries. Outwardly the front was maintained and the continued and uncontrolled use of Contergan was even promoted through massive representations made for its being completely innocuous. In the sales district of Dortmund a report of 3 September 1960 reads: 'In some pharmacies the liquid formulation is very much appreciated as "Cinema-juice", by which is meant that before visiting the cinema in the evening parents give Contergan to their children in liquid form.'

Disrespect for the potential dangers of a drug, which was no harmless vitamin pill but a sedative, promoted among the consumers by unrestrained advertising, is demonstrated by the following note made by Dr Sievers at the end of 1960: 'On the other hand, we have already heard that the liquid preparation of Contergan, for example, is often taken without using a spoon. An appropriate gulp is taken direct from the bottle.'

The serious side-effects made the leaders of Chemie Grünenthal aware of the danger that sooner or later thalidomide would be made a prescription drug, and in their internal memoranda the mention is made of the importance of taking 'precautions against the danger of prescription'. Doctors intending to produce unfavourable reports should be approached in a proper way, e.g. 'to visit Professor Amelung, from the clinic where critical comment is expected, and without previous warning attack him'. Sales propaganda had to be revised to cope with the new situation and it was even suggested 'primarily to take out the concept "atoxic" from all advertising material'.

On 21 November 1960 Dr Sievers of Grünenthal paid a visit to Professor Laubenthal's clinic, which, several times, had reported cases of polyneuritis to the Stolberg factory. Professor Laubenthal and his head physician, Dr Raffauf, made no secret of their opinion that they considered the nerve damage unusually severe, and that there was absolutely no doubt that it was being caused by Contergan. When Dr Sievers was told that Dr Raffauf intended to publish his results he tried to persuade Raffauf to refrain. Laubenthal and Raffauf did not comply and urged the company to make arrangements to notify physicians about this type of side-effect.

When the Grünenthal people heard that Dr Horst Frenkel, the neurologist in Königstein, intended to publish his observations of about twenty cases of nerve damage caused by thalidomide, Dr Sievers and Dr Kelling also visited him to prevent publication. Dr Frenkel refused and declared that he intended to publish in *Die Medizinische Welt*. As there seemed little possibility of influencing Dr Frenkel, Grünenthal tried to stop publication at the editorial board level of the journal. With this aim in mind Dr Kelling started negotiations with Dr Matis in Stuttgart, editor-in-chief of *Die Medizinische Welt*. In his monthly report for September 1960 Dr Michael wrote, 'In the long run we will not be able to stop publication of the side effects of Contergan ... In Stuttgart Dr Kelling and I visited Dr Matis, the editor in chief of *Die Medizinische Welt*, to discuss preventive measures against the article he has received about Contergan.'

When questioned during the Alsdorf trials Dr Paul Matis admitted that he had forwarded the manuscript of Frenkel to Chemie Grünenthal for comments. He denied categorically that he had ever let himself be influenced.

Later in the spring of 1961, Dr Michael made similar approaches to Dr Stamm, an editor of *Deutsche Medizinische Wochenschrift* about the publication of an article by Dr Raffauf concerned with polyneuritis caused by thalidomide. Dr Stamm was of the opinion that the article was 'absolutely objective and without exaggeration'. Dr Michael's report adds 'publication was scheduled for January and will be postponed until the end of April, to meet my wishes, and that under no circumstances will the reports appear before the Internisten-Kongress'. As a result Dr Werner could write in his monthly report for March 1961, 'The appearance of negative articles has been delayed so far, but they cannot be avoided during the next month.'

Meanwhile Raffauf and his chief, Professor Laubenthal, were surprised at the delay in publishing the article which had been sent to the journal in September 1960. On several occasions Laubenthal had complained to the editorial board. A representative for the journal excused himself – there were so many obituaries to be printed. Raffauf told the court during the Alsdorf proceedings on 12 May 1969 that 'this appeared frankly grotesque. In our clinic we actually discussed whether the journal was dithering for so long because it was worried that if it was published, it would get less advertising.'

When in November 1960 Dr Homann, superintendent of the Drug Commission of the German Medical Association in Göttingen, took up the question of the side-effects of Contergan, Grünenthal now had to adopt a new defensive front – against the various administrative institutions concerned with public health. Grünenthal representatives visited officials in the ministries concerned to try to convince the authorities of the 'complete harmlessness' of Contergan. 'We intend to fight for Contergan to the bitter end,' exclaimed a Grünenthal document. From July to October the company salesmen paid 30,382 visits to physicians. The sales promotion material was not modified, Contergan was still represented as nontoxic. Not until 2 November was a new label designed which contained the following comment: 'As with most drugs, a more or less prolonged use of Contergan may evoke hypersensitivity reactions in certain predisposed patients ... After immediate withdrawal of the drug, these allergic reactions will disappear.'

Not only does the text minimize the severity of the reactions, but it was also false and misleading, since a number of neurologists had pointed out to Grünenthal representatives that the nerve damage was often irreversible, and no improvement at all could be noted after medication had been stopped. Further, the damage was not of an allergic type but was generally diagnosed as a form of 'toxic polyneuritis'. An internal CIBA report reads, 'It is thus unequivocally established that thalidomide produces severe neurotoxic damage ... The German manufacturer (Grünenthal) tries to emphasize ... that this damage is a skin reaction of an allergic nature (which also occasionally occurs after Doriden).'

The amended labels for Contergan were dated September

1960, which Dr Sievers made a point of in a letter written on 23 December to a physician: 'Since I have the unfortunate impression that you are not confident that we are genuine in our efforts to explain the side-effects scientifically, I enclose a Contergan package label which we have been inserting in all of our packages since the end of September.' These package labels were purposely predated two months.

In fact, the Grünenthal people were themselves not at all convinced that the nerve damage was of an 'allergic' type. In January 1961 Dr Sievers wrote to Professor Custodis in Dusseldorf, 'At the moment we are therefore still not able to decide whether these effects are of allergic nature ... It seems more likely that a disturbance of metabolism is involved.'

On 31 December 1960, a letter appeared in an issue of the *British Medical Journal* entitled 'Is Thalidomide to Blame?' by Dr A. Leslie Florence. Dr Florence briefly described his observations of four cases of thalidomide polyneuritis and inquired 'whether any of your readers have observed these effects after long-term treatment with the drug'. This was the first description of nerve damage to appear in any medical literature.

At the end of February 1961 Chemie Grünenthal learned of more than 400 suspected cases of polyneuritis associated with Contergan. Besides the nerve damage a large number of 'paradoxical effects' had been reported and a total of several thousand cases of various kinds of side-effects had by then reached Stolberg. In a letter to Wm. S. Merrell Co., Ohio, Grünenthal claimed only to have heard of one single case of polyneuritis during 1960 and information of more cases in Germany was said to have been obtained for the first time at the Dusseldorf lectures on 15 February 1961.

That the staff at Stolberg were now convinced themselves that thalidomide did cause nerve damage is demonstrated by

the fact that the internal documents did not discuss *if* thalidomide was the cause of these effects but *why* and *how* thalidomide provoked such reactions.

In December 1960, Dr Oswald and Dr Nowel undertook
to visit officials at the various health authorities to prevent
any attempts to put Contergan on prescription.

December, 1960: Dr Oswald and I (Dr Nowel) were sent on a
journey to point out to the ministries that the attacks were unjustified, and that no side-effects were known which could be
connected with Contergan.

In a report for April 1961 Dr Nowel gave further details
of these visits to Leufgens and to von Schrader-Beielstein:

To maintain the maximum turnover of Contergan Dr Oswald
and Dr Nowel . . . have visited the superintendents of the Health
Departments of the Ministries for Interior Affairs and given
special prominence to the following points:

(1) Contergan is as good as atoxic.
(2) Side-effects have practically never occurred.
(3) Arguments from the Ministry for Interior Affairs concerning the necessity of prescription enforcement were refuted,
by underlining:

(i) that such rumours could possibly be due to a mix-up
with Doriden (the competing sedative marketed by CIBA),
(ii) that until now only rumours, but no facts are known.
(4) Suicide attempts with Contergan had so far not been
successful.

Similar discussions were held with the Federal Health Board
in Berlin in December 1960, and with the pharmacist in
charge of the Federal Ministry for Interior Affairs in January
1961.

The sales promotion men, for their part, were kept busy
mounting a front against the doctors and the pharmacists.
One salesman wrote, 'My happy laughter and appropriate
references to the completely harmless properties of the drug

were apparently successful in putting the often anxious pharmacists' minds at rest.' Trials were encouraged in an attempt to secure favourable comment. For this purpose doctors were approached in the county asylums (*Landes-Heilanstalt*) where positive results were usually obtained. Patients in this kind of hospital were often quite unable to communicate with their surroundings, and were far from able to describe the symptoms of polyneuritis. One of the doctors using Contergan for the treatment of mental illness pointed out to Grünenthal that 'from a scientific point of view the documentary value of such patients is not very high'.

On 7 December 1960 the sales office in Dusseldorf wrote to Hermann Wirtz and Winandi: 'Do we actually know, then, how many side-effects have been caused by Contergan? We have certainly been informed by some doctors that Contergan-patients with side-effects are being treated. However, we must ask ourselves how many other patients are there whose damage has not been recognized.'

In December 1960 objections were received from the sales area of Dusseldorf:

We do not believe it is constructive to make a report to the Public Relations Section about a 'campaign initiated by competitors' when, in fact, strong criticism against Contergan has been brought forward in some well-known clinics in Nordrhein-Westfalen as well as by a lot of doctors. We have reported these cases to you.

One salesman, Dr Goeden, writes on 23 February 1961 about his visit to the neurological university clinic in Cologne: 'I declared our standpoint on the problem of polyneuritis and Contergan, and sought above all to cause confusion.'

The company policy may thus be summarized as follows,

the method used in individual cases being determined by the situation :

(1) To deny all causal connection between thalidomide and polyneuritis.

(2) If there is no possibility of denying that thalidomide has caused nerve damage

(i) To associate the nerve damage with allergic reaction;

(ii) To minimize the severity of the polyneuritis;

(iii) To withold information about the true number of cases which are known to the company;

(iv) To ascribe the rumours of toxic effects of thalidomide to slander campaigns from competitors;

(v) To 'cause confusion' as to the real nature of this damage.

It should be emphasized that, as thalidomide was claimed to be a completely innocuous drug which could be taken without any restrictions, the polyneuritis was frequently not recognized by physicians as being caused by thalidomide and the nerve damage was often ascribed to quite different causes. And, of course, the kind of propaganda sponsored by the producers made correct diagnosis still more difficult. Years after thalidomide had disappeared from the market many patients in Sweden with severe polyneuritis caused by thalidomide met with incredulity from doctors when they suggested that their affliction was due to thalidomide. All physicians knew by then that this drug caused foetal damage but many of them had never heard about any nerve damage. The relationship was only established when these patients came to a specialist who had previously seen such a case. The number of cases published in medical literature, or reported to the manufacturer, is merely the tip of the iceberg, with the majority of cases remaining concealed. As long as the side-effects of thalidomide were not generally known, the manufacturers must have realized that the number of cases reported to the company were only a fraction of the true number. Still, the number of reported cases was considerable and amounted to around 1,300 by the end of May 1961.

The situation suddenly worsened for Chemie Grünenthal when they learnt that the neurologist Dr Ralph Voss intended to present several typical cases at a postgraduate course for neurologists, on 15 February 1961 in Dusseldorf. It now seemed unavoidable that thalidomide polyneuritis would become known to a wider circle. Dr Sievers paid a visit to Dr Voss to try to persuade the Dusseldorf doctor not to mention this damage in his lecture. Dr Voss for fear of being misquoted had arranged that a colleague should be present as a witness during the meeting with Dr Sievers. Previous experience with Grünenthal had indicated a need for such precautions.

Dr Voss did not allow himself to be influenced, but declared that he thought it quite essential that the medical profession should be informed about the thalidomide-polyneuritis which so far had resisted all forms of therapy. He thought it all the more important since the company had refused to show any willingness to give accurate information on the matter. He considered that the clinical picture and its cause was not recognized in the majority of cases, and was usually ascribed to disturbances in the blood circulation.

After the Voss lecture the Grünenthal staff became nervous. Dr Günter Nowel wrote in his file of note cards, 'After the medical symposium in Dusseldorf on 15 February, everyone lost his head. Winandi immediately wanted to put it on prescription. No uniform policy existed any longer.'

Dr Mückter was on vacation, and when he was contacted by telephone argued against all 'rash decisions' in his absence and would not hear of any prescription control. At the most, a mild warning might be issued. The fight for Contergan must go on! The effects of the Voss lecture must be neutralized! Dr Goeden visited the University neurological clinic in Cologne to see the head physician, Dr Paul Bresser. Excerpts from Dr Goeden's report are revealing:

On the basis of this evidence I gently hinted to Voss that neither the personal feelings of colleagues who were for or against the product, nor the interests of other firms, should be left out of account when making a judgement on it.

During the Alsdorf trial Bresser said that on 13 May 1969 he was under the impression that the representative of Chemie Grünenthal was not willing to discuss his findings but rather to force upon him his own opinion. He remarked that 'You could discuss things quietly with the representatives of other pharmaceutical firms.' In his report to his employers Goeden characterized Dr Bresser as '... our most aggressive and skilful adversary'.

By February 1961 the Chemie Grünenthal staff had to recognize the possibility that Contergan would suffer prescription control. A certain restraint in their propaganda within Germany could be detected. However, the export material was not revised in most cases and slogans 'non-toxic', 'no danger from toxic damage' were used as before. There was even a tendency outside the country to intensify the propaganda campaigns.

In March the situation worsened still further. A company report stated: 'In St Anna Hospital, Cologne-Lindenthal, 271 (Contergan) has been banned as a result of a decision made by the chief physician.'

Another report reads:

Dr Paukert said, 'I have stopped Contergan immediately in the treatment of all my patients. It is irresponsible to continue to market this drug. I shall suggest to my colleagues that they also stop using Contergan.'

Professor Heymer, director of the medical university clinic in Bonn, had at that time heard of ninety cases of polyneuritis after using Contergan . . . He has now prohibited all use of this drug in the University clinic and has further demanded that Contergan should be taken off the market. Putting it under prescription would be insufficient and irresponsible. He wishes to have no further discussion with the manufacturers.

The domestic department of Chemie Grünenthal seemed to be overwhelmed by the number of reports of side-effects which were pouring in. To cope with the situation Winandi wrote in his monthly report:

In this department we have above all to avoid following up every little report [of side-effects] or paying too much attention to them. We must not bother our colleagues and physicians too often with perpetual queries and interruptions. The wider knowledge of possible side-effects from the use of Contergan will be best promoted by the accurate reports whose publication we anticipate. It is no longer possible to concern ourselves with each individual case or to attack every single trouble centre.

The possible financial consequences of this 'wider knowledge' were considered in the Sales Department, in March.

The discussions in Dusseldorf and Cologne concerning presumptive side-effects have not had any influence on turnover. This will surely change, if – as a counteraction – Contergan is put under prescription.

During March and April the scientific department devoted a lot of time to speculation about the mechanism underlying the neurotoxic action. They discussed whether thalidomide affects the function of important vitamins (e.g. vitamin B_1) in the metabolism of the body, or if thalidomide is an anti-metabolite which blocks important enzyme reactions. Some tentative approaches were made to a few specialists. It was made clear to the Grünenthal staff by these specialists that the clarification of these questions on a biochemical level would involve considerable cost and would be very time-consuming. The company took no serious initiative in carrying out any scientific investigations into the matter.

Chemie Grünenthal made great efforts to try to ascribe the polyneuritis to other causes, for example, misuse of alcohol. Information sent out by the company to doctors and pharmacists on 3 March 1961 (60,154 copies) looked superficially exactly like their previous brochures. There was no special indication that this particular brochure contained hints of new side-effects. For most physicians and pharmacists the leaflets went straight into the wastepaper basket, as they assumed it contained the usual sales promotion stuff. Anyone reading through the brochure would have come across the following passage:

It has become known that in occasional cases after long or exaggerated use, sensoric polyneuritis may develop; in the majority of cases this is evidently due to a previously administered sedative or to misuse of alcohol.

Chemie Grünenthal staff were well aware that the neurologists concerned with these reported cases had carefully excluded such causes in their reports and had made this point clearly to the company representatives at all times. The clinical picture was also quite characteristic and not at all like that seen in alcoholism. In a lecture at the University of Cologne on 11 March 1961 Professor Scheid said, 'The neurological symptoms of the Contergan polyneuritis may already be distinguished from other polyneuritis syndromes and characterized as specific. We do not know of any other polyneuritis which gives a similar clinical picture of varied subjective symptoms.' He continued: 'I do not believe that

67

alcoholics are especially predisposed. I consider this quite improbable. Alcohol plays no part whatever in the cases I have seen myself. . .'

Three physicians connected with Chemie Grünenthal and a representative of the company staff were present at that lecture.

4

Later Stages of the Struggle

During March the Grünenthal management was for the first time confronted with the worrying question of possible legal consequences arising from the damage caused by their 'completely harmless' drug. As a result the company's law department hired a private detective, a Mr Ernst Günther Jahnke from Essen, to report on physicians who displayed a hostile attitude to Contergan and to report on the individual patients with damage who might raise compensation claims against Grünenthal. Mr Jahnke made notes on details of the private life and family circumstances of certain physicians. One report says, 'The father of Dr B is an ex-communist and nowadays a member of SED.' Their primary aim was to prevent any civil law suit coming about which would cause irreparable damage to the company's reputation from the ensuing publicity. Discussions were also held with representatives from the Gerling company with whom Grünenthal was insured.

At a meeting on 29 March between the staff of Grünenthal and representatives from Gerling it was pointed out by the insurance company that 'the statement on the package-inserts, "even extreme overdosage will not be toxic", would not be without risk'. Grünenthal themselves would have to take full responsibility and bear all the risks involved for any nerve damage caused by Contergan since the lecture by Dr Voss on 15 February 1961.

The Drug Commission of German Physicians (Arznei-mittelkommission der deutschen Ärzteschaft), a section of the Federal Medical Board without strong powers (*hoheitliche Gewalt*) but able to make recommendations, was not properly informed by the company as to the side-effects of Contergan. On 8 March 1961 a letter from the Drug Commission was received:

> While we have been considering our decision about Contergan, it has been pointed out to us during recent weeks from several sources that polyneuritis of a sensoric type has been observed after long-term use ... I very much deplore that I was informed about these observations by your company in a general letter to physicians, which I received only yesterday ...

As a result of this letter Dr Michael visited the chairman of the Drug Commission, Dr Homann, in Gottingen on 20 March 1961. A report of the discussions given to the Stolberg staff stated:

> Dr Homann's exact words were: 'This whole business has caused Grünenthal great damage, since a number of the members of the Drug Commission took a clear stand against Contergan and Grünenthal.'

I explained to her [Dr Homann] that there was no reason for us to have made any proposition to the Drug Commission when the first reports of polyneuritis reached us at the end of last year, since at that time we had no success in obtaining proof that the reports were more than rumour. We had our first opportunity of discussing the question with people who had actually seen such cases only after the evening in Dusseldorf; this was the first occasion on which we were able to convince ourselves that poly-neuritis might appear. After a discussion which lasted for over half an hour ... Dr Homann pointed out emphatically that our measures to put the drug under prescription should be speeded up as far as possible to enable the drug to be medically controlled ...

We were also strongly reproached for having stressed the lack of acute toxicity and the unsuccessful suicide attempts but not the important matters relating to polyneuritis. Members of the Drug Commission regarded this simply as misrepresentation of the facts.

The increasing pressures on Chemie Grünenthal are reflected in the instructions sent on 2 March to staff concerned with public relations:

We have to come to terms with some reports of side-effects which will be certain to cause trouble as they are being canvassed in an exaggerated or distorted manner. We must expect published comment. The (apparently) organized circulation of reports of side-effects also produces completely unjustified claims and controversial attacks. We are concerned to put things right again ... There have been reports of occasional, but not very important, side-effects of dermal and neurological types after the use of Contergan. There is no reason to concern ourselves at all with this matter, as it has been excessively exaggerated ... In cases where nothing is really known about side-effects, these should be mentioned casually because of the published reports we must expect. Where something is actually known, interest should be displayed. In cases where possible prescription is discussed one should refer to the sense of responsibility at head office and mention that appropriate measures have just been initiated in this respect.

(In fact at that time no steps to bring Contergan under prescription had been taken by the company.)

As to the claim that polyneuritis appeared only occasionally, in reality more than 400 suspected cases were known to the company at that time. It was also well aware that mention of side-effects would escape the attention of most physicians. In the monthly report for March, Dr Kelling wrote,

'One can estimate that, at the most, a quarter of all physicians who received the first information letter have since read about the side-effects of Contergan ...'

The unfavourable reports were growing. On 8 April the Dortmund sales area reported: 'You have already been informed in a special report that seven hospitals in our area have turned down Contergan in general terms ... In the future other hospitals will surely abstain from its regular use. All hospitals which have generally turned down Contergan are meanwhile partly treated by special measures.'

The Grünenthal management made great efforts to co-ordinate the defence of Contergan. 'Motto: We must succeed at any cost.'

Dr Mückter tried speeding the marketing of their new combination-drug, Noctosediv. In addition to thalidomide this drug also contained a barbiturate. Grünenthal had for years been waging an intensive campaign against barbiturates because they assumed them to be less safe than thalidomide; now they themselves were including a barbiturate in one of their own preparations. Many of the company's physicians were clearly against the marketing of such a drug for both medical and tactical reasons.

During the Deutschen Internistkongress (conference on internal diseases) in Wiesbaden at the beginning of April, Professor Hoff from Frankfurt, a well-known specialist on drug-induced diseases, and Professor Amelung, gave an account of nerve damage caused by thalidomide. On the same occasion Professor Kimmig of Hamburg described cases of purpura also caused by thalidomide. Despite the increasingly sharp criticism from specialists against thalidomide Grünenthal continued to use the same misleading labels as before. Winandi even suggested a change in the label wording to a more non-committal style since he found the existing labels were 'too detailed' in their information about negative effects. Great efforts were made to obtain favourable articles about thalidomide. One such article came from Dr Winzenried, an old friend of Dr Sievers from his time as a soldier during the war. The article was, however, rejected by the *Deutsche Medizinische Wochenschrift*.

The doubtful value of investigation on psychiatric patients appears to have become quite clear to Grünenthal and on 21 April 1961, Tachezy, the manager of the Sales Department, wrote to Stolberg from Hamburg, 'In psychiatric departments with a heavy 271 (Contergan) consumption no side-effects at all are reported (perhaps the patients are enjoying themselves when it's itching !).'

At the end of April Jahnke, the private detective, wrote a detailed report about some neurologists who were critical of Contergan:

As far as I have heard Chemie Grünenthal's competitors are showing malicious joy over Contergan's now established faults. But on the other hand, they have evidently not provoked this situation. They haven't needed to since the damage has been confirmed by physicians and widely discussed by experts in professional circles.

Meanwhile the Stolberg firm concentrated on stopping hostile publications. In the monthly report for April, Dr Werner wrote, 'We have managed to bring further delays in unfavourable publications, but after May this will no longer be possible.'

Attempts to conceal the real situation from the authorities were stubbornly continued, to avoid thalidomide being put under prescription. An account has already been given of attempts to influence the Berlin authorities in December 1960 and again in January 1961.

In April Dr Nowel and Dr Oswald from Grünenthal visited Professor Gerhard Kärber, the director of the Federal Health

Department in Berlin, to assess the situation. Professor Kärber later declared before the court in Aachen that Grünenthal had completely failed to mention the polyneuritis caused by Contergan. Grünenthal's policy had less success in the Ministry of Internal Affairs in the state of Nordrhein-Westfalen since Dr Voss, the neurologist, immediately gave his observations to Dr Tombergs, one of the pharmaceutical experts of the ministry. Dr Voss concludes in his letter to Dr Tombergs: 'We are concerned with a severe and widely distributed disturbance to health. If the authorities do not intervene swiftly and energetically a scandal will be unavoidable.'

Dr Tombergs then wrote a detailed letter to Chemie Grünenthal on 10 April 1961, in which the symptoms were described and the irreversibility and severity of the effects were pointed out. Before proceedings to enforce prescription Dr Tombergs asked Grünenthal to comment immediately on his observations. Chemie Grünenthal did not reply to his letter until 17 May.

The Grünenthal PR staff were often in an increasingly unpleasant and difficult position and some of them began to react against the company's policy. In a report from Essen of 10 April 1961, can be found:

... at today's conference we came to the certain conclusion that investigation of patients with Contergan damage being conducted by the central office, in which the co-workers are asked to collaborate, cannot be reconciled with professional medical ethics, and by doing this we are making many angry enemies amongst physicians.

Some of those working with Grünenthal were quite critical of the manner in which physicians and pharmacies were informed of side-effects; in April Winandi received the following comments from Münster:

Our letter to physicians and pharmacists in which we announced our application for prescription control was too non-committal. If we know about the side-effects, then an objective presentation of all observations together with medical interpretations and explanations must be clearly revealed. The physicians out here in general practice and in clinics surely know much more already, partly through congress lectures in Wiesbaden and discussions at regional meetings, and partly through reports from colleagues who were present on these occasions . . .

In my opinion we should take up a clear position. I have given up the initial tactics of not mentioning Contergan to regular users especially to small-scale consumers. Sooner or later the situation is bound to become acute and prevention is better than a cure.

In a circular letter of 30 April to 'Colleagues across the World' no mention at all was made of the much-discussed side-effects of thalidomide, and propaganda was carried through without any inhibitions. Although the word 'atoxic' disappeared from advertisements for Contergan as a sedative, it was smuggled into propaganda for some thalidomide combinations. This was demonstrated in an advertisement for Algosediv which appeared on 12 April and 14 April saying: 'The additional inhibition of the pain centre by the atoxic spasmolytic sedative Contergan.'

Dr Sievers and Dr Kelling also instructed the representative in Hanover to keep a watchful eye on doctors in health-resorts since 'a health-resort could be a horrible spreading place for the whole Federal Republic'.

Some representatives of the medical profession were evidently quite immune to the Stolberg Company's diplomacy. Professor Friedrich Tiemann, director of the Medical University Clinic in Bonn, wrote to Stolberg on 26 April: 'I sincerely regret this publication . . . The current discussion found there about the side-effects of Contergan cannot be minimized by your letter of 17 April. It seems to me that your letter tries to circumvent the central issue of the discussion and you apparently assume that receivers of your circular letter are so unintelligent and uneducated that they can be impressed by such simplified propaganda ... your letter constitutes a monstrous imputation and is unworthy of a serious enterprise.' At the Alsdorf hearings on 7 May 1969 Professor Tiemann stated that he had never received any answer to this letter.

Dr Hubert Gigglberger of Regensburg also wrote to Stolberg at the beginning of May in connection with his reporting cases of nerve damage. He considered it quite 'irresponsible to have still not withdrawn such a questionable drug from the market'. In view of the behaviour of Chemie Grünenthal he would not again prescribe any other of the company's products. In his opinion the trustworthiness of the whole enterprise was open to doubt.

Dr Gigglberger was henceforth labelled 'trouble-maker No. 1' of the South German area. A Grünenthal representative wrote to head office, 'We have to pull out this sick tooth before the infection spreads.'

By the end of May Grünenthal had received reports of about 1,300 cases of polyneuritis. That the incidence of polyneuritis could be quite high was illustrated by a physician from Nuremberg who claimed that half of his patients treated by Contergan Forte were now suffering from paraesthesia. Physicians demanded over and over again that thalidomide should be taken off the market, but in vain.

On 4 May Leufgens and von Schrader-Beielstein met the licensees in London, Distillers Ltd, who reported seventy-five to ninety cases of polyneuritis. It was now clear to the Stolberg company that the polyneuritis was not isolated to certain geographical regions in the Federal Republic as they had previously claimed. Meanwhile investigation by private detectives of physicians and damaged people was extended to

Professor Laubenthal, Dr Voss, Dr Buchholz, Dr Helsper, Dr Finke and Dr Frenkel. However Jahnke the detective could only report : 'In any case the whole action is not initiated by the industry but by the physicians.'

The situation was aggravated when in May three extremely unfavourable articles appeared in the medical literature. On 6 May Dr Frenkel's article 'Contergan – Side-Effects' appeared in *Die Medizinische Welt*; on 12 May an article 'Polyneuritic Syndrome after Long-Term Thalidomide Administration' by the neurologist, Professor Scheid, appeared in *Deutsche Medizinische Wochenschrift* and in the same number of that journal an article by Dr Raffauf of Essen was published 'Does Thalidomide (Contergan) Cause Damage?'

It is sufficient to give here the following passage from the Raffauf article :

Note Added in Proof : The latest prospectus distributed by the Chemie Grünenthal enterprise states, in addition to their earlier sales promotion material in which the drug was described as 'non-toxic', that after a shorter or longer use of Contergan oversensitivity reactions may appear. Sudden skin rashes, or continuous restlessness, trembling, itching or sensation of numbness in the hands or the feet may be indications of such side effects. After immediate withdrawal of the medication these allergic phenomena will disappear. We have seen more than twenty cases of the type described and heard of many others. In these cases we are concerned not only with harmless or transitory paraesthesia but with exceedingly persistent disorders of the type described, which certainly remain for a long time after the Contergan medication has been stopped. We very much question the claim that these effects can be considered as purely allergic.

Grünenthal resorted to denigration of the scientific competence of the authors of these articles, and described their reports as 'one-sided' and 'narrow-minded'.

Three new extremely critical articles appeared in the

German medical literature and at the end of May Dr von Schrader-Beielstein sent copies of these articles to the National Drug Company in Philadelphia and to Merrell in Cincinnati. In an enclosed letter von Schrader-Beielstein added deprecatingly: 'We regret that these authors have not taken an objective view of the problem.'

Obviously Dr Sievers had quite a different private opinion of Dr Raffauf, as seen from a report of December 1960 written by Dr Sievers: 'Dr Raffauf ... is a very sympathetic, serious and undoubtedly very objective man scientifically and I do not believe that he could be promoting the interests of another firm.'

The letter from the Ministry of Interior Affairs for the state Nordrhein-Westfalen still remained unanswered, which induced Dr Michael to make a written statement about the situation on 10 May.

Every day reports are accumulating of polyneuritic side-effects, which physicians set in relation to the use of Contergan. After Wiesbaden [a conference] and after the hostile publications the opinion is being publicly advanced that Contergan is responsible for such side-effects, some of which are serious. It is impossible for us to maintain that we are dealing with evil and insufficiently founded attacks against Contergan.

I now think that there is no doubt whatever that under certain circumstances, which I am at present unable to survey or explain, Contergan can cause nerve damage. I am convinced that the rest of the management of this firm will also have to subscribe to this view. If we start from this premise there is, in my opinion, only one possibility open to us in answering the letter of the Ministry of Interior Affairs in Dusseldorf: we cannot continue to claim as in earlier drafts of our reply that interpretations of these effects are incorrect; we must first make our standpoint clear, that in the present situation we have to accept that Contergan causes polyneuritic disturbance ...

I consider it quite impossible for the firm to officially adopt the standpoint that these reports are exclusively a matter of unqualified polemics. In the public interest members of the medical profession can and must have the right to follow up such matters in an accurate manner. With the means at our disposal it is impossible to continue to fight against 'official opinion'. Since requests for prescriptive control now exist in Dusseldorf, we should not for one minute delay in submitting a priority notification from our firm. I realize that prescription control will involve a considerable decrease in turnover for Grünenthal. However I must assume that such a loss will occur in any event if we avoid taking a decision …

In the present developmental stage of our firm I consider it an exceedingly heavy set-back if we appear to be more concerned with our turnover than with our responsibility as producers of pharmaceuticals. The reputation of our firm is as important on the positive side of our balance sheet as is the Contergan turnover in Deutsch marks.

We should immediately request prescription control from our side as any delay from us now could mean a greater loss than we can imagine at the moment.

The letter to the ministry of Nordrhein-Westfalen signed by Dr Werner and Dr Sievers did not contain any request for prescription enforcement. On the other hand, the letter contained a misrepresentation of the facts. Chemie Grünenthal claimed to have received no reports of polyneuritis before 15 February 1961, when in fact at that time over 300 such reports were known to the company. The etiology of the polyneuritis is treated in a very elusive manner.

We would like to assume on the grounds of the observations made up till now, that relatively few patients in the Federal Republic are to be found who show disturbances that with a high degree of probability can be connected with a long-term use of Contergan.

On a further visit to Dusseldorf Dr Nowel perceived that the letter had had little success in changing the ministry's unfavourable attitude; he therefore suggested that the following steps should be taken:

Submission of an application (for prescription control) *within the next 10 days;* i.e. Dr Tombergs can enclose our application to the records sent to Professor Kärber.

Advantage: Our application can then be back dated *officially* to February and it will then be dated before that of Dr Voss's presentation.

By this means we avoid Dr Voss's petition being the *first official record* at the Federal Health Board.

... We can also delay matters by discussing certain side-effects with Dr Tombergs ... if we make an application in the form recommended here and follow the timing plan I suggest then we are already in a better position where *Professor Kärber* is concerned and we shall be able to intervene by *delaying the discussions* about side-effects. *In this way we have the time factor in our hand.*

The legal department was extremely critical of these manipulations. Dr von Veltheim, the firm's legal representative, tried in vain to point out the dangers of the situation to Dr Hermann Wirtz, the director. A memorandum of 26 May 1961 reads:

At present we have twelve separate cases in which patients damaged by Contergan have already made compensation claims. In six cases we are on the verge of a law suit ... It is in our most urgent interests to as far as possible prevent every single law suit ... What the results will be can never be judged in advance. If we lose just one trial *that could be the first crack in the dam.*

Here is another memo from the legal department on 30 May:

'Critical Points' caused by Chemie Grünenthal's attitude until now. Our behaviour in relation to prescription enforcement could under circumstances be interpreted to our disadvantage – as incriminating Grünenthal.

In relation to possible legal complications, contact was made between representatives of Chemie Grünenthal and Gerling-Conzern, an insurance company. A memo of 12 June describing such a meeting reads:

With our consent, on 9 June, Dr Hubert (of Gerling) visited Professor Scheid, who has for long been engaged as medical expert for Gerling. On this occasion Scheid stated:

Cases of damage after Contergan occur regularly.

The damage is irreversible.

The directions for use enclosed in the Contergan-packages are in his opinion inadequate. They explain too little and they make no mention of the degree of severity of possible damage. According to Professor Scheid, Contergan should not be administered for more than three weeks under any circumstances. This should be stated on the labelling.

Prescription enforcement should anyway be indispensible.

In a circular letter sent out to 61,369 physicians and 9,000 pharmacists just after the articles by Frenkel, Scheid and Raffauf appeared, the word 'polyneuritis' is not mentioned at all. On the other hand, it claims that 'adverse effects of any kind are very rare, but the therapeutic effect is almost always attained to the desired degree'. Enclosed with this circular letter was a reprint of a work by Pogge entitled 'Review of Clinical Experience in 3,140 Cases' (see pp. 124–5). No mention was made of the fact that Dr Pogge was an employee of a licensee, nor was it made clear that the 3,140 cases described could not be used to support the claim of safety for long-term medication as was clear from the nature of the work itself. The areas of indication, as well as the conditions for use, were usually not comparable with those described in the recently published critical articles in Germany. On 8 June Dr Körbel in Cologne-Lindenthal wrote to Chemie Grünenthal saying, 'I thank you for your letter of 19 May 1961 [this was the letter directed to physicians in which the work of Pogge was enclosed]. I have to confess that I was somewhat surprised by the contents. Just one week before *Die Deutsche Medizinische Wochenschrift* published two articles about Contergan. Have you overlooked these articles or are the "3,140 investigations" cited in your letter supposed to wipe out the impression made by results from well-known clinics?'

During June it became clear that although most cases of polyneuritis occurred in elderly patients, younger age groups could also be damaged. Physicians aware of polyneuritis became more and more irritated by the sales promotion material sent out by Grünenthal. The sales centre in Dusseldorf reported : 'Most doctors blame us for not being more cautious in our circular letters and package inserts despite the medical profession's view that there are many aspects of Contergan which have not been clarified.'

Meanwhile Grünenthal's research department tried to reproduce polyneuritis in animal experiments, but without success. On this matter Dr Mückter had discussions with Dr Simon the neurologist and Professor Schimert in Munich. Both pointed out to Dr Mückter that the Contergan labelling was inadequate and that the producers must make clear that the drug was not suitable for long-term medication. Dr Mückter mentioned the negative results of animal experiments, but Professor Schimert declared that no conclusions about the nerve-damaging properties of thalidomide in man could be made from the fact that no damage had been found in animal experiments. Even in the chicken, which is very sensitive to such neurological effects, it is very difficult to demonstrate paraesthesia objectively. Dr Mückter also visited the neurologist, Dr Voss, and Professor Bay in Dusseldorf, and confirmed that 'both view these matters objectively and are evidently influenced by our competitors very little or not at all'.

Chemie Grünenthal also contacted a specialist on allergies, Professor Max Werner, who agreed to make a medical examination of several cases. He came to the conclusion that the Contergan-Polyneuritis could not be of an allergic nature under any conditions.

The Stolberg enterprise had more luck with the cooperation of Dr Winzenried in Hamburg, an old friend of Dr Sievers. His publication 'Concerning Disturbances of Sleep' was finally accepted by *Medizinische Klinik* and published on 16 June. The author stressed the safety of the drug which he claimed was illustrated by a suicide attempt in which a forty-year-old woman had taken 140 tablets of Contergan Forte. 'The patient slept soundly for ten hours and then remained in a state of somnolence for a further six hours. No disturbance of respiration or circulation was observed . . .'

This description corresponds very poorly with what actually happened. The patient in question was immediately transferred from Dr Winzenried's psychiatric clinic to the neurological clinic as her case was judged to be serious. In the neurological clinic her stomach was pumped and she was treated with the circulation stimulant Cardiazol. The figure of 140 tablets was never checked and in this case Dr Winzenried relied only on the information given by the patient. The woman succeeded in committing suicide a year later.

Winzenried also stated in his article that Contergan had proved to be efficient and safe during a three-year period, and that among 200 patients treated every night for more than a year no single case of polyneuritis had ever been observed. In this particular investigation no records were kept. The patients were not systematically examined by Dr Winzenried nor even questioned by him. The director of the clinic, Professor Burger-Prinz, further revealed in a letter to the Ministry of Interior Affairs of the State of Nordrhein-Westfalen on 29 May 1961 that the patients were never given

Contergan continuously for more than four to six weeks. When asked if he himself had ever tried Contergan, Winzenried testified before the court in Aachen that he had tried the drug on one occasion, but he refrained from all further experiments since the next day his skin itched and he was constipated. Winzenried further testified that the day after his article was published he observed a case of Contergan polyneuritis. By the end of August he had observed more cases which he reported to Chemie Grünenthal. Nevertheless the Stolberg company continued to use reprints of his articles for purposes of sales promotion, as evidence against the neurotoxic action of thalidomide.

On 8 June Dr Nowel of Chemie Grünenthal had a meeting with the Privy Councillor, Dr Hans Tombergs, at the State Ministry for Interior Affairs in Dusseldorf. Dr Tombergs seriously reproached Grünenthal for not having kept the Ministry informed in an adequate manner. He also resented the 'strange attitude of the firm' in formulating the application for prescription control. Dr Tombergs guessed that these 'manipulations were intended unjustly to transfer responsibility for the belated application to the Ministry'. On this occasion Dr Nowel had to admit that he had been given incomplete information by the management. Dr Nowel describes this doubtlessly unpleasant meeting in his report :

In contrast to all our previous visits, the atmosphere was chilly if not even icy from the beginning of the meeting ... To begin with Dr Tombergs on his side observed that the much greater extent of side-effects which had meanwhile come to his knowledge, as well as the circular letter to physicians which Dr Voss had mentioned, constituted 'confirmation that we had by no means kept the ministry sufficiently informed about the Contergan problem'.

During the conversation that followed, which lasted for an hour, Dr Nowel tried desperately to defend his company and to calm Tombergs down. He assured Dr Tombergs that the first correspondence between Dr Voss and Chemie Grünenthal concerning polyneuritis dated from the autumn of 1960. Dr Nowel continued :

On returning from the meeting with Dr Tombergs an inspection was made of the records as well as the documentation of Dr Sievers because of the hints of an alleged existing correspondence between Grünenthal and Dr Voss. *Regrettable result.* An exchange of correspondence had in fact taken place during the period October to December 1959. In this first letter Dr Voss pointed out that polyneuritis could be diagnosed in patients after a long use of Contergan.

Dr Nowel was furious with the company management.

Such a case of making an inadequately informed representative responsible for negotiation with the ministries results in the undermining of the firm's reputation as well as the reputation of the representative himself.

It should be pointed out that the effects on possible recourse demands will under certain conditions be incalculable.

Besides his written report Dr Nowel also protested verbally to his superior Leufgens, and said that he 'personally felt disavowed'. Leufgens replied, 'This question does not revolve around the good name of a colleague. The firm is our sole concern in this case.'

A visiting salesman reported to Stolberg on 14 July about a physician who had a number of patients with polyneuritis. This doctor showed special concern since 'he had recently had a patient in whom severe paraesthesia had occurred. In addition a depression developed which resulted in a suicide attempt'.

More and more hospitals which had previously used Contergan refused to use the drug any longer and sales showed a definite tendency to decline. While the turnover for May gave a net income of DM 1,373,806 the sales had gone down to DM 1,088,647 in July. Hostile articles continued to appear. An article entitled 'Polyneuritis after Contergan' by Dr Becker was published in *Der Nervenarzt*. In it it was stated:

At all events there is no longer any doubt that Contergan Forte induces a 'toxic polyneuritis' which is surely widely independent of dispositional and other exogenic factors, and it may even develop, not as a result of overdosage, but evidently in a relatively short time after administration of superficially inoffensive daily doses.

In as far as we have been able to investigate our patients we have to count on permanent damage.

Similar conclusions can be found in the article of Dr Voss which appeared in *Munchener Medizinische Wochenschrift*. And finally, during the same month, the theme was taken up by C. J. Rübsaam in the Dutch medical journal *Nederlands Tijdechrift vor Geneeskunde* on 22 July.

Doctors and scientists were now losing confidence in the firm in still wider circles. A letter from Professor Laubenthal to the head office on 12 July may be cited as characteristic as it expresses the resentment felt by many members of the medical profession at that time:

It appears still more remarkable to us that Grünenthal should itself refer to polyneuritis-like symptoms in the circular letter of 7 April, implying that these symptoms are of a transient nature which will disappear shortly after interruption of the medication; this is absolutely contrary to our own results. We find it so utterly impossible to reconcile this with our own findings, of which we have notified you, that we ... cannot consider that objective cooperation is any longer warranted, and we must assume that you and your firm do not in reality consider our cooperation to be of any value ...

I sincerely regret that your action has made trustworthy cooperation on our part quite impossible.

In July the risk of law suits increased and the legal department made great efforts to settle all questions out of court. The Grünenthal lawyers wrote, 'In any case we must recognize that the question pertaining to the works dealing with chronic toxicity may be a weak point.' The memo continues:

In any case our arguments ... would not be satisfactory in explaining why we made no changes in the package inserts ... until September 1960. Until that date it had said, among other things, 'Chemically this N-phthalylglutamic acid-imide, which under the name of Contergan and Contergan Forte respectively, is at your disposal, being an efficient, tasteless and atoxic sedative and hypnoticum.' It is obvious that we shall be accused of contributory negligence in omitting to give any kind of warnings on the package insert, in case a patient has taken Contergan between May and September 1960 and has developed polyneuritis as a result.

Regarding the change of the package inserts in November 1960 von Veltheim pointed out that in a possible future trial the opponents would argue that the change in the package insert should have been stated on the package itself, since a patient who has been buying the drug for a long time would not bother to read the package inserts any more ...

We have also to consider that medical experts will raise serious doubts about the last sentence in which allergic reactions are said to disappear after immediate interruption of medication.

However, the package insert of April 1961 could be considered as a retrograde step since the warning about side-effects which until then had been included under the heading 'Notice' was now transferred to the extensive section 'Mode of Action and Tolerance' ...

The lawyers conclude:

It is quite clear that the trial risk in relation to our guilt is far larger than we could have foreseen in the first instance. Under these circumstances we do not seem justified in going through a trial on this matter.

Following this advice Chemie Grünenthal, for the first time, paid out compensation to prevent a public legal dispute. On 28 July 1961 Dr Kersten-Thiele, a minister in Dusseldorf received the sum of DM 750.

Nervousness spread rapidly amongst the Grünenthal staff when in July they heard that *Der Spiegel*, the pugnacious, active and widely circulated magazine, had begun to turn its attention to Contergan.

Even Dr Mückter, who until the end of June had been a 'hawk' about the question of prescription, now seriously doubted that it was any longer possible to delay its enforcement. It was at a staff meeting on 14 July 1961, that Dr Mückter declared: 'If I were a doctor, I would not prescribe Contergan any more. Gentlemen, I warn you. I will not repeat what has already been said before. I see great dangers.'

With the export business a careful policy was undertaken not to alarm unduly the foreign partners 'but', it is stated in the instructions for the foreign section, 'we have to take into account that the side-effects mentioned above will also be known in other countries'. Accordingly, licensees and representatives outside Germany were informed in stages and new propaganda material was printed.

Dr von Schrader-Beielstein, who spoke for continuing the hard line, was upset by the pessimism of some of the staff members. 'The draft for a tightened up package insert is tantamount to helplessness. Dr Mückter will ruin Chemie Grünenthal with this text,' von Schrader-Beielstein exclaimed.

At the end of July the old package inserts were still in use.

Meanwhile visiting salesmen were having a tough time. One salesman reported: 'My discussion with Dr Zeh, the head physician, was very depressing. At least at the beginning. He advocated rather queer ideas and was sharply blaming partly me personally and partly blaming the firm ... The head physician said he would prescribe whatever he chose and he did not owe the industry any account whatever when he stopped using a drug.'

Dr Michael of Grünenthal visited the University Neurological Clinic in Münster on 1 August in a desperate attempt to engage Dr Max Engelmeier's support for a favourable statement about thalidomide. Dr Engelmeier had already observed Contergan polyneuritis and firmly declined.

Favourable statements were still to come from a group of Austrian doctors, Rett, Schober, Roth and Birkmeyer. These physicians still supported the safety of thalidomide and claimed to have observed no nerve damage. When Rett published his paper he sent it first to Chemie Grünenthal for approval. In a statement to the Austrian Ministry of Social Welfare Dr Birkmeyer wrote on 3 August:

To the aforesaid question, I should like to say we have clinically tested Softenon (Austrian brand name for thalidomide) tablets and Softenon Forte in the local department for three years and six months ... Disturbances of the liver and blood picture could not be observed by us. Furthermore, no (poly)neuritic effects were noted using this dosage.

Two weeks later Dr Birkmeyer wrote about his experiments to Chemie Grünenthal:

In this case of the disturbances observed we are concerned with a toxic polyneuropathia ...

My personal opinion is that Softenon, similarly to other chemical compounds, may cause toxic neurological damage when used in high dosages and over long periods.

Finally it should be added that the type of patient studied by these Austrian doctors consisted to a large extent of cases who already had nerve or brain damage. It is clear that objective diagnosis of polyneuritis would be difficult to make in such cases.

The busy life of most overworked practising physicians does not give them time to follow the literature continuously, and a visiting salesman reported on 18 August: 'Most doctors did not know anything about the critical publications. Nor have I called these gentlemen's attention to the same.'

The responsibilities of a drug manufacturer in Germany were well realized by the legal department as evidenced by a letter of 5 July to Coles, the commercial partner in Brussels.

In Germany it is the duty of the manufacturer to inform the physician in an objective way of the advantages and side-effects of a prescription drug. The responsibility for the use of such a drug then rests with the physician. However if this is neglected ... the physician is freed of his responsibility for the use of the drug and consequently the manufacturer is responsible for possible damage.

In another memo the legal representative, Dr von Veltheim, warned:

When the need for a product, which has apparently caused damage to health, to be on prescription is for one reason or another not announced, the entire responsibility as well as the giving of compensation lies with the producer ...

It is well known we have not managed to produce a single publication in the field of neurology capable of refuting the findings of the authors mentioned [i.e. the five critical articles published by Scheid, Frenkel, Raffauf, Voss and Becker].

Dr von Veltheim was in close touch with Jahnke, the private detective, who reported regularly on physicians and damaged patients. During August Heinz Gehde, the governmental official from Dusseldorf who had bitterly attacked Grünenthal, was carefully watched.

In the same month several indemnifying payments were made to individually damaged persons in sums varying from

DM 200 to DM 2,000. The payments were deducted from a special 'Contergan damage account'.

Dr Mückter soon regained his courage and at an internal meeting on 31 August declared that 'up to now Contergan is the best sleeping pill in the world'.

On 1 August all drugs containing thalidomide were put under prescription enforcement in the states of Nordrhein-Westfalen, Hessen and Württenberg. On 16 August Contergan polyneuritis was made known to a wider sector of the lay public, for the first time, by an article in *Der Spiegel*. Chemie Grünenthal evidently considered it too risky to continue publicising the 'atoxicity' of thalidomide even in the less developed countries. In a letter of 21 August to the Astra SA in Argentina Grünenthal urged the company to stop using such expressions as 'non-toxic' (*atoxico*) in view of the widespread knowledge of neurological side-effects caused by the drug.

During September 1961 the reports of nerve damage exceeded 2,400. The true number was concealed from representatives of the licensees of USA, England and Sweden at a meeting held in Stolberg on 4–5 September. At this meeting the English reported about 109 cases, whereas Astra of Sweden had so far only heard of one case. On 30 September a new article appeared with reports of polyneuritis, this time in the *British Medical Journal*, which has a wide international circulation. Through Grünenthal's efforts to minimize the risk and seriousness of nerve damage, many pharmacies still continued to sell Contergan freely in spite of the prescription duty.

On 1 October Dr von Schrader-Beielstein, Dr Sievers and Dr von Veltheim reported that in seven states the drug could still be purchased freely, but that so far eighty-nine demands for compensation had been made. Of these cases fifteen had been settled, including one case outside Germany. In the fourteen cases inside Germany a total of DM 32,013.45 had been paid out. In spite of the serious situation general feeling at the time was optimistic. The application for prescription had created a good impression with many physicians and better times could be hoped for again.

Dr Frenkel, regarded as the company's most dangerous enemy, was given special attention. A woman was smuggled into Dr Frenkel's clinic on the pretext of suffering from Contergan polyneuritis. She was unable to report anything incorrect in the neurologist's behaviour which could be used against him.

During October Grünenthal became more and more concerned about the legal aspects of thalidomide damage. Serious efforts were now made to put the drug on prescription in all states. Positive legal medical reports from cooperative doctors and scientists were also collected and reviewed with a view to use in possible future criminal law suits. Intensive investigations of the legal literature for precedents also took place, but it was discovered that up till then no verdict had ever been pronounced by a German court in a similar case.

Cooperation between Grünenthal and certain physicians and scientists was not going very smoothly. Professor Laubenthal complained to Professor Scheid in a letter of 3 October: 'However, I am strongly opposed to such cases being deliberately directed by Grünenthal to a north German clinic, when people of their own accord have not noticed any Contergan damage. The behaviour of this enterprise is in several respects exceedingly strange and remarkable.'

The information given to business partners outside the country varied considerably, depending on what was thought to be the extent of general awareness in the area concerned. In the general propaganda for thalidomide in West Africa the drug was still described as completely harmless. At the end of November about 3,000 cases of nerve damage were known to the company.

In a note of 19 April 1962 von Veltheim estimated that a maximum of 4,000 persons were suffering from nerve damage within the Federal Republic and that Chemie Grünenthal had to face the possibility of compensation claims amounting to a total of about DM 12 millions. According to some German specialists the estimated number of affected people given by Dr von Veltheim was far too low a figure. Professor Lenz thought some 40,000 people would be nearer to the truth.

But worse was to come. Evidence began to accumulate of a far more devastating effect – the birth of deformed children to mothers who had taken thalidomide during the early stage of pregnancy.

5

Thalidomide Babies: Chemie Grünenthal Withdraws the Drug

In October 1960 Dr W. Kosenow and Dr R. A. Pfeiffer, members of the staff of the Institute of Human Genetics in Münster, exhibited two grossly deformed infants at the annual meeting of paediatrics held in Kassel. The two physicians had never seen such a combination of malformations in a single infant. Because the long bones of the arms were stunted, the arms were so short that the hands seemed to project almost directly from the shoulders. The legs were less affected but showed similar distortions. A large hemangioma (abnormality of the blood vessels of the skin) was disfiguring the face of both children and in addition one of them had a duodenal stenosis (constriction of the first part of the small intestine). At this meeting the malformation picture was considered as a new clinical syndrome.

This type of malformation of the extremities is known as phocomelia (from the Greek *phoke* = seal, and *melos* = limb). There was no indication in the family history of either child to indicate that heredity had played a part in the condition. Phocomelia is normally so rare that few physicians had ever seen such a case before in their lives. The exhibit did not attract a great deal of attention, however, which in retrospect seems surprising, since by that time many paediatric clinics in West Germany had recently come across several cases of this rare malformation.

A clue to the actual frequency of this type of malformation, observed before the introduction of thalidomide, may be found in the monograph 'Congenital Deformities of the Upper Extremities' by Birch-Jensen (Copenhagen, 1949). This material may be regarded as almost complete concerning deformities of the extremities in the Danish population. Only *one* bilateral phocomelia-like case is included with three fingers on each hand and a congenital heart deformity. This single case was found in a survey of the population of 4 million. Nor does any other investigation indicate that before the introduction of thalidomide this type of congenital malformation was more frequent than one in 4 million in other countries.

With the growing recognition that thalidomide could produce grave side-effects in adult human beings (as we have seen in the previous two chapters), it was natural to wonder if it could affect the foetus when taken in pregnancy. The first inquiry of this kind passed on to Chemie Grünenthal seems to have come through the National Drug Company (a subdivision of Richardson-Merrell) in a letter dated 23 February which was answered very vaguely by Dr von Schrader-Beielstein on 23 March 1961 :

We have read the memorandum of Dr Stevenson with great interest and would like to inform you that we ourselves have no experience regarding the question of Contergan and pregnancy and the transplacental passage of Contergan to the foetus. Our experience until now in the field of gynaecology is mainly reviewed in the work of Blasiu, and will be extended in a second work to appear this year. Animal experiments relating to the passage of Contergan to the foetuses may perhaps be very valuable, although we do not assume any influence on the foetus, judging from what we know of animal experiments.

In spite of their having no information whatever on the possible effects of thalidomide on the foetus, Grünenthal had been *specifically recommending* the use of the drug during pregnancy. (Covering letter of 1 August 1958.)

During July 1961 Chemie Grünenthal was again confronted with the question of the safety of thalidomide during pregnancy. This time the question was taken up by the head physician of the gynaecological department of the hospital in Heilbrunn. Dr Werner and Dr Sievers replied, 'On the basis of experience obtained so far we should like to say that there is no evidence that Contergan passes the placental barrier to the foetuses.'

Similarly, Hypia, a visiting saleswoman from Finland, forwarded to Grünenthal the following questions from a Finnish doctor:

(1) Does Softenon (Finnish brand name for thalidomide), when given to female patients, pass the placenta?

(2) If the drug passes the placenta to the embryo, can it exert harmful effects on the child?

(3) In which part of the organism is Softenon broken down?

Dr Mückter gave the following answer to each of these questions:

To (1) not known.

To (2) unlikely.

To (3) evidently by the liver.

These questions were later taken up in 'internal reports' by Dr Werner. He asked von Schrader-Beielstein, 'Are any of our licensees making any investigations about these questions?'

Dr von Schrader-Beielstein replied, 'No!'

During the early part of 1961 the Stolberg company was told of a Dr Davin Chou in Singapore who had successfully used thalidomide for the treatment of pregnant women. No details were given about the stage of pregnancy treated, the dosage used or the frequency of therapy. Finally, and most significantly, the brief report was concerned only with the effects on the pregnant women themselves, and no mention was made of any possible effects on the foetuses. This lack of any specific detail did not deter Dr Werner from distributing a circular letter to 'co-workers throughout the world' saying, 'In a private clinic in Singapore Softenon was given to pregnant women who tolerated the drug well.'

Even if the responsible medical staff at Chemie Grünenthal had really overlooked the extensive material already existing in medical literature, and had consequently no knowledge of the possible hazards to the foetus associated with the drug treatment during pregnancy, their attention was drawn to this possibility by sources outside their company in specific relation to thalidomide on at least three separate occasions: by Richardson-Merrell in the USA in connection with the FDA's request for evidence for safety of the unborn child; by the doctor in Heilbrunn; and lastly in the letter from Hypia in Finland.

During 1961 increasing attention was paid to the sudden increase of this phocomelia in West Germany. Studies were started in a number of research centres, by Lenz in Hamburg, by Weicker in Bonn, by Wiedemann in Kiel and by Pfeiffer and Kosenow in Münster, each undertaking special studies. Some doctors assumed that the cause was radioactive fall-out from nuclear weapon tests. When in September 1961 Wiedemann presented a paper describing twenty-seven cases in the Kiel area, he suggested that amongst the constant flow of new drugs thrust on the market one chemical might have been involved. However Wiedemann had obtained incorrect information that no case of phocomelia had been found in the Bremen area, and he had no access to the correlated figures for the consumption of various chemicals and the frequency of these malformations. Dr Widukind Lenz, then active as a paediatrician in Hamburg, had been investigating the possible causes of these curious malformations for some time. 'I was convinced that the cause must be some chemical sold by drugstores or food shops,' he told Dr Nilsson, 'and I thought for some time it could be a detergent.'

Initially the results of the inquiries were depressing and at the beginning of November Lenz concluded that drugs could be eliminated as the cause. 'We had not found any drug in our case records up to that time which was common to all cases,' Dr Lenz said. The whole investigation could have ended right at that point. 'Then, one day a mother of a deformed child told me that she had taken Contergan during pregnancy. We started to question the other women again and it soon became apparent that, indeed, most of them had taken this drug. Checking of receipts and medical records gave additional support.'

At a meeting of West German paediatricians held at Dusseldorf on 18 November the awareness of the mysterious outbreak of phocomelia was widespread. Dr Lenz disclosed that he had tentatively traced these malformations to the intake of a widely distributed, newly introduced drug. After the meeting Lenz told some of his colleagues engaged in collecting information on the causes of phocomelia from the University clinics of Dusseldorf, Bonn, Münster and Cologne, that the drug in question was identical to Contergan, the German trade name for the sedative thalidomide produced by Chemie Grünenthal GmbH in Stolberg. Dr Wiedemann and Dr Kosenow had been notified of Lenz's suspicions some days earlier. At the meeting Lenz stated that he had definitely been able to trace the intake of this specific drug during early pregnancy to fourteen of the twenty-one cases of grave deformity of the extremities. In three cases it was very likely that intake of this drug had occurred, and in one case Dr Lenz had obtained information from the hospital that another mild sedative, Doriden (Gluthetimide), had been consumed.

However, an inspection of the original hospital records showed that in this case also Contergan, and not Doriden, had been prescribed to the woman. In the remaining three cases no clue was yet available to a possible consumption of the suspected drug. (In fact, at a later date, Contergan intake could also be virtually proved in these three cases.) Dr Lenz's original material had to be considered as strong circumstantial evidence for a causal relationship between Contergan and phocomelia.

At the Dusseldorf meeting Lenz stated: 'Both as a human being and a citizen I cannot take the responsibility of keeping silent about my observations. In view of the incalculable human, psychological, legal and financial consequences I have, after consultation with a paediatrician and a pharmacologist, informed the manufacturers of my observations and told them of my personal opinion that the drug should be immediately withdrawn until its harmlessness is firmly established,' and added finally, 'Each month's delay in sorting this out means the birth of perhaps fifty to one hundred horribly mutilated children.'

On the 15 November 1961, before his report in Dusseldorf, Dr Lenz had been in touch with Dr Mückter, the medical director of the research laboratories of Chemie Grünenthal, who gave the impression of showing little interest in taking any immediate action about Contergan, despite the fact that Dr Lenz made no secret of his concern that every day of delay in withdrawing the drug was a deliberate experiment in human teratology (science dealing with the induction of malformations to the foetus). Lenz therefore sent a letter dealing with the problem, which began:

Yesterday in a telephone conversation with your scientific adviser, Dr Mückter, I informed you of certain observations. Because of the importance I attach to this matter, I invited a colleague to be a witness of the conversation. Since I got the impression that

Dr Mückter did not seem to attach the importance to the matter which I feel it has, I would like, in my own defence, to repeat here a short account of my observations.

Then comes a summary of his observations, and the letter ends:

Naturally I fully realize that these details do not amount to complete proof of an etiological connection between the medicament and the malformations. Nevertheless, such a connection is conceivable. In view of the incalculable human, psychological, legal and financial consequences of this problem it is, in my own opinion, indefensible to wait for a strict scientific proof of the harmfulness or harmlessness, as the case may be, of Contergan. I consider it necessary to withdraw the medicament from sale immediately until its harmlessness as a teratogenic agent in man is conclusively proved.

Dr Lenz was cautious about the final proof of the teratogenecity of Contergan. This is understandable since such an accusation might have involved considerable personal risk. When Grünenthal took no immediate action Dr Lenz decided to make his observations public at the meeting in Dusseldorf. On 20 November Dr Lenz was visited by three representatives from Grünenthal, Dr von Veltheim, Dr von Schrader-Beielstein and Dr Michael. They gave Dr Lenz the impression that they were more interested in certain legal aspects of the problem than in the material collected so far. They also made it clear that Chemie Grünenthal could take legal action against Dr Lenz to protect the company's reputation. However, on that occasion it was decided that the issue should be taken up with the health authorities in Hamburg. At that meeting, which took place at 2.30 on 20 November 1961, Dr Lenz stated: 'I will show you my material and explain it in detail. I will refrain from any conclusions but leave these entirely to you.' The three representatives of Chemie Grünenthal firmly refused to listen to a detailed presentation of Dr Lenz's material, but insisted instead that he should hand over all his records. One of the officials deplored 'the form in which the questions were directed to Dr Lenz' by the company representatives. The Grünenthal people described the issue as 'murdering a drug by spreading rumour'. When asked directly whether the company planned to withdraw the drug from the market, their reply was that no such action was planned.

As a result of the meeting the Hamburg health authorities sent a cable to the Ministry of the Interior for Nordrhein-Westfalen in Dusseldorf giving the essential details of Lenz's suspicions. According to West German law legal responsibility for the activities of Chemie Grünenthal came under the jurisdiction of the authorities for the area where Grünenthal had its factory. On the same day as the meeting with the Hamburg health authorities, Grünenthal sent out 66,957 copies of a sales promotion leaflet in which the advantages of Contergan were again underlined : 'Contergan is a safe drug.'

The next morning Dr Lenz presented a detailed documentation to Chemie Grünenthal which showed that in his cases intake of Contergan during early pregnancy could be proved by hospital records. Lenz also gave von Veltheim and Dr von Schrader-Beielstein photocopies of all his records, from which every name had been deleted. Lenz made these deletions as he was afraid that undue pressure might be exerted on the families involved.

Dr Lenz said that 'he would not give Contergan any chance to be freed from suspicion (of causing malformations) and that he would make the same statement to the health authorities'.

On 21 November 1961 contact was made between Grünenthal and Professor Soehring and Dr Winzenried, to discuss Dr Lenz's observations. Both men pointed to the scientific integrity of Dr Lenz. Winzenried further urged the firm to withdraw the drug. Two days later the medical-scientific department began preparations for new propaganda material for the use of Contergan in paediatrics.

On 24 November at 10 a.m., a meeting took place at the Ministry for Interior Affairs of the State Nordrhein-Westfalen in an atmosphere of bitterness. Officials from the ministry were present, and representatives of Chemie Grünenthal, Dr Nowel and Dr von Schrader-Beielstein, as well as Dr Lenz and a solicitor, Schulte-Hillen. The Grünenthal employees arrived first. When Dr Lenz later arrived with the solicitor, Dr von Schrader-Beielstein asked if Schulte-Hillen was to represent Dr Lenz. The solicitor replied that he had no connection with Dr Lenz but was solely representing himself since he had a deformed child. Von Schrader-Beielstein immediately objected to the presence of the lawyer, who was forced to leave the room. Outside the room Dr Tombergs of the ministry explained that the authorities had to be very cautious in the present situation. During the conference that followed Dr Karl underlined the severity and possible implications of the disclosures made by Dr Lenz, and tried to induce the company to withdraw the drug immediately. The Grünenthal representatives stated that they had no authority to do so but that they would contact their superiors for further instructions during the lunch break. After lunch the company attitude considerably hardened. The Grünenthal representatives even threatened that the company might raise compensation claims if the authorities prohibited the drug. They then demanded that Dr Lenz should leave the conference. After he had done so it was declared that the company would be prepared to supply the packages containing Contergan with a special notice reading, 'Not to be taken during pregnancy'. The authorities pointed out that such measures would be inadequate, but Chemie Grünenthal were not willing to make any further concessions. However, the authorities were confident that suspicion of the horrible properties of Contergan would leak out to the lay press and create great pressure on the company from public opinion.

At an internal meeting in Stolberg on 25 November, Dr von Schrader-Beielstein declared that in his opinion the withdrawal of the drug could not be postponed any longer. Dr Mückter held the opposite opinion, in spite of the fact that he had information from the British licensee that another physician in Australia, quite independently from Lenz, had established a possible causal relationship between thalidomide in pregnancy and certain malformations. The delaying tactics of Chemie Grünenthal were put an end to when on 26 November the newspaper *Welt am Sonntag* disclosed the catastrophe to the public under the headline 'Malformations from Tablets – Alarming Suspicion of Physician against World-Wide Distributed Drug'. *Welt am Sonntag* cited most of the arguments put forward by Dr Lenz in his letter to Chemie Grünenthal of 16 November: 'Every month's delay in clarification means that fifty to one hundred horribly mutilated children will be born.' Lenz's demands that the drug should immediately be withdrawn were also repeated by the journal. It continued: 'Immediate withdrawal of the preparation! So far it has not been withdrawn! Should this warning, prompted by a sense of medical responsibility, be ignored? It is high time that the authorities intervened and without delay too!'

This article in *Welt am Sonntag* revealed that 'pharmacological bomb' for the first time to a horrified public.

On the same day Chemie Grünenthal decided to withdraw the drug from the market. They gave their reason for doing so as fear of the strength of public opinion which might be created by the *Welt am Sonntag* article, rather than the actual damage itself. On the 27 November Chemie Grünenthal wrote to the Drug Commission of the German Medical Association: 'Because press reports have undermined the basis of the scientific discussion, we have decided to withdraw Contergan from the market immediately.' A letter of 22 December 1961, to the licensee in Japan, reads: 'Due to continuous pressure from Dr Lenz on the health authorities, and above all, because of the press campaign in Germany which we feared might break out, and which in fact did break out, we were finally forced ... to withdraw Contergan from the market on the 25 November.'

On 27 November the withdrawal of Contergan was carried out, and with it at the explicit demand of the Ministry for Interior Affairs of Nordrhein-Westfalen the other thalidomide-containing drugs.

Simultaneously the West German Ministry of Health issued a firm but cautious statement that Contergan was suspected as the major factor in causing phocomelia. Radio and television stations and the front pages of newspapers promptly spread announcements warning women not to take the drug.

At the beginning of 1961 Professor Hans Weicker had already been busy collecting information from the University Paediatric Clinics in Bonn, concerning the sudden increase of phocomelia. Weicker had information from fifty families with children with these malformations. The mothers were asked which drugs they had taken during pregnancy. 22 per cent stated they had taken Contergan during early pregnancy. When, on 18 November, Weicker heard about Lenz's conclusions he again got in touch with the same mothers on the telephone and instead of asking which drug they had taken, he mentioned the names of some common drugs on the market, including that of Contergan, and inquired whether they had taken any of these. 70 per cent of the mothers then said they had taken Contergan, whereas of the mothers in a control group with normal children only 2 per cent stated they had used Contergan. The result clearly demonstrates some of the difficulties associated with such a retrospective inquiry. It was difficult for the women to remember the names of drugs, but when certain names were mentioned to them it was easier to identify which pharmaceuticals had been taken.

On the other side of the world Dr William G. McBride, a young doctor at Crown Street Women's Hospital, Sydney, Australia, saw his first case of phocomelia on 4 May 1961. McBride, 32 at the time, had received a postgraduate grant to study foetal salvage, the causes of miscarriage, and the effect of hormones on abortion. On looking through the mother's records he could find no clue to the cause of these malformations. Within three weeks he came across another case exhibiting the same kind of abnormalities. Since McBride was aware that this type of malformation was thought to be exceedingly rare, the birth of two babies suffering from phocomelia at his hospital within the same month struck him as more than mere coincidence.

McBride began a detailed study to find a common exogenous cause of the malformations. Fortunately both mothers had visited the hospital clinic regularly, and every medication received during pregnancy was included in the records. A closer inspection revealed that in both cases Distaval (the trade name for thalidomide in the Commonwealth) had been administered during the early stage of pregnancy, when it is known that the embryo is quite sensitive to disturbances of development. Dr McBride had actually been conducting a study on thalidomide as a drug for treating morning sickness in early pregnancy. Although he had strong suspicions that there might be a causal relationship between the intake of this drug and phocomelia, he had little material evidence to support this idea. Since the drug had been advertised as a completely harmless drug lacking any kind of toxicity his colleagues met his inquiries with scepticism.

Another deformed baby was born – and again an inquiry into the mother's records showed that Distaval had been consumed. McBride now succeeded in convincing his superiors of the possible relationship between the 'completely harmless' sleeping pill and phocomelia; the drug was withdrawn from use in the hospital in May 1961 and investigations carried out on the women who had taken the drug.

As early as April, McBride notified the representatives of Distillers in Australia about his suspicions. Dr McBride's observations never reached head office – at least Distillers in England claim to have first heard of the Australian phocomelia cases as a result of a visit made by the company's representatives to McBride, and a letter was sent to London which arrived on 21 November 1961.

In October and November McBride saw three more cases which also gave positive indication that the mothers had been taking thalidomide during pregnancy. After the Distillers branch was again notified, officials from head office visited McBride, and as Distillers of England had received information about similar observations in Germany, the head office decided to withdraw thalidomide from the British market on 27 November 1961. On 16 December 1961 Dr McBride's observations were published in the *Lancet*, and the *Australian Medical Journal* published a similar article on 23 December.

In contrast to Chemie Grünenthal, which was only forced to withdraw the drug as a result of public opinion, the staff of Distillers showed quite a different attitude to the possible consequences to their consumers. This is demonstrated by a letter of 11 December 1961 from the Distillers' medical adviser to Dr C. N. Brown.

Thank you for your letter of the 5 December in which you refer to the reasons for our withdrawing Distaval from the market.

We took this action after receiving two reports, one from Australia and the other from Germany, that foetal deformity was thought to be associated with the administration of the drug in early pregnancy. These reports were passed on to us from commercial sources in the countries concerned and the data available to us is still incomplete. However, the type of deformity in the six cases from Australia and the eight from Germany follows the same pattern, in that they all involved limb deformities. In addition, the six Australian cases had associated duodenal atresia. It is still far from clear what other drugs were taken during the relevant period, but we felt that the coincidental report of such an effect, even though it is no more than suggested at the moment, was so serious that we had no alternative but to withdraw the drug immediately.

During a meeting of 7 December between Grünenthal and Distillers the representatives again mentioned the possibility of resuming production of Contergan on 11 December 1961. Dr Dennis Burley of Distillers wrote to Dr Struthers at Southern General Hospital in Glasgow:

I realize that even if it is proved that Distaval can cause congenital malformations it scarcely affects your own usage and it may be possible for us shortly to re-introduce Distaval in a limited way to hospitals. Whether we do so will to some extent depend on representations made both to this Company and to medical journals. But I am sure you will agree that it would be most unwise to make the drug generally available as one would then not have the remotest idea who was getting it.

During 1961 Dr A. L. Speirs of the Stirling Royal Infirmary and Falkirk and District Royal Infirmary had observed ten cases of children with limb malformations in Stirlingshire. In September Dr Speirs started to analyse these cases to find a common factor which might be the cause.

The results were reported in the *Lancet* on 10 February 1962 :

> The appearance of so many cases of a very rare condition within such a small area virtually amounted to an epidemic and some noxious factor was obviously operative. As the limb buds usually appear at the sixth to seventh week and have formed by the eighth week, this factor would operate about this time. The mothers were questioned particularly about exposure to radiation, nutrition, infection, and drugs. At this time no positive results were forthcoming.

> With the announcement of the withdrawal of thalidomide further investigations were immediately started despite the fact that several of the mothers denied having had drugs during the first three months of pregnancy. Three lines of approach were made. Firstly, all the patients' family doctors were contacted. Secondly, the mothers themselves were visited and shown tablets of both strengths of thalidomide to see whether they could remember having taken these. Finally, with the permission of the family doctors, the clerk to the local executive council was approached and he agreed to have his staff search the year's prescription forms for the area. By this method it was hoped that documentary proof would be obtained of the drugs prescribed, the dosage, and the dates when they were taken.

Speirs continued with his results :

> Evidence was obtained that of these 10 mothers 8 took thalidomide during pregnancy. One had a sedative, the nature of which is unknown, and in one case there is no evidence that the mother had any drug at all. However, it became apparent early in the investigation that statements by the patient or the doctor that no thalidomide had been taken could not necessarily be accepted. In view of this, it remains quite possible that the 2 mothers for whom there was no proof did in fact have this drug.

In Germany during the period following the withdrawal Chemie Grünenthal tried by all possible means to minimize the effect of the catastrophe. Scientists, physicians and pharmacists who did not conform to the official Grünenthal line were described as 'demagogues', 'trouble-makers', 'opportunists' or 'fanatics'. In a memo of a meeting of 27 December 1961 the attack on Dr Lenz continued:

When considering how many countless psychic traumas have been produced by the contribution to the discussion of Dr Lenz and still more by the sensational reports of the irresponsible gutter press, I cannot regard Dr Lenz's behaviour as responsible. What Goethe once has stated applies to him as well as to Dr Frenkel: 'Idiots and clever people are both equally harmless. Those halfwits and half-educated people who always recognize only half-truths alone are dangerous.'

When Dr T. Jones and Dr R. T. Stormont of Richardson-Merrell and Dr L. Mitchell of Frank W. Horner Ltd (Canada) were on an emergency visit to Stolberg on 1 December 1961, the manner in which Chemie Grünenthal tried to distort facts and cast doubt on Dr Lenz is illustrated by the report of Leonard Mitchell dated 19 December 1961. A footnote in the report reads as follows

Dr Lenz is associated with the paediatric clinic of the University of Hamburg and has been interested in genetics for a long time. His father was a famous and popular geneticist in Nazi times, since he had 'proven' the validity of the master race concept on genetic grounds. He first broached his suspicions to them [Grünenthal] on 16 November, but was unwilling to give any details of the cases that had come to his attention. He simply wanted them to take the drug off the market immediately and is supposed to have told Grünenthal that he had a 'vision' indicating Contergan as the cause of all these deformities ... Although it had been Grünenthal's intention to send out a warning letter, and their local health authorities (Rheinland) had agreed that this was all that was required, the furore in the newspapers grew so quickly and violently that Grünenthal felt they had no choice but to take the product off the market until the question had been resolved.

In a memorandum written in January 1962, Dr Werner relates that he had managed to engage a journalist specializing in medical questions. During a forthcoming congress this journalist was supposed to 'influence the press for our purposes'. He was to write articles for daily newspapers and technical journals in order to 'promote' and 'direct' the news service.

In the Grünenthal internal monthly report for February 1962 may be found:

In a joint consultation with the heads of the domestic section (Winandi) it was decided that all doctors, and especially those in a position to influence public opinion, who make critical statements must be persuaded by the strongest possible means to change their minds or at least must be neutralized.

It is extremely important that our PR department in the future should make even greater efforts than in the past to keep in close touch with important scientists and leaders of public opinion.

After the first articles by Lenz, McBride and Speirs in the *Lancet*, reports of similar observations started to flow in from all over the world. The relationships between thalidomide and malformed babies became an established fact, recognized by scientists and drug-controlling authorities in all the developed countries.

Another important clue was obtained when, during the months of February and March 1962, Dr Somers of Distillers succeeded in producing similar malformations in rabbits to those seen in man. This, of course, was a very strong argument against Grünenthal's thesis 'that the question of the malformations was still a relatively open one'. Consequently, Dr von Schrader-Beielstein in a letter to Distillers of 21 March suggested the company did not publish these results for the time being. The British company, however, took no notice. During the same period preparations were begun against possible future law suits. The Chemie Grünenthal legal adviser wrote on 4 April 1962, 'To summarize, there is the strongest probability that we will lose most of the civil law suits brought against us.'

Dr von Veltheim underlined this in an internal memorandum: 'The measures with regard to these affected by Contergan must be accompanied by an intensive, but very careful and tactful, "public relations" exercise which unobtrusively shows the Grünenthal position in the best possible light in the medical and trade press.'

One of the few people at Chemie Grünenthal who was personally involved in the development of thalidomide and expressed a deep concern was Dr Keller. 'When I heard this [that thalidomide was suspected of causing the malformations] I had a terrible shock. I felt like a bus-driver who has run into a group of children and has killed and injured many of them.'

In West Germany the news of the suspicion that thalidomide could cause malformation undoubtedly reached the vast majority of the people. The news in the mass media did not reach everyone, however, as some later cases of malformed births have proved. Many women required extensive psychiatric treatment for a long time after their malformed children were born and there were a number of suicides.

At the time of the withdrawal of thalidomide in Germany thousands of malformed babies had been born throughout the world.

6

The Results of Vigilance:
Thalidomide in the United States

On 12 September 1960, Richardson-Merrell Inc. submitted material for an application of registration of thalidomide to the US Federal Food and Drug Administration, but they were unable to convince the officials that the product was safe for use, especially during pregnancy. Nevertheless, they continued to make great efforts to secure positive reports from clinical investigators throughout the USA to bring about registration by the FDA; their campaign is outlined in a manual entitled the 'Kevadon-Hospital Clinical Program'. ('Kevadon' was the name used by the Merrell company in Canada for the drug.) This 'Program' was used in connection with meetings for its employees, arranged by the firm 25–26 October 1960:

'The objectives of the Kevadon Hospital Clinical Program are threefold' the manual explained:

1. To contact Teaching Hospitals ... and the chief and senior members of the department of surgery, medicine, anesthesiology, and obstetrics-gynecology, for the purpose of selling them Kevadon and providing them with a clinical supply.

2. To eventually accumulate a series of clinical reports on Kevadon's indications, as they apply within different departments of a hospital.

3. To perfect and develop the best possible detail story for a national introduction of Kevadon.

The manual then proceeded to instruct 'how to influence people':

Contacting your doctors

In contacting the physicians you have selected, it is advisable to start with the chief of the department; if you meet with success – fine. However, regardless of whether you sell the chief, you may wish to contact another influential man within the department; by all means do so . . .

What kind of clinical material Richardson S. Merrell Co. was out for was clearly expressed in the section entitled:

A WORD OF CAUTION

Bear in mind that these are not *basic* clinical research studies. We have firmly established the safety, dosage and usefulness of Kevadon by both foreign and U.S. laboratory and clinical studies. This program is designed to gain widespread *confirmation* of its usefulness in a variety of hospitalized patients. If your work yields case reports, personal communication or published work, all well and good. But the main purpose is to establish local studies whose results will be spread among hospital staff members. You can assure your doctors that they need not report results if they don't want to but that we, naturally, would like to know of their results. Be sure to tell them that we may send them report forms or reminder letters, but these are strictly reminders and they need not reply. Their reports or names would not be used without getting their express permission in advance.

At the beginning of your interview, don't be secretive – lay your cards on the table. Tell the doctor that present plans call for Kevadon to be marketed early in 1961. Let them know the basic clinical research on Kevadon has been done. Don't get involved by selling a basis [sic] clinical research program instead of Kevadon. *Appeal to the doctor's ego – we think he is important enough to be selected as one of the first to use Kevadon in that section of the country.*

Richardson-Merrell wrote to Grünenthal on the subject of thalidomide introduction on 4 January 1961: 'Probably you have already heard from Merrell that the FDA has postponed the acceptance for introduction of the drug in that it requires still more data concerning the toxicity.'

During the same month von Schrader-Beielstein and Leufgens made a visit to England and took the opportunity of criticizing their British licensee for putting a warning about polyneuritis on their labels. 'The open reference to polyneuritis in view of the worldwide importance of K17 [code name for thalidomide] is not at all to our taste.' Leufgens and von Schrader-Beielstein pointed out the possible detrimental influence such a policy might have on the new drug application, which was being considered by the FDA in the USA.

Dr Kelsey's suspicions had been aroused when she heard about the reports of peripheral neuritis published by Leslie Florence in the *British Medical Journal*. A memorandum in the Food and Drug Administration File of 23 February 1961 reads:

Dr Murray called (9.03 a.m.) to inquire about status of Kevadon. I explained we were concerned about chronic toxicity and lack of animal studies (histology etc.) – He inquired as to what I meant by chronic toxicity so I mentioned recent British reports and he said they had seen them too and had written for further information. He said that the English company was merely adding a warning on their brochure. I explained that we would be reluctant to release the product until we had a little more information since essentially nothing was known of the metabolism of the compound.

In a letter to Merrell the reasons for Kelsey's reluctance to clear thalidomide are further expanded:

Gentlemen: Reference is made to your new drug application dated January 17, 1961, submitted pursuant to section 505(b) of the Federal Food, Drug and Cosmetic Act for the preparation of 'Kevadon tablets'.

The application is incomplete under section 505(b) (1) of the act as follows:

It fails to report the animal studies in full detail. In particular we note the incomplete nature of the long-term animal toxicity experiments which are still in progress. It is felt that complete autopsy reports, including appropriate histologic studies of the central and peripheral nervous system, should be available on these animals after they have received the drug for at least 1 year. This seems particularly indicated in view of the recent reports, (*Brit. M.J.* 2, 1954, 1960; *Brit. M.J.* 1, 291, 1961) that prolonged use of this drug may give rise to peripheral sensory neuropathy in patients. We also feel that further information relevant to this reported toxicity should be presented, particularly as it applies to the clinical evaluation of the drug. In this connection, we are asking you to submit a complete list of investigators to whom the drug has been furnished so that we can ascertain whether similar adverse effects have been recorded with shorter term use of the drug.

Since the application is incomplete under section 505 (b) (1) of the act, it may not be filed as an application provided for in section 505 (b).

On 27 February 1961 Dr Murray of Richardson-Merrell was in touch with von Schrader-Beielstein on the telephone. He told him, 'The FDA has referred to a publication in the *British Medical Journal* both on the telephone and in writing, and we are considering whether to carry out toxicity trials over a longer period or to include a polyneuritis warning in the package inserts. In the latter case discussions must first be held with the FDA who must then give authorization.'

Schrader-Beielstein added a note to the memo of this telephone interview: 'This telephone conversation may well have offset the negative impression caused by the British article and by our own silence concerning these cases.'

Under the existing law the FDA had to make a decision

on a new drug application within sixty days, otherwise approval was automatic. If the medical officer found the application incomplete, however, the FDA could ask for additional data and thus postpone the final decision. This made it possible for Dr Kelsey to look further into the question of the safety of thalidomide. As a consequence Richardson-Merrell had to resubmit the application several times. Between 3 March and 15 March Dr Murray and another representative of Richardson-Merrell visited England and Germany to obtain further information about the cases of polyneuritis which had been published. Meetings were arranged with representatives of the Distillers Co. in which Dr von Schrader-Beielstein of Grünenthal also participated. Von Schrader-Beielstein wrote in his report:

Dr Somers (of Distillers) also participated in the discussions, during which he (Dr Somers) not only gave a detailed and completely unsolicited account of his toxicity investigations but also handed over a report to the Americans. [See pp. 183–4]. This situation was unpleasant for us since in view of the divergent results in Germany and England and the future exchange of mouse strains, this matter could not be considered as finished and in consequence had not yet been communicated to the Americans. We had to give a short review in order above all to prevent the Americans from receiving the impression that we had purposely or otherwise suppressed important results.

During their journey the Merrell representatives were also in touch with some physicians in England and in Germany who had observed neurological side-effects from thalidomide. Dr Leslie Florence and Dr Kremer were contacted in England, Professor Wieck in Cologne and Dr Winzenried in Hamburg. The Associate Director of Medical Research at Merrell received a report of eight cases of polyneuritis at the beginning of March from Dr Thomas L. Jones, Senior Lecturer in Neurology at the Neurological Unit of Northern

General Hospital in Edinburgh. The Scottish physician wrote: 'My feeling is that this is a genuine toxic effect.' Writing to Dr D. M. Burley of Distillers on 27 March Dr Jones admitted: 'Since returning home I am more than ever convinced that peripheral neuritis from thalidomide is certainly a clinical entity, albeit a bizzare one.' From the Merrell correspondence it seems clear that on this occasion Chemie Grünenthal only admitted knowledge of thirty-four cases in West Germany. Several reports of polyneuritis also came from American doctors associated with the Brown-McHardy Clinic in New Orleans, the Veterans Administration Center of Los Angeles, and the Nutrition Clinic of the Hillman Hospital, Alabama.

In March on his return from his trip to Europe, Dr Murray telephoned Dr Kelsey to say that he had found that neurological symptoms did occur with the prolonged use of thalidomide. He claimed that if discovered in time the effects were evidently reversible. Kelsey informed him that she considered the toxicity to be serious.

However Dr Murray never seems to have mentioned anything to Dr Kelsey about Dr Somers's experiments, in which an increased toxicity of thalidomide had been observed. A memo of an interview on 30 March signed by Dr Kelsey reads:

SUMMARY OF SUBSTANCE OF CONTACT

Drs Jones and Murray came in to discuss the Kevadon application in view of their recent visit to England and Germany. They maintained the toxicity incidence was low and rapidly reversible. Brief perusal of a report by Cohen in California indicated that this was not always the case. They displayed British and German labelling that draws attention to the toxicity. They kept urging me to say we would pass the drug with similar cautions. I pointed out that we would have to study the submitted material in detail before reaching any conclusions as we felt that the field of usefulness of the drug was such that untoward reactions would be highly inexcusable. I had the feeling throughout that they were at no time being wholly frank with me and that this attitude has obtained in all our conferences etc. regarding this drug. I may have been partly prejudiced by their advance publicity (*Medical Sciences*, 25 March 1961) in which they featured work by Lester which we indicated was inadequate and in which they compared Doriden and Kevadon chemically after they had previously mentioned that they were entirely different drugs, and by their failure to notify us of the British reports of toxicity.

In retrospect it seems quite clear that Chemie Grünenthal withheld information about the number of cases known in Germany and also minimized their severity. The German company's lack of frankness must have been clear to the licensees, especially where it concerned the reversibility of the nerve damage. In the reports published in the literature during 1961 it was emphatically pointed out that in many cases these symptoms had not disappeared after withdrawal of the medication. The German neurologist, Raffauf, wrote in an article in May 1961 :

In most cases the neurological symptoms were unusually persistent. Those patients who have been observed for the longest period of time, (until now ten months after the beginning of their symptoms) complain of the same intensity of their affliction as at the beginning. It is quite possible that we have to count on certain lasting damage ... We want to stress the fact that in none of the cases described had there been any (or very little) misuse.

Similar observations were published by the neurologists Scheid, Wieck, Stammier, Kladetzky, Gibbles and Frenkel who had also published articles in the German medical literature during the month of May.

In November Carl A. Bunde of Merrell visited Drs Voss, Wieck and Frenkel in their offices in Germany and was told of their experiments as physicians. The continuing clinical trials in USA also clearly demonstrated that polyneuritis did appear as a consequence of thalidomide medication.

When one of the clinical investigators wrote to Dr Kelsey about polyneuritis he obtained the following reply on 5 May 1961:

I very much appreciate your letter of April 4, 1961, concerning the new drug application submitted by the Wm S. Merrell Co. for thalidomide, Kevadon tablets.

We agree with your view that the only serious complication with respect to the safety of the drug is peripheral neuritis. The fact is that we do not as yet have sufficient information with respect to this toxic effect of the drug to permit a complete evaluation of its safety. Among other things, we do not have sufficient information to share your conclusion that this toxic effect of the drug is completely reversible. Further, from other reports it appears that the incidence of peripheral neuritis may be very much greater than suggested in your letter.

It is the responsibility of this Administration to be satisfied that a new drug has been demonstrated to be safe before it may be released for general marketing in the United States. The fact that the compound has been available in other countries for some years has no particular significance except as a source of additional information with respect to the properties of the drug. It will be our purpose to consider any reliable information that can be obtained, particularly with respect to the problem of peripheral neuritis in those areas where the drug has been employed.

At about this time irritation began to be felt between Dr Kelsey and the representatives of Richardson-Merrell, and this is well documented by the record of a telephone interview of 14 April, taken down by R. G. Smith of the FDA:

SUMMARY OF SUBSTANCE OF CONTACT
(Handwritten:) Dr Murray asked if there were any new developments on the Kevadon application. I told him that no decision on it had been reached.

He related that his management thought that he had failed to get the application through by the usual methods and that there should be some pressure exerted. Accordingly, Mr Woodward, their vice-president, intended to see Mr Larrick if nothing was going to be done. He said that they would like a 'yes' or 'no' decision so that they could prepare to go to a hearing if necessary.

I told him that I couldn't give him a decision at this time, since as I had told him before, I believed that Dr Kelsey wished to talk to some of the investigators.

He said that since no action had been taken since their report on the peripheral neuritis he believed that Dr Kelsey was avoiding a decision. I told him that this was not true since she wanted to investigate further. I also told him that we may be misled about the low incidence of peripheral neuritis since there might have been many occurrences which were not attributed to the drug because it wasn't suspected. It often happened that side effects of drugs were not reported until they had been on the market for some time.

Since there seemed to be little more to be said the conversation ended at this point.

It should be added here that the number of cases of nerve damage reported to Chemie Grünenthal up to the end of April had now reached over 400. Dr Kelsey did not yield to any threats and wrote a sharply formulated letter on 5 May, in which she again found the application faulty:

In our opinion the application as it now stands is entirely inadequate to establish the safety of Kevadon tablets under the proposed labelling. In particular, the application does not include complete reports of adequate animal studies nor sufficiently extensive, complete and adequate clinical studies to permit an evaluation of the toxic effects of the drug which have been manifested by reported cases of peripheral neuritis. On the present evidence we cannot regard Kevadon tablets as safe in the sense that its usefulness as a sedative-hypnotic outweighs the toxic effects indicated by the cases of peripheral neuritis. Detailed case reports with adequate follow-up studies will be required to determine whether the condition is reversible. Animal studies should include appropriate neurological studies of the central and peripheral nervous systems.

We have taken appropriate note of your contention that it has not been proved that Kevadon tablets actually cause peripheral neuritis, and the fact that the labelling of the drug proposed in your letter of 29 March 1961 fails to make a frank disclosure that the drug has been found to cause peripheral neuritis. In the consideration of an application for a new drug, the burden of proof that the drug causes side-effects does not lie with this Administration. The burden of proof that the drug is safe, which must include adequate studies of all the manifestations of toxicity which medical or clinical experience suggest, lies with the applicant. In this connection, we are much concerned that apparently evidence with respect to the occurrence of peripheral neuritis in England was known to you but not forthrightly disclosed in the application.

Dr Murray of Richardson-Merrell regarded this letter as 'somewhat libellous' as he told Ralph G. Smith of FDA on the telephone a few days later. He inquired of the FDA whether his firm was dealing personally with Dr Kelsey in this connection and, if so, whether Dr Kelsey's letter was subject to reconsideration. Dr Smith told him that the letter should be considered as coming from the FDA, but that regardless of who had signed it, it could be reconsidered if the applicant thought he had sufficient reason.

In anger and desperation the Merrell Co. tried to bypass Dr Kelsey by demanding an appointment with the medical director of the FDA, William H. Kessenich, and this took place on 10 May. On that occasion Dr Murray and the vice-president of Richardson-Merrell Inc., Mr Woodward, complained about the handling of the thalidomide business. Their new drug application had been presented in September 1960 and there had been two subsequent submissions, all of which were deemed incomplete and inadequate. Dr Murray and

Mr Woodward felt they had supplied what was required and asked Dr Kessenich what they should do now. Dr Kessenich gave his visitors no specific remedy and promptly referred them back to the Division of New Drugs, i.e. to Dr Kelsey, and arranged for a conference to be held on 11 May. During this conference Dr Murray explained that communications between his company and the European companies had failed regarding the neurological toxicity of thalidomide. Dr Kelsey was then inclined to accept Dr Murray's statement that he had only learnt of these effects when he read the article by Leslie Florence in the *British Medical Journal*.

At this same conference Dr Kelsey brought out a new aspect of toxic potentialities of the drug. Could the company furnish evidence that thalidomide was safe when used during pregnancy? If the nervous systems of adults could be damaged by thalidomide, what about the sensitive tissues of the foetus?

The problem of the effect of thalidomide on the foetus was evidently not new to the Richardson-Merrell Co. On 5 December 1960 the following letter had been sent to a Dr Linton in Knoxville, Tennessee.

Dear Dr Linton: I have heard from our representative in your area Mr J. Walker with regard to your question on the possible effect of Kevadon on the foetus. Unfortunately, I am unable to answer this question, since it has not been established whether or not there is any transfer of Kevadon across the placental barrier. However, we feel that, even if transfer does occur, it would be completely safe since Kevadon produces no respiratory depression and has no effect on vasomotor pathways and thus would not affect the cardiovascular system.

Should you have any other questions relative to this compound I should appreciate hearing from you.

Sincerely yours,
THOMAS L. JONES, M.D.
Associate Director of Clinical Research.

On 31 May 1961, Dr Murray of Richardson-Merrell submitted amendments to the FDA containing material which was supposed to give evidence of safety for the use of thalidomide during pregnancy. However, these studies, carried out by Merrell's investigator Nulsen, were conducted during late pregnancy and gave no proof of safety during the first three months. This fact was pointed out by Dr Kelsey. She would have been even more reluctant to accept the findings, had she known the circumstances in which the investigation had been carried out. This was revealed in the deposition of Dr Nulsen taken by Attorney Spangenberg before the Eastern District Court of Pennsylvania, Cincinnati, Ohio, in June 1964, in the case of Diamond versus William S. Merrell Co. and Richardson-Merrell Inc.

Dr Ray O. Nulsen was a physician of Cincinnati, Ohio, who had no special formal training in obstetrics. Nulsen began testing thalidomide on pregnant patients in the late spring of 1959, and continued to do so until instructed to stop in late 1961. Dr Nulsen is listed as the author of one of the two articles published involving the drug's possible effect on unborn children, articles used extensively in sales promotion by the producers of thalidomide. The article appeared in the June 1961 issue of the *American Journal of Obstetrics and Gynecology*. It states that thalidomide had no deleterious effect upon the babies delivered of the mothers he had studied who had been receiving thalidomide late in pregnancy.

When the side-effects of thalidomide became known, some of Dr Nulsen's patients, who had participated in the clinical investigation and had subsequently given birth to deformed babies, made it known publicly that they intended to bring suits for damages against the firm. Dr Nulsen was the defendant, along with Richardson-Merrell (the Wm. S. Merrell Co. is a division of Richardson-Merrell), in two million-dollar suits brought by two Ohio women who claimed that the doctor gave them thalidomide in early pregnancy. Both women gave birth to deformed children. Over the years Dr Nulsen had done clinical research in experimental drugs for several large firms, including Merrell. He admitted that he did not know whether the drugs which he had been testing for Merrell were approved by the FDA or not. On 20 April 1959 Dr Raymond C. Pogge, then director of Merrell's department of medical research, wrote Dr Nulsen a letter asking whether he would be interested in testing a new sedative, 'rather widely used in Europe for the symptomatic treatment of nervous tension'.

Dr Nulsen said he never received any fees for his test work on thalidomide, nor fees or honorarium for his subsequent article.

'I note, doctor,' Spangenberg said in taking Dr Nulsen's deposition, 'that he (Dr Pogge) asked you to start testing promptly and to send in reports. Do you have copies of the reports you sent in?'

'No, it was all verbal,' Dr Nulsen replied.

Dr Nulsen later said he had passed on the testing information to Dr Pogge 'by telephone, or it may have been that we had lunch together, or it may have been when we played golf'.

Spangenberg asked Dr Nulsen about the details of his research.

Spangenberg: 'When you started giving patients doses of thalidomide at the hour of sleep, Dr Nulsen, did you keep a record of who these patients were?'

Nulsen: 'Yes.'

Spangenberg: 'And how much you gave them?'

Nulsen: 'Yes.'

Spangenberg: 'Did you have any means of making any direct observation from the patients? By that I mean this: I know some clinical researchers wrote papers in which they said they would give the drug, and every thirty minutes they would look at the patient and make some physical observations on what the patient seemed to be doing.'

Nulsen : 'No, this was not done, the people took these in their own home.'

Spangenberg : 'And would report back to you how often?'

Nulsen : 'When they came in for a visit or if they called by phone.'

Spangenberg : 'Did you obtain consent from the patients in written form during this clinical investigation?'

Nulsen : 'No.'

Dr Nulsen explained, 'We didn't give people this thing against their will. We always explained to them that this was something we were trying and it wasn't obtained, it couldn't be obtained in the drugstore, and that they should let me know how they liked it, how it worked.'

By late 1960, Dr Nulsen said, he had given thalidomide to some eighty-one pregnant women in their last three months (third trimester).

This information was eventually collected in an article published under Dr Nulsen's name in the June 1961 issue of the *American Journal of Obstetrics and Gynecology*, entitled 'Trial of Thalidomide in Insomnia Associated with the Third Trimester'. This rather detailed publication put forward the conclusion : 'Thalidomide is a safe and effective sleep-inducing agent which seems to fulfil the requirements outlined in this paper for a satisfactory drug to be used late in pregnancy.'

Spangenberg : 'Who wrote the article, Dr Nulsen?'

Dr Nulsen replied, 'Dr Pogge. I supplied him with all the information.'

At another point the attorney asked, 'All right. In your article you cite many other researchers, and I will confess, if I may, when I asked you if you read German, your article cites about half a dozen German magazines and German texts. [Dr Nulsen had earlier admitted during the questioning that while he studied German in college he no longer read it.] Did you ever read these articles?'

Nulsen: 'No. That was supplied to me.'

Spangenberg: 'You also cite Mandarino, another doctor, and footnote the citation, and the footnote reads, "To be published". Did you ever see his article?'

Nulsen: 'I don't remember having seen it.'

In his deposition, Dr Nulsen said he did not keep any detailed records of the number of pills he had received from Merrell, nor the exact totals he had dispensed. He could not remember how many the company had given him all told. Spangenberg asked him for more details on the testing records: 'In the Kevadon programme generally, doctor, there were certain report forms that the doctors were supposed to send, a standard form, or a standard form of case report form that would list a patient's name or initials, the age, the drug used, and then a table of checklists as to whether it is better than the barbiturate or equal to it or less effective, whether side-effects were experienced, and the indications for its use, that is, the reason you gave it, associated with or resulting from a list of disorders, including obstetrical conditions. Are you familiar with that report form?'

Nulsen: 'We never filled out – so far as I know, I believe we never filled out anything like that so far as Kevadon is concerned.'

Spangenberg asked, 'Doctor, you recall your article, which you said they wrote for you in draft form, listed a study of cases, and, as I remember reading that article, there was quite a bit of detail as to the age groups and the effects and percentages of those who got as good relief and so forth. What kind of reporting or written detail was there to support those statements in the draft of the article Merrell wrote?'

'I don't remember,' Dr Nulsen said. 'It may have been we filled out those original report things Dr Pogge suggested or it may have been I put figures down on paper and stuck it in my pocket and gave those figures at lunch one time. I don't remember.'

One cannot help admiring the frankness of the witness.

During the summer the problem of neurotoxicity came under discussion in view of a number of new articles appearing in print. At a conference on 7 September, arranged by Dr Murray, the FDA representative met a group of clinical investigators brought in by Merrell. The purpose of the conference was to make a complete review of the properties of thalidomide. The clinical investigators reported cases of polyneuritis in their clinical material, although it was claimed that the incidence was low. However, one of the investigators, Dr Cohen, admitted that one case of peripheral neuritis was still not cured after over a year. The FDA officials were still not convinced that the symptoms were reversible, as claimed by the Merrell staff. It was also noted that the group said, when asked, that they had no knowledge of what the drug might do to the foetus if used by pregnant women. The cases of polyneuritis mentioned at this conference prompted Dr Kelsey to ask for detailed reports, and on 26 September the FDA informed Dr Murray that in addition to a warning against polyneuritis their labelling should also include advice against administration of the drug during pregnancy.

The increasing number of reports being published about the neurological side-effects continued to worry the FDA, and Dr Kelsey became aware of the fact that the incidence of these side-effects was higher than had been previously believed. The general safety of the drug was questioned in relation to its proposed use.

On 30 November 1961, Dr Murray telephoned Dr Kelsey

and informed her that thalidomide was suspected of causing congenital malformations in West Germany and had been withdrawn from the market. Dr Murray expressed the hope that this association was only coincidental. On 8 March the FDA received a request for the withdrawal of the Richardson-Merrell application.

False claims were made by the Swedish Health Authorities and the Astra Co., and spread by the mass media, that Dr Kelsey was prepared to allow thalidomide in the USA just before Dr Lenz demonstrated that thalidomide was the cause of phocomelia. On the contrary, in view of the neurological damage Dr Kelsey was by then seriously questioning the general safety of the drug. Quite apart from the assessment of the toxicity for adults, Dr Kelsey would never have allowed the drug to be used during pregnancy. She explicitly demanded that a warning against use by pregnant women should be included in the labelling, until clinical evidence for the safety of the drug during the *whole* of pregnancy was presented.

Certain sources have in retrospect claimed that Dr Kelsey, in fact, had few objective reasons for postponing the introduction of thalidomide in the USA, and that it was merely a piece of good luck that this country was saved from a disaster. Besides the evidence cited already, such allegations are refuted by the fact that the FDA of the USA was *not the only* state authority in the world which would not allow the introduction of the drug on grounds of its apparent lack of safety. In a deposition to the Swedish court given by Professor Jung, chairman of the Control Advisory Committee for Drug Commerce of the German Democratic Republic, on 19 October 1966, it is stated (Documentation: SCM, Vol. V, 1081):

The admission of thalidomide as a drug in the DDR was the subject of an expert meeting (clinical physicians, pharmacologists and pharmaceutical chemists) in the beginning of 1961. On this occasion it was established:

(1) The information found in the international literature concerning thalidomide and the scientific results published by the Chemie Grünenthal A G are inadequate to motivate the introduction of this sedative for long-term use by a wide circle of consumers, especially since thalidomide cannot be considered as an indispensable drug ...

(2) Occasional reports concerning a neurotoxicity of the drug seem to indicate that the compound is not as harmless as claimed by the producer. Before the new compound is to be introduced, extensive animal testing as well as clinical investigations would have to be made by qualified scientists.

(3) A very experienced pharmaceutical chemist has pointed out that the chemical structure ... would possibly indicate that surprises could result upon long-term use.

In view of the questionable scientific quality of the testing of the possible neurotoxicity as well as the clinical dispensability of the drug, the expert committee concluded that any import as well as domestic production of thalidomide should be rejected. The state authorities of the DDR were on this occasion also recommended not only to stop official imports but also to take measures to prevent the introduction of the drug by private routes. This decision and recommendation was made at a time when the expert committee was unaware of the thalidomide-embryopathies.

The problem still remained of dealing with the tablets that had been sent out to doctors in the USA 'for experimental purposes'. Merrell sent a drug warning letter to the doctors they had asked to test the drug. A press release issued by the Department of Health, Education and Welfare stated that Merrell had distributed 2,528,412 thalidomide tablets, in a variety of colours and sizes, to 1,267 doctors, who had given them to some 20,000 patients, in containers that bore nothing more than directions for use. The Food and Drug Administration had been unable to track down ninety-nine of the physicians, the release said, and of the rest 410 had made no effort to get in touch with the patients to whom they had given thalidomide – in many cases because they had kept no record of doing so. The Food and Drug Administration, the release continued, had no idea how many tablets were still around. Most of the doctors had received the manufacturer's warning to stop using the drug in March 1962, but eighty-five of them said they had not been notified of the product's side-effects, and forty-two others said they had received no warning at all. The Food and Drug Administration had asked the doctors whether they had signed statements to say that they were qualified to test the drug; 640 said that they had, 247 said they had not, and the rest couldn't remember or didn't answer the question.

7

The Results of Negligence:
Thalidomide in Sweden and Canada

Up to the withdrawal of thalidomide in Germany in November 1961, a very similar pattern of events took place in Sweden. The Astra Company of Scandinavia did very little. Although they were informed about the work of German neurologists during the summer of 1961, they made no effort to contact the research centres where these investigations were being carried out. The Astra Company was even urged to introduce warnings of polyneuritis by Chemie Grünenthal. Astra admitted before the district court of Södertälje that they had no doubts whatever about the competence of the German neurologists Frenkel, Raffauf and Scheid. On 8 November the Swedish Medical Board urged Astra to inform the doctors about the risk of polyneuritis. Despite this they did not introduce *any* kind of warning against polyneuritis in their propaganda material until 30 November 1961, by which time the drug had already been withdrawn from the market in Germany. Even then their warning was misleading: 'If side-effects of the type mentioned above [polyneuritis] do appear the medication should be discontinued and the symptoms will disappear.' It was quite evident to the Astra Company that these reactions were *not* always reversible. The Astra medical director wrote in the journal *Opuscula Medica* at the beginning of 1962:

During 1961 certain established and certain suspected side-effects were described in the English and especially in the German literature, with the consequence that the drug is no longer on the market. It seems appropriate to give a more detailed report of these complications.

Occasional cases of sensoric neuritis were principally found localized in the peripheral parts of the extremities ... In the milder forms complete restitution was obtained, while in the more severe cases a certain improvement was observed but not always a complete restitution.

Once the drug had been withdrawn in Germany, it should have been a fairly simple matter to see that it was also withdrawn in Sweden. But this was by no means the case.

We have already seen (pp. 39–41) the large number of trade-names under which thalidomide was sold. Dr Per Olov Lundberg wrote with some emotion in an article in the *Swedish Medical Journal*, 1965 :

At the end of November 1961 some of my colleagues at the Academic Hospital (Uppsala) were sitting reading a small notice in a Stockholm newspaper concerning a German drug called Contergan, which at a recent congress had been reported to have a possible teratogenic action. We naturally wanted to know if this was something to remember and if the drug in question existed in Sweden. A telephone call to a chemist resulting in an intensive study of the literature gave us the answer : neither Contergan nor any similar drug seemed to exist in our country. Unfortunately, this was not true.

In an article entitled 'The Evils of Camouflage as Illustrated by Thalidomide' (*The New England Journal of Medicine* 269, (1963) p. 92) Professor Helen B. Taussig of the Johns Hopkins Hospital in Baltimore attacked the 'masquerade' of drugs where one and the same pharmaceutical appears under different names even within the same country :

The many different names under which the drug has been marketed makes it difficult to determine whether the woman has taken thalidomide. Indeed, almost every firm that makes or is licensed to sell the drug sells it under a different name. Such a policy is in all probability financially advantageous to the firm, but it presents a real difficulty to the doctor and the patient. What makes things even worse in some countries, like England, is the fact that the name of the drug is withheld from the patient by the pharmacist who only provides a label with the name of the patient and a number.

Taussig tells of one unfortunate woman who took Distaval during two successive pregnancies and has two children with phocomelia because the bottle was unlabelled. Although there is no law in the United States regarding the withholding of the name of a medicine given by prescription, the custom is firmly established that prescriptions are filled in by number and the name of the drug is omitted. This is a dangerous custom since it means that a large amount of unlabelled medicine is accumulated by everyone. There is danger not only that a medicine that has been withdrawn from the market may remain available but also that when medicines are taken by mistake, especially by children, the doctor may be at a loss to know what has been taken.

Common sense seems to call for an amendment to the law in these countries, enforcing obligatory labelling of medicine bottles by the pharmacies with the name of the drug concerned. Such regulations have existed for a long time in Sweden and some other European countries.

When the two Stockholm newspapers, *Svenska Dagbladet* and *Dagens Nyheter*, published the news on 27 November 1961 that Contergan had been withdrawn in West Germany, not even physicians suspected that Contergan was another name for the fairly wide-spread sedatives Neurosedyn and Noxidyn, marketed by the Astra Co. However, *Expressen*, the liberal evening newspaper, was better informed and on 5 December had traced the true identity of the drug. In an interview with a representative of the Astra Co. the information was given that a warning letter had been sent to all physicians in Sweden, in which administration of thalidomide during pregnancy was 'advised against'. The warning letters in question were in no way distinguished from other types of information and advertisement sent out by the pharmaceutical companies, of which every Swedish doctor receives about 55 kg. per year, and which in most cases goes straight into the waste paper basket. Most members of the medical profession were first made aware of the problem only several months later through articles in the lay press. By comparison, when the producers of thalidomide in Canada sent a warning letter to physicians on 7 December these were sent by first class mail, and the envelopes were clearly marked 'Drug warning'.

In an interview published on 7 December in the Communist newspaper *Ny Dag*, Astra's medical director Dr Svedin and Dr Ake Liljestand of the Medical Board of the Swedish State stated that no measures to withdraw the drug from the Swedish market were being considered. When the *Ny Dag* journalist referred to the withdrawal of thalidomide in England announced in an article in *The Times* on 3 December Dr Liljestrand dismissed this action as being 'too drastic'.

The Swedish Medical Board chose to make as little publicity out of the matter as possible in Sweden. This resulted in the tragic consequence that several deformed children were born in Sweden because mothers with thalidomide in their homes, which had been previously prescribed in good faith by the physician, were not informed about the drug's dangerous properties.

Thalidomide was not withdrawn from the market until 12 December 1961. This was not revealed to the public until two months later in an article in the small daily newspaper, *Dagen* (21 February 1962). The article was taken up by the

Swedish Broadcasting Corporation in its news comment, and by 23 February all Stockholm newspapers were relating the news. The general director of the Swedish Medical Board, Dr Arthur Engel, still considered that suspicions of thalidomide side-effects were 'unconfirmed', as there were no clear cases in Sweden. This was despite the existence of several articles containing new and extensive material published in the international medical literature.

The Swedish Medical Board did not change attitude until 14 March 1962 when Arthur Engel gave a short official statement on Radio and TV in which the horrible effects of thalidomide were acknowledged. The reason for the silence was explained by Dr Karl-Eric Linder, the Medical Board representative, in an interview with *Dagens Nyheter* published on 18 March. 'If we had sent out an official message (in connection with the withdrawal of the drug in December 1961) and caused a furore the results would have been traumatic.'

Dr Linder still found clear proof lacking concerning the cause of the malformations. Yet on 6 January 1962, and again on 3 February, Dr Lenz had published detailed material in the *Lancet* which Dr Kelsey of the FDA described as 'overwhelming evidence to support his [Dr Lenz's] belief that thalidomide is teratogenic in man'. The difference in their judgement may be based on the fact that while Kelsey managed to save the USA from disaster by virtue of her insight and knowledge, the responsible persons in the Swedish Medical Board failed to do so.

The press reaction became rather violent during the weeks that followed Dr Engel's announcement. One paper spoke of an international catastrophe. How was this possible? From the start the Astra public-relations machinery worked effectively and the largest Stockholm newspapers were advocating the view that the manufacturers could not be blamed since the tragedy was surely quite unexpected and unforeseeable. The Astra Co. gave out optimistic assurances that no legal action was anticipated. Thalidomide had been tested exhaustively both in animal experiments and on humans.

In July 1963 the Medical Board estimated that 153 thalidomide-damaged children had been born, of whom sixty-six had died.

Information about the situation in Canada can be obtained from a compilation of the correspondence between the Federal Government and the drug companies, beginning on 1 January 1957, which was sent over to the House of Commons on 17 October 1962 from the Department of Health and Welfare and the Prime Minister's office.

On 8 September 1960 William S. Merrell Co. submitted data for thalidomide to the Food and Drug Directorate in Ottawa. A note of compliance to sell the drug under the name of Kevadon on prescription was obtained from the authorities on 22 November 1960. The marketing of Kevadon was initiated on 1 April 1961. From the very beginning Merrell included a warning about polyneuritis, but this was formulated in a misleading way, since it was stated that the symptoms immediately disappeared upon withdrawal of the medication. This misrepresentation of the facts was retained in the instructions for use until the drug was withdrawn, in spite of the fact that numerous written reports did not give any indication that the nerve damage was always reversible. On the contrary, many investigators repeatedly stressed the persistency and lack of improvement after the drug was discontinued.

On 1 September 1961 another firm, the Frank W. Horner Company, informed the Food and Drug Directorate of their intention to distribute thalidomide under the name of Talimol. Horner was authorized by Merrell to refer to their New Drug

Submission for Kevadon, and on 11 October 1961 Talimol was cleared for sale. From 12 December 1961 Strong Cobb Arner of Canada Ltd was manufacturing Kevadon tablets for Merrell as an alternative source.

Thalidomide had, therefore, only been on the market for a quite short time when on 29 November 1961 the William S. Merrell Co. learned about Dr Lenz's suspicions associating certain malformations with thalidomide. At a meeting with representatives of the Food and Drug Directorate a letter was agreed containing a warning against the use of thalidomide by pregnant women and by pre-menopausal women who might become pregnant. The letters in envelopes clearly marked 'Drug Warning' were sent to all physicians in Canada on 5 December. The drug continued to be sold on the market and as additional reports of thalidomide-induced malformations appeared in medical literature, Merrell sent out a fresh warning letter on 21 February 1962.

On 23 February 1962 *Time* magazine published an article entitled 'Sleeping Pill Nightmare'. A short account of the story of thalidomide was presented which included the findings of Lenz as well as those of a Dr A. L. Speirs, of Stirling-shire, and was evidently based on the scientific articles which had appeared in the well-known medical journal the *Lancet*. *Time* did not add any 'sensational' speculations of its own but F. J. Murray of William S. Merrell Co., Cincinnati, writing to Dr Morrell, the director of the Food and Drug Directorate (FDD), declared that he was 'shocked by the sensational approach and the lack of objectivity' of *Time*. The American magazine stated quite correctly that the drug had been taken off the market in Germany and in Great Britain whereas Merrell had only sent out a warning letter to physicians. The Canadian press reacted – why was the drug still available in Canada? Dr Morrell of the FDD informed the *Toronto Star* that Canada 'had no cases yet' and that the evidence for a connection between thalidomide and malformation 'is only statistical'.

A few days later, on 27 February, Dr Gordon Hewitson, a physician in Pointe Claire, Quebec, wrote to Dr Morrell:

Six weeks ago I saw an infant with the congenital abnormality of phocomelia (seal limbs).

In the first eight weeks of her pregnancy this mother took a daily tablet of thalidomide (Kevadon).

This drug as you are well aware has been removed from the market in Great Britain and never licensed for use in the United States.

The firm marketing the drug in Canada sent out a warning notice to doctors in December and a follow up notice was distributed last week. This hardly seems enough for such a hazardous drug; it should certainly be removed forthwith from further use.

On 1 March a head physician wrote to Dr Morrell: 'I am afraid that there can be little doubt with the accumulating literature on the subject, of which I know you are well aware, that there is more than a casual relationship between this drug and the occurrence of serious abnormalities in newborn infants.'

The number of reports increased in medical literature connecting phocomelia with thalidomide, and on 2 March Dr Morrell was forced to request the manufacturers of thalidomide to withdraw the drug from the market. He wrote to the manufacturers:

A meeting was held at this Directorate on Wednesday, March 1, 1962, to discuss the advisability of temporarily withdrawing the drug thalidomide from the Canadian market.

In view of increasing demands from Canadian physicians, as well as certain other pressures, we have decided to ask you to withdraw your product Talimol from the Canadian market until such time as we can be certain of its possible association or lack of association with congenital deformities in newborn children.

I regret very much having to take this course of action and can only hope for an early resolution of the problem.

According to *MacLean's* magazine of 19 May 1962, six weeks later, on 10 April, thalidomide was still being sold over drugstore counters. A *Maclean's* reporter phoned seventy-seven drugstores in eleven Canadian cities. None still sold the drug in any of the stores that were asked in Victoria, Vancouver, Regina, Winnipeg, Quebec City, Fredericton or Halifax. Winnipeg pharmacists were upset by the question; they were refunding customers who brought back partly empty bottles. However, of the twenty-four drugstores asked in Toronto, five were still selling thalidomide; in Edmonton three out of eight; in Montreal three out of thirteen; and in the Ottawa-Hull area three out of eight. One Toronto pharmacist was asked why thalidomide was still on sale. He answered, 'Why not? It is safe for the adult male isn't it?' When it was pointed out that any medicine lying at home might be taken by a woman, he replied, 'That's not my problem. I'm not sending back the rest of the supply until people stop asking for it.' The Food and Drug Directorate, who had taken no measures to ensure that the withdrawal was effective, was told of the situation by the newspaper.

Dr Morrell hurriedly sent further instructions to the William S. Merrell Co. and to Frank W. Horner Ltd:

With the withdrawal of this acceptance thalidomide returns to the status of a new drug and must not be sold except to qualified investigators for the purpose of obtaining scientific and clinical information that could be used to support the safety of its use under conditions to be recommended by the manufacturer. Such sale does not include its sale through pharmacies.

Violation of the new drug regulations, e.g. sale of this drug by a pharmacist, may result in seizure of the product and/or prosecution of the seller.

The Department of Health also threatened substantial

penalties, up to $5,000 fine and three months' imprisonment. The Canadian Pharmaceutical Association wrote to the registrars of the Provincial Pharmaceutical Association in a letter of 10 April 1962:

It is understood that the Frank W. Horner Ltd. and the William S. Merrell Co. took immediate steps to recover all supplies of their products 'Talimol' and 'Kevadon' respectively. Moreover, faced with some refusals to relinquish stores, their activities were supported by a letter from the Food and Drug Directorate. There is still evidence that such refusals are continuing, although it is most difficult to understand why an individual pharmacist or practitioner would take such a stand. There may, therefore, be considerable stocks of this potentially dangerous drug still available and being dispensed on the prescription order of, presumably, an unsuspecting physician.

Meanwhile public opinion raged against the policy of the Food and Drug Directorate under Dr Morrell. On 30 March the *Globe and Mail* reported a session in parliament: 'Three months elapsed between a manufacturer's warning a sedative might be dangerous to pregnant women and a Government request it be withdrawn from circulation, the Commons was told today.' Outside the House, Health minister J. Waldo Monteith was pressed. He denied there had been any delay in obtaining withdrawal of the drug, thalidomide, which caused a Winnipeg woman to give birth to a deformed child. 'The department had to check reports that were of a sketchy nature; little more than rumours,' he said. In the House he declared: 'The information supplied was statistical in nature in that the instances of certain malformations in the group of children born to mothers taking the drug were somewhat higher than in a group of children from mothers not taking the drug.' We know that this declaration was indeed a grievous distortion of facts. On 3 February 1962 Dr Lenz had written in the *Lancet*:

Sir ... I am afraid I have not made my point sufficiently clear in my letter of January 6. I have conclusive evidence that 'Contergan' (thalidomide) is teratogenic in man. The evidence includes (1) 6 cases in which the mother disclosed before delivery that she had taken thalidomide in early pregnancy and in which the infant showed major malformations at birth of the same type as seen in retrospectively ascertained cases. 4 of these cases are part of three unselected series of hospital births in which (a) no case was found in which the mother of a normal infant had taken thalidomide between the third and eighth weeks after conception, and (b) no case of the thalidomide type of malformations was found in which the mother had *not* taken the drug.
(2) 55 cases in which the exact date of the prescription and/or intake of thalidomide is known and coincides with the time of development of the malformed organs.
(3) Five series of consecutive cases collected independently from hospitals outside Hamburg and communicated to me by gynae-cologists and paediatricians.

The number of cases known to me of malformations and a history of thalidomide intake during the first two months of pregnancy is increasing at present at a rate of 3–10 per day.

Merrell's Robert H. Woodward stated in a letter to Dr Morrell that Lenz would not release details of the case histories on which the conclusions in his article in the *Lancet* of February 3 were based. In view of this claim the following passage by Lenz is revealing :

Any medical person seriously interested in the aetiology of human malformations and with sufficient knowledge of German to be able to read case-histories and letters in German is cordially invited to study my entire material for critical evaluation.

While I agree with Dr Burley [of Distillers] (Jan. 13) that it is desirable that the problem should be solved without undue emotion and alarm, I can hardly imagine that any person will be able to face the facts without emotion and alarm.

According to Professor Lenz, the William S. Merrell Co.

did not even try to get into contact with him, let alone make any request to take part of his basic material.

The violent reaction of the public made the pharmaceutical industry concerned about their general reputation and all firms made a clear effort to stick together in support both of the manufacturers of thalidomide and of the unfortunate authorities who allowed thalidomide into their respective countries. Geigy Pharmaceuticals of Canada rushed to the aid of Dr Morrell.

P. B. Stewart of Geigy wrote in a letter of 13 April:

I am enclosing a newspaper clipping from the *Globe and Mail*, which you most likely have already seen, about thalidomide. I think the headline is extremely unfair and I wondered whether you could not counter this by releasing a statement to the press indicating that the drug was only withdrawn in Europe after approximately three to four years' experience, whereas it was withdrawn promptly in Canada and had been on the market less than a year when the connection between ingestion of this drug and congenital malformations was discovered. I think you should make more of the fact that experience in Europe had extended over three years before suspicion was cast on the drug, and that your Directorate acted as fast as was consistent with accuracy in protecting the Canadian public.

The following editorial was read over the Montreal radio station CKGM on 15 April 1962:

Last December two US companies reported to Ottawa that the drug was dangerous. On February the twenty-third the Director of the Food and Drug Directorate in Ottawa discounted this report, but on March the second he ordered the drug withdrawn. At the end of March the third, babies whose mothers had used thalidomide were born without arms and legs. Doctors warn there will be more. Our Food and Drug Directorate is gravely negligent here. Who knows how many human tragedies will result from it?

Frank W. Horner sympathized – they were all in the same boat now. 'Needless to say, we all wish you well during this difficult period, Dr Morrell' (letter of 17 April).

Not all physicians welcomed the withdrawal of thalidomide since many had had positive experience with the drug. Dr Morrell's attitude is revealed to the full in a letter to such a physician on 27 April:

I think if the medical profession would take a stand, such as you have taken, that there is every possibility that thalidomide could indeed be reinstated on the Canadian market and to this end I would encourage you to urge strongly your colleagues to express themselves to us on this question.

In conclusion I feel certain that if the majority of Canadian physicians want to have this drug, it will make a strong case for its reinstatement.

In retrospect, it is remarkable that the responsible officials of the authorities in countries like Canada and Sweden never made any attempt to contact those research centres in Germany and England in which a number of cases had already been accumulated and were under study. Instead they relied completely on the vague and evasive policy of the drug manufacturers, who in view of the situation could naturally be expected to show a defensive attitude. By their lack of initiative and decision these authorities soon came to sit in the dock with the accused in the eyes of public opinion.

The psychological situation must have been difficult for a physician who had prescribed thalidomide in good faith to a woman who later gave birth to a deformed child. In spite of not having for a moment suspected such terrible results from this 'completely safe drug' the meeting with mother and child must have produced feelings of guilt. Natural suspicion of 'wonder drugs' at the time saved many physicians from such a situation. Dr M. W. Black of Grand Rapids Hospital, Manitoba, wrote to Dr Morrell on 14 April:

For your information, it is my habit never to use new drugs where old ones have been of proven efficacy. In the case of thalidomide for instance I saw no conceivable advantage of risking the use of a new drug with its possible side effects which had yet been undetermined, when I had at my disposal a very wide range of sedatives and tranquillizers of proven efficacy, and where the side effects were known, of minor consequence, and could be reasonably anticipated. Therefore, I did not at any time attempt to use this drug.

In the case of drugs which have some apparently highly desirable effects which are not available with older and proven remedies, I try and make very sure about my literature first. In particular, I *never ever* rely on reports given to me by the drug manuturers. Experience has long taught me that the drug manufacturer in the North American continent can put out biased reports which are unreliable, misleading and frequently dangerous.

As a counter-measure the drug industry began a massive campaign, through their public relations departments, usually through the medical correspondence of the big newspapers. For example, an article in the London *Times* of 1 August 1962, denying all responsibility on the part of the manufacturers of thalidomide for what had happened, was distributed to people in the administration of the Canadian government, because, as Robert F. Daily, the general manager of Smith, Kline and French of Montreal expressed it: 'We did not ourselves manufacture or sell the drug, but as a major pharmaceutical company we are naturally interested in fostering public understanding in our industry.' It did not seem to bother Daily that the article in *The Times* was misleading with regard to tests for the teratogenic property of drugs. On this problem *The Times* wrote:

This is not a matter in which a commercial firm has omitted tests which professional pharmacologists with no commercial interests would infallibly have carried out. They would infallibly not have carried them out ... In retrospect it is natural to ask: Why were no tests made of the teratogenic effects (the production of congenital malformations)? The answer quite simply is that the need for such tests has never been made evident, before.

Daily should have been well aware that his own company had in 1957 already tested a tranquillizer pro-chlorperazine (Compazine) both in animal experiments and in clinical trials for its effect on the foetus.

On 8 September in the *Winnipeg Free Press*, the following passage may be found:

It was inevitable that in the aftermath of the thalidomide tragedies there should be some panic over drugs. The danger now is that, as thalidomide itself, the side effects of the treatment could be more harmful than the disease.

The hazards are several. First, patients, grown suddenly suspicious of all 'wonder drugs' may refuse to take medication genuinely necessary to their health. Thousands of doctors have had to contend with this situation in past weeks.

Second, governments may be forced by public pressure into writing restrictive laws that could inhibit the development of needed new drugs, while providing no real safeguards against a repetition of the thalidomide episode.

Again the misleading statement is repeated:

It was not tested for possible teratogenic (the causing of congenital malformations) effects, simply because the need for such tests had never before become evident. In short, nobody even thought of that possibility.

In Canada a parliamentary investigation was made of the handling of the thalidomide case by the Food and Drug Directorate but their findings were never made public. The Rokeah Pharmaceutical Association in Toronto wrote to Dr Morrell on 28 August:

We are writing to express our concern over what we feel can

only be described as your department being very lax in its responsibility with regard to thalidomide.

A letter sent by Morrell states that your department was informed of the possibility of malformed births due to the drug in November of 1961 yet it was not until March of 1962, nearly four months later that it was ordered to be withdrawn from the market. Certainly it appears to us that November of 1961, when the first reports appeared and you were informed of them, was the time to act to either withdraw the drug, or at least to prevent further marketing of it pending investigation into the reports.

Dr Morrell answered on 4 September, 'Existing regulations do not authorize us to prohibit the sale of a drug in Canada.'

On 16 August 1962 F. Hugh Wadey, the Canadian managing director of the William S. Merrell Co., claimed in a letter addressed to doctors: 'At no time did Kevadon literature suggest usage of the drug for nauseas of pregnancy.' In the brochure called 'Kevadon – Merrell safe, sound sleep' printed in Canada for Merrell the following passage is found under the heading 'Safety Data': 'Nulsen administered 100 mg. Kevadon to 81 expectant mothers and Blasiu to 160 nursing mothers. In both instances all of the babies were born or nursed without any abnormalities or harmful effects from the medication.' There is no doubt whatsoever that the producers of thalidomide and their licensees were aware of the fact that this drug was used by the doctors for treatment of pregnant women.

In October 1961 Distillers issued an advertisement containing this passage: 'Distaval can be given with complete safety to pregnant women and nursing mothers, without adverse effect on mother or child.' Although 'nausea of pregnancy' was not mentioned, the important matter is that thalidomide in a general way was recommended for use during pregnancy.

Dr Helen Taussig, professor of paediatrics at the Johns

Hopkins University, Baltimore, gives further examples of the difficulties encountered in detecting the production and sale of drugs containing thalidomide. She cites a report in the Brazilian magazine *Ocruziero* of 6 September 1962. The birth of a child with phocomelia prompted a journalist on this paper to investigate. He was, however, told that thalidomide was not on sale in Brazil, but through his own inquiries he learnt that fifty other infants had been born with phocomelia. He then visited a pharmacy and purchased a drug containing thalidomide. Later he discovered that other such drugs were also manufactured in São Paolo and distributed all over Brazil. The health authorities then instituted an investigation and found that thalidomide was sold under five different names. Moreover, in a ten-day long, unannounced search, they confiscated nearly 2,500,000 pills, 46,000 bottles containing thalidomide and 96,000 kg. of the pure substance in the pharmacies and pharmaceutical firms of São Paolo. This was during the summer of 1962.

In Italy thalidomide was sold under ten different trade names. In spite of an outbreak of phocomelia in Turin in June 1962 some of these products were not withdrawn in Italy until September 1962.

In Argentina Astra did not take the thalidomide-containing drugs off the market until March 1962.

According to an article by Tadashi Kajii and Mamoru Shinohara, 'Thalidomide was first made available to the public in Japan under the trade name of Isomin by the Dainippon Pharmaceutical Co. on 20 January 1958, some two months later than Contergan'. Subsequently thalidomide and compound substances containing it were produced by fourteen firms under fifteen trade names and sold without prescription. The largest among these was Dainippon and its products Isomin and Pro-Ban M held more than 90 per cent of the Japanese market before their withdrawal.

On 17 May 1962, in view of reports they had received from Europe associating the drug with congenital malformations, five of these fourteen firms voluntarily determined to stop producing and providing thalidomide. News about thalidomide babies in Europe had frequently appeared in medical journals and in newspapers in Japan; but the name thalidomide was almost exclusively used and not the more familiar Isomin with the result that not all doctors were aware of the connection. On 13 September 1962 these five firms finally declared that they were withdrawing thalidomide-containing drugs from the market and the withdrawal was completed by January 1963, more than one year after Grünenthal's withdrawal of the drug.

Thus in Japan hundreds of malformed babies have probably been born as a result of thalidomide consumption by pregnant mothers *after* Lenz, McBride and others had revealed the teratogenic effects of the drug.

8

The Proof that Thalidomide
Caused the Disaster

At the present time every drug-controlling authority in the developed countries of the world, with the possible exception of Japan, has recognized as a fact the damaging effects of thalidomide on the unborn child, and in most cases this has led to a considerable tightening of drug regulations. In the light of the thalidomide catastrophe most authorities now require that every new drug put on the market should be tested for its effect on the foetus. Even some of the manufacturers who produced thalidomide, for example the Richardson Merrell Co. of the USA and the Astra Co. of Scandinavia, now admit that thalidomide was responsible for the outbreaks of phocomelia observed in countries where the drug was distributed. The reason for the attitude of the Japanese authorities is surely to be found in the fact that leading Japanese officials are now faced with civil law suits for taking no measures to enforce the withdrawal of thalidomide from the market for a year or more after being informed both of Dr Lenz's revelations and of the withdrawal of the drug from other countries. The only rational explanation for the attitude of the Japanese authorities is that before their court proceedings they must plead that it has never been shown that thalidomide does in fact damage the embryo. Any other excuse would be tantamount to a confession of guilt.

More or less fantastic stories have been circulated in the lay press about the reasons for these very special kinds of malformation and this has undoubtedly confused the public. A closer inspection of the facts seems justified.

At a time when our society is so scientifically based, and so fully dependent on science for its existence, it is surprising how few people in other fields, such as politicians or lawyers, are acquainted with the principles underlying scientific thought. Many such people are often involved in decisions about science on administrative levels; this is not only disconcerting but also dangerous for society itself and for individual security.

Medicine is one of the biological sciences and as such it is an empirical science, i.e. it is based on observation. The facts of medicine are gained by the application of the *scientific method*, one of the basic tenets of which is the *rejection of authority* – the refusal to accept a statement just because someone has written it down or said it is so. The true scientist wants confirmation of any statement by an independent method of verification.

Since the ultimate source of all facts in science is observation, the manner in which observations are collected is of the first importance. An observational error is carried through into everything that follows and the whole scientific effort may thus be defeated before it has properly begun. The difficulty largely lies with unsuspected bias. People often see what they *want* to see or observe what they think they ought to observe. The more descriptive and non-quantitative the particular branch of science is, the greater the scope for this kind of influence. In astronomy or in a highly exact science like physics the investigator may be less influenced by personal bias. But in a semi-quantitative, less exact branch of natural science, like clinical medicine, in which complex processes are described which are sometimes difficult to measure with any precision, the danger of personal factors influencing the observations becomes much greater.

After an observation has been made, the second step of the scientific method is to define a *problem*. What is it that makes such and such things behave as they do? To be valuable scientifically such a question must be both relevant and testable. Thus philosophical questions like 'why do we exist?' or 'what is the purpose of our lives?' fall outside the domain of science.

The third step in scientific method after the proper questions have been asked is to postulate a hypothesis. Hypotheses cannot be accepted until they are verified by some form of testing, and this is the fourth step in scientific method. Further experiments and investigation may prove or disprove the original 'working' hypothesis. In this way they are constantly being refined or changed.

Despite ingenious design and careful execution the result may still not be a clear 'yes' or 'no'. This is especially true of biological experiments like the testing of a drug in man or in animals, where there is *biological variation* among individuals. In a drug-testing experiment in which a certain pharmacological activity of a drug is being tested it is virtually certain that not all members of the experimental, drug-treated group will be affected to the same extent. Some will be more affected while others will perhaps be not at all affected. The actual results may be something like seventy out of a hundred patients exhibiting the effect, ten patients showing doubtful effect and twenty patients in which no effects could be detected, in comparison with the control group in which twenty patients out of a hundred showed the effect and five cases were doubtful.

If the experiment does not give a clear 'yes' or 'no', the next step is to use mathematical-statistical methods to show whether the difference observed between the experimental group and the control group is true, or whether it could be due to chance variations. It can be fairly generally stated that statistics alone applied to given biological data can never, as in a geometrical theorem of Euclid, give absolute proof of anything. The statistical treatment leads to an estimate of the *probability* that a certain hypothesis is correct. In fact, empirical science as a whole can never furnish absolute proof in this sense, but is merely concerned with the probabilities of different degrees of order.

When a hypothesis has been supported by a large body of different types of observation and experiment, it will be considered as a *theory*. A good theory not only relates, from one point of view, facts which previously appeared unrelated and which previously could not be explained on a common basis, but also predicts new facts. It prophesies certain results. The *scientific prophecy*, however, does not say that something will certainly happen, but only that something is likely to happen with a stated degree of probability.

When theories have been shown to be universally valid and have a very high degree of probability they are considered as *natural laws*. It is a matter of universal experience that the mixing of a hot gas with a cold one is irreversible. No one has ever observed that the molecules of such a gas spontaneously divide into one hot part, containing the faster moving molecules, and one cold part, containing the slower moving molecules. Similarly we have never seen water by itself flow up a hill. Consequently, *natural laws* have been formulated to cover these situations (for example the second law of thermodynamics and the law of gravity). However the predictions of such laws are not absolute but rest on a statistical basis. A stone of quartz weighing 1 kg. contains about 10^{25} molecules of SiO_2. The statistical chance that all these molecules should *simultaneously* move in a direction against gravity, although it exists, and can even be calculated, is so infinitesimally small that it can virtually be considered never to occur. However, if we consider *individual* molecules the situation becomes quite different.

It is important to realize these facts, since there are few concepts which have been misused to such an extent as 'scientifically proven' and 'scientifically not proven'.

When the producers of thalidomide used the scientific method for promotion purposes they were often satisfied with material which on statistical grounds would not even suffice to provide a decent working hypothesis. When Chemie Grünenthal later said 'scientifically not proven' when confronted with the disastrous effects of thalidomide they used the term in the sense in which not even the gravitational laws would have met their requirements.

In relation to the phocomelia outbreak in various countries the goal, as in many other scientific studies, was to explain the *cause* of a certain phenomenon. To obtain hard-and-fast proof that a cause-and-effect relationship exists between two events may not be so simple. If the circumstances leading to a certain effect always have some factor in common in a variety of cases, that factor may be the cause of the event. It is, however, no proof since there may also be some other common factor operating.

It would be wrong to conclude, for example, from the finding that scotch and soda, gin and soda and bourbon and soda all produce intoxication, that soda was the cause of the intoxication. The method of discovering a common factor (the method of agreement) can often be used as a first step, but seldom gives binding evidence.

In the case of the outbreak of phocomelia people tried to find in several places a factor common to all the cases. Lenz tracked down thalidomide in fourteen out of twenty cases, and in three cases thalidomide intake was suspected. The figures are not impressive unless you compare them with the frequency of this special type of malformation in a population where no thalidomide has been consumed. In biological experiments one considers, in more rigorous situations, a statistical difference as significant if the probability of such a difference arising by chance is less than 0.1 per cent i.e. only one in a thousand. This factor was already fulfilled in the original material of Weicker, Professor of human genetics in Bonn, which consisted of fifty families in which deformed babies were born and fifty families where normal children were born. The probability that there was no causal relationship was less than one in ten thousand. When the data from university clinics in Bonn, Dusseldorf, Cologne, Kiel, Mainz and Münster had been collected at the beginning of December 1961 (by the expert committee of the Health Department of the Ministry for Interior Affairs of the state Nordrhein-Westfalen), it could be estimated that the probability that the difference observed could be ascribed to chance was less than one in 10,000,000. By early 1962 this had increased to one in 10^{40} (i.e. 10 followed by forty noughts).

This method of unravelling cause-and-effect relationships in which two sets of circumstances differ only in one factor, and the circumstances containing the one factor lead to an event and the other does not, is called the *method of difference*.

In the case of thalidomide direct experiment on man was, of course, excluded. Nevertheless, several cases are known which in scientific terms could be considered equivalent to planned experiment.

Professor Lenz related a case in February 1962, i.e. three months after thalidomide was taken off the market, in which a pregnant woman, because of a cold, received a package of the thalidomide-containing drug Peracon-Expectorans from a physician. The administration of this drug was noted down on the doctor's file card. Lenz does not say whether the physician in question knew that Peracon-Expectorans contained thalidomide or whether he did not believe the claim that thalidomide could cause malformation. The second alternative seems quite probable in view of the intensive propaganda launched by the Chemie Grünenthal representatives claiming that there was no proof whatever that thalidomide had such effects, and that it was the sensational articles in the press which had forced the company to withdraw the drug. Passed on by certain cooperative members of the press and other news media this argument bore fruit, and no doubt accounted for the birth of several malformed children after the drug had been withdrawn. The woman described by Lenz in October 1962 gave birth to a baby with malformations of the extremities.

During the famous Lüttich murder trial in Louvain, Professor Hoet from Louvain gave evidence concerning the teratogenic properties of thalidomide. During the days of the trial a woman who was present visited Hoet and asked him if thalidomide was really so dangerous – she was pregnant and had just taken a few tablets. Professor Hoet reproached her and told her to destroy the rest of the pills immediately. Eight months later she gave birth to a deformed baby.

There are actually many cases recorded in which the intake of thalidomide during the sensitive phase of pregnancy could be ascertained before delivery, and special clinical attention could be paid in advance, before the outcome of the pregnancy was known. The results of these studies were no different from the retrospective ones.

In Sweden medical abortion was allowed in a few cases where thalidomide intake had occurred during the sensitive phase and it could be ascertained that the foetus was malformed.

That thalidomide caused the malformations in question is further proved by several other lines of evidence.

(1) The frequency of the epidemiologically occurring malformations in Germany followed the absolute sales of thalidomide with a time-lag of a little less than one year (see the figure below). Eight to nine months after the withdrawal of thalidomide from the market the wave of typical malformations disappeared as suddenly as they had appeared, after the same time-lag as followed the introduction of the drug.

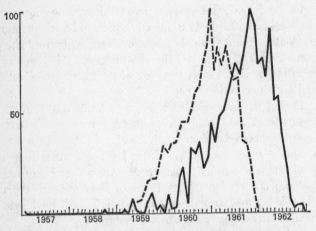

Graph showing the relation between malformations of the thalidomide type and the sales of thalidomide (figures for Germany excluding Hamburg).

- - - Thalidomide sales (January 1961 = 100)
——— 845 abnormalities of the thalidomide type (October 1961 = 100)

(2) The geographical distribution of phocomelia-like malformations of the thalidomide type coincides with the sales area for thalidomide. In countries where the substance was not on sale, such as France, the USA and Eastern European countries, with some exceptions, no increase of such malformations has been seen. In most of the exceptional cases where such malformations were found in these countries, it

has been established that the mothers had taken thalidomide brought from places where thalidomide was on sale, or that the drug had been used for investigational use (as in the USA). The frequency of malformation in various countries is related to the degree of market success of the drug. After West Germany, Japan and Great Britain have had the largest number of cases. Thereafter come Ireland, Canada, Australia and Sweden.

(3) Careful studies have shown that the exact timing of thalidomide intake and the severity and type of resulting malformations follow the recognized sequence of organ development, established by medical embryology. Intake of thalidomide between the thirty-fourth and thirty-eighth day after the last menstruation is usually associated with ear malformations, abnormalities of some of the cranial nerves, and sometimes with duplication of the thumbs. Complete absence of arms does not seem to have occurred where thalidomide was taken before the thirty-ninth day. Severe abnormalities of arms and legs have been associated with thalidomide intake between days forty-two and forty-eight. Absence of gallbladder and abnormalities of the duodenum (the first portion of the small intestine) as well as most heart malformations were produced between the fortieth and forty-fifth day, whereas minor defects of the thumb and sometimes constriction of the rectum (the final section of the large intestine) was the result of thalidomide intake at about the fiftieth day, the end of the sensitive period. At a large symposium on teratology, supported by the Wellcome Trust and the CIBA foundation, which was held in London in 1965, Professor Lenz discussed the relationship between the timing of the intake of thalidomide and the malformations observed: 'I consider these data to be the final proof of the existence of a causal relationship between the ingestion of thalidomide by pregnant women and their giving birth to malformed

offspring. At least I cannot think of any other acceptable explanation which would account for such a consistent and biologically meaningful correlation between time of intake of thalidomide and the type of malformation.' Nobody opposed this conclusion. At this symposium experts in teratology and medical embryology from throughout the world were assembled, with representatives from the drug-controlling authorities of many countries and scientists from many well-known pharmaceutical companies.

(4) In animal experiments it has been possible to produce malformations by thalidomide in a number of animal species: rabbits, mice, rats, dogs, pigs and monkeys. In the case of monkeys the results are especially suggestive since the type of malformations are very similar to those seen in man.

(5) Professor Weicker finally gives the following convincing evidence:

Weicker reasoned that the section of the population concerned with the actual manufacture of the teratogenic agent which was responsible for the wave of phocomelia seen in West Germany must have had more opportunities of access to the agent in question and would thus be affected to a greater extent. As soon as suspicion fell on thalidomide, Weicker made an analysis of the frequency of extremity and ear malformations among children born by women working in Chemie Grünenthal and among women whose husbands were employed in the factory, and found that in fact the frequency was more than twenty times that of the rest of Nordrhein-Westfalen.

According to specialists, in the realm of medicine there are few pathological conditions in man with the exception of infectious diseases for which the cause has been explained in such detail and with such accuracy as the thalidomide-embryopathies (phocomelia-like syndrome produced by thalidomide). The fact is unequivocal that thalidomide was the cause of the outbreak of phocomelia in West Germany and other countries and this is universally accepted in medical science today.

The objections advanced can, without exception, be easily refuted. The most familiar arguments and speculations raised by the manufacturers of thalidomide and by persons affiliated with their interests, are as follows:

(1) Other exogenous factors than thalidomide may have been the possible cause of the typical malformations.

In a survey of more than 100 substances (food additives, detergents, etc.) only thalidomide shows a correlation with these special malformations. No positive correlation with other drugs, smoking or alcohol was ever found.

(2) The malformations have occurred predominantly in families where mothers have very frequently watched television. The X-radiation from the television screens could possibly have been responsible for the malformations.

X-rays from television tubes are so soft (low energy) that almost nothing passes through the glass of the television screen. The radiation dose in question is negligible in comparison with the background exposure from the presence of low concentrations of radioactive isotopes in building materials, cosmic radiations, etc. Apart from these physical considerations, this wild speculation is refuted by the fact that no malformations of this kind were seen in countries where thalidomide was not on sale but where television sets of the same construction were in use. Finally, West German mothers were watching television a good deal, both before and after thalidomide, apparently without any adverse effects.

(3) The malformations could have been caused by radioactive fall-out from atomic bomb tests.

If this claim were accepted it remains a mystery why in the West the Federal Republic, but not France, was hit by the wave of phocomelia, and the German Democratic Republic and Czechoslovakia escaped in the East, although radioactive fall-out has been fairly evenly distributed over Central Europe.

(4) The malformations could have been caused by unsuccessful abortion attempts.

No support exists whatever for this cynical allegation. In the majority of cases these malformed children had been wanted. There was no new abortion technique, or abortifacient in the criminal or medical fields which was in especial use between the years 1958 to 1962. Abortions have been attempted before and after the period when thalidomide was on the market without these special types of malformation being observed.

(5) Certain constitutional, psychological or hereditary factors in the organism of the mother could have triggered off these malformations.

It should be particularly stressed that the mothers of these malformed children came from all social groups and from different parts of the world. They belong to several races and to all fertile age groups. Most of the pregnancies ran a completely normal course without any pathological symptoms. In the absolute majority of cases there was no record of hereditary abnormality in the family. Further, many of these mothers gave birth to normal children both before and after thalidomide. It has not been possible to link the incidence of these malformations with any kind of pathological change in the mother during pregnancy. The only factor common to all these women during pregnancy was the intake of thalidomide.

(6) Such malformations had been observed even before the introduction of thalidomide.

As pointed out in the introductory chapters, the frequency of this particular type of malformation was no higher than one in four million. Before thalidomide very few doctors had ever in their lives seen such a picture of malformations.

(7) It has been claimed that mothers were giving birth to

children with typical phocomelia in Germany in the years 1958–62, without having taken thalidomide.

The cases mentioned have since been re-examined. It is now clear that these mothers were amongst those who could not remember which drugs they had taken during pregnancy. In some cases they agreed that they had taken some tranquillizer or hypnotic but could not remember the name of the actual drug. By intensive investigation into the files of pharmacies, doctors and hospitals, it could even be established that in the majority of these cases thalidomide had in fact been taken. Often the mother was unaware of the fact that the drug contained thalidomide since it had been sold under a name other than Contergan (Grippex, Peracon-Expectorans, Algosediv, etc). A few women admitted that they had deliberately not answered the questions because of a 'feeling of guilt'.

Finally there have been some objections which were supposed to cast doubt on the causal relationships between thalidomide and malformations, but which actually have no relevance to this question. Since they have undoubtedly caused a lot of confusion they will be discussed here:

(8) Mothers who claim to have taken thalidomide during the critical phase, have given birth to absolutely normal children:

It is not known in how many cases this has occurred and the power of thalidomide to produce malformations is still being discussed. However, all seem to agree that thalidomide is an extremely potent teratogen, producing malformations when taken during the sensitive period in 60 to 100 per cent of the cases. In monkeys, where malformations remarkably similar to those seen in man have been produced, and where a controlled test can be made, the malformation frequency is almost 100 per cent, which supports its high effectiveness found in man. It is, for obvious reasons, sometimes quite difficult to check in retrospect, for example, that thalidomide really was consumed during the sensitive period and not a short time before or after. In some of these cases although the children had no striking, easily visible malformations, they were later found on thorough examination to have minor defects of the thumbs or internal organs.

If thalidomide caused these special malformations it is in principle of no importance whether thalidomide resulted in malformed children in 70 per cent, 80 per cent or 95 per cent of the cases where the drug was taken during the sensitive phase. Every biologist knows that within a group of living organisms there is *always an individual variation* in the sensitivity towards, for example, a poison or a drug. Because of natural biological variation some individuals are affected more than others and some are perhaps not affected at all. If about 0·5 mg. of strychnine is given by intraperitoneal injection to a certain strain of rats, approximately 50 per cent of the animals will die. The fact that the other 50 per cent survive cannot, of course, be taken as evidence *against* a causal relation between the intake of strychnine and death in rats.

(9) The detailed mechanism of the action of thalidomide is unknown and hence it cannot be proved that thalidomide caused these malformations. This point of view was advanced by Professor Erich Blechschmidt of the University of Göttingen when testifying as one of the expert witnesses called by Chemie Grünenthal during the Alsdorf trial.

This argument is logically false. To establish the relationship between cause and effect it is not necessary to know the exact pathway by which the cause finally gives the observable effect. None of the pharmaceutical industries selling the drug seem to have doubted that thalidomide was indeed a good sleeping pill although the mechanism of the sleep-inducing action of thalidomide is unknown. With most drugs the detailed mechanism of their action is still unknown, but no physician will doubt their effect in clinical use because of this.

In the case of barbiturates it is still not at all clear how these compounds elicit sleepiness. But no physician in his senses would ever dream of doubting this effect as being caused by barbiturates. The events leading from the absorption of ionizing radiations, like gamma-rays, to the final manifestation of radiation sickness are largely unknown, but no scientist would therefore be in doubt that such radiation when given in a certain dose would be able to bring about radiation damage. The conclusion that barbiturates or thalidomide cause sleep is based on experience. Thalidomide did not cause sleep for *every* single patient, but in a large percentage of patients with sleeping difficulties thalidomide gave a beneficial effect. In an individual case one cannot say that a consumption of fifty cigarettes per day will necessarily lead to production of circulatory complications or lung cancer. What may be asserted is that the probability that such an individual will acquire these afflictions is so and so many times greater than if he did not smoke at all. In the case of drugs where mostly very small amounts of the active substance is administered – in the range of order between fractions of a milligramme up to a gramme – the added compound is distributed among the innumerable cells of the organisms. Every single cell represents a complicated machine built up by intricate structural elements (mitochondria, ribosomes, lysosomes, nucleus, cell membranes, etc), mainly composed of proteins, carbohydrates and nucleic acids. A single cell may contain tens of thousands of separate enzymes, each regulating a specific chemical process. These separate processes form functional units controlled by feed-back systems like an unbelievably intricate electronic computer. The separate cells are in turn themselves organized in tissues forming organs of various complexity which in turn are controlled by various stimuli such as hormones, neurological transmittor substances, etc. To this comes the mechanism of the operation of the entire organism of man which is also influenced by psychic factors and the environment.

The notion 'to clarify the mechanism of action' is necessarily very undefined. The analysis of a physiological or biological process may be proceeded with indefinitely. Strictly speaking, it is unusual ever to reach the point in the analysis of a complex biological phenomenon when one can be said to have 'fully' clarified the mechanism of action. There is sure to be some detail overlooked, or some chemical process at the molecular level which is not properly understood. Although the detailed mechanism of the action of thalidomide still remains unknown, it can be said that thalidomide acts by passing from the bloodstream over the placental barrier to the foetus, where between day 34 and day 50 after the last menstruation the substance produces malformations by inhibiting the cell division of specific organs undergoing development.

All testing of pharmaceuticals, whether done on experimental animals or on man, is essentially based on the observations of a desired *end* effect of some kind, the incidence of which may even be evaluated statistically. If this method of approach was considered non-conclusive, we would not only be without most of the valuable drugs we use to combat disease, but we should also lack most of our modern biological science.

(10) A hypothesis about the mechanism of action of thalidomide which has been given considerable attention in the lay press and other news media, originated from experiments in animals done by the English scientists Duke, Hellman and Tucker in 1965. These research workers observed that thalidomide inhibited the rejection of transplanted tissue due to inhibition of the normal immunological reactions. On the basis of this observation it was suggested that thalidomide did not cause malformation of the foetus but prevented the spontaneous abortion of already deformed foetuses. Thalido-

mide would have a 'life-promoting' effect on deformed embryos which under normal circumstances would not survive. This hypothesis was advanced by Karl Ferdinand Kloos, a professor of pathology in Berlin and an expert witness at Alsdorf for Chemie Grünenthal.

Whereas there is little reason to doubt the experimental results of Hellman and his fellow workers – the 'immuno-suppressive' activity of thalidomide has been confirmed by other scientists – the conclusions drawn are completely erroneous: the property of inhibiting the rejection of transplanted tissues by suppressing the immunological response of the recipient is known to occur with a number of chemical compounds as is also irradiation with high energy radiations like X-rays and gamma-rays. Examples of such compounds are amethopterin (methotrexate), aminopterin and azaserin. In general they are also teratogenic in mammals – one of them, aminopterin, has been demonstrated to be also teratogenic in man – and give toxic reactions similar to ionizing radiations (radio-mimetic compounds). The immuno-suppressive agents, including radiations, are far from being 'life-saving'; they usually inhibit the cell divisions in growing tissues. Thus the observation that thalidomide inhibits immunological response is in agreement with its teratogenic action. It is difficult to understand why only foetuses which exhibit the malformations typical in 'thalidomide-embryopathias' would be protected from abortion but not those having other types of malformation. If the speculations of Hellman, Duke and Tucker were correct, the malformed foetuses which are normally aborted (without intake of thalidomide during pregnancy) should show the same high frequency of malformations of the extremities and ear as are found in 'thalidomide-babies'. This is not so. The thalidomide malformations are found as rarely as they are among babies delivered normally at full term.

Even if these speculations were correct they are clearly irrelevant from a legal point of view – they do not change the basic question of the possible responsibility of the producers for what had happened. Thalidomide would also in this case remain as the ultimate cause of the malformations, i.e. without intake of thalidomide no such deformed children would have been born.

9

Could Foreknowledge Have Prevented the Disaster?

The pharmaceutical firms responsible for the distribution of thalidomide defended themselves by claiming that before the thalidomide disaster nobody considered the possibility that drugs could damage the foetus, with the exception of certain anti-cancer agents. No pharmaceutical industry in the world carried out any kind of testing to ensure the safety for the unborn child of a drug given during pregnancy. It was only the thalidomide disaster which revealed these types of side-effect and initiated intense research in the field. The drug houses were unfortunately quite successful in communicating their ideas to the press, assisted by the statements of various 'experts', and even today public opinion in general accepts this version of the 'unavoidable' disaster. Their credulity has naturally been increased by the action of the authorities in countries where the use of thalidomide was permitted. These authorities now share a great moral responsibility for what happened. The fact that the Food and Drug Administration of the USA was considerably more alert has been extremely embarrassing. The Swedish Medical Board has claimed that it was a matter of pure chance that thalidomide was not cleared by the FDA. The gold medal of the President's Award for Distinguished Federal Civilian Service was not given to Dr Kelsey by chance, as is clearly proved by the FDA files. Dr Kelsey's reasons for concern about what thalidomide might do to the unborn infant were based at that time on certain relevant theoretical considerations.

Dr Kelsey's interest in the effect of drugs on the foetus dated back to her time as a young student in 1943 when she, in co-operation with Frances K. Oldham, conducted studies on the breakdown of quinine. The team demonstrated that, whereas the liver of adult rabbits quickly breaks quinine down, the rabbit foetus has little or no ability to do so ('Studies on Antimalarial Drugs: the Influence of Pregnancy on the Quinine Oxidase of Rabbit Liver', by Francis K. Oldham and F. E. Kelsey, *Journal of Pharmacology and Experimental Therapeutics* 79 (1943) p. 81). A drug circulating in the blood stream of a pregnant woman penetrates the placenta and reaches the foetus, where it may persist since the developing foetus cannot break the drug down as efficiently as the adult can. As is well known the general sensitivity of developing tissues is increased towards all external agents, and the foetus is at greater risk than is the adult from damage by a toxic drug.

The study of deleterious influences on the embryo caused by external agents began much earlier than 1943. From earliest times man has blamed external events for the birth of monsters or deformed children. Hippocrates advanced mainly mechanical theories, such as the crippling of the child by the mother's fall or a contusion in the mother.

Such ideas, usually connected with superstitions about witchcraft and the Devil, have survived from the Middle Ages to our present times. In certain parts of southern Europe the birth of a deformed child is still considered to be punishment for the sins of the parents. Italian doctors told us that such attitudes probably contributed to the fact that so many thalidomide babies born in Italy and Spain had been hidden away by the parents. Any kind of legal action due to the failure of the authorities and the producers to withdraw the drug from the Italian market until almost one year after it had been shown to be teratogenic was considered unthinkable.

The first really scientific approach, in a modern sense, in the science of teratology (the study of monsters, from the Greek *teratos* – a monster) seems to have begun in the experimental studies of Dareste, published in a monograph entitled *Recherches sur la production artificielle des monstruosités ou essai de tératogénie expérimentale* in 1891. Dareste was able to produce a variety of congenital abnormalities in chickens by means of various poisons. At that time the scientists extrapolated such experimental findings to man, and in the second edition of the Swedish Encyclopedia *Nordisk Familjebok*, published in 1913, chemical factors are mentioned as possible causes of malformation in man. The possible effect which lead poisoning of the father might have on the offspring was tested on fowl and rabbits by Cole and Bachhuber in 1914, and on guinea pigs by Weller between 1914 and 1916. In an article called 'Keimverderbnis und Fruchtschädigung', published in *Medizinische Klinik* in 1924, Müller discussed the possible role of toxic agents such as alcohol, morphine, lead, mercury and iodine for the induction of malformation in man. In the fourteenth volume of *Handbuch des normalen und pathologischen Physiologie*, Broman of Lund, Sweden, wrote in his chapter 'Allgemeine Missbildungslehre': 'In man one should especially consider diseases which produce chemical changes of the blood (e.g. diabetes, nephritis) as well as intoxication by alcohol, morphine, sedatives or different drugs as causes of malformations.' During the thirties considerable attention was paid to the possible deleterious effect of quinine on the foetus. In 1934 H. Marshall Taylor wrote: 'That the placenta is permeable to drugs has long been recognized. The obstetrician has for many years accepted this fact and since it has become recognized that quinine, when administered to the mother, may be toxic to the foetus much research work has been done on the subject.'

When sulphonamides came into clinical use they were also investigated for their effects on the foetus. A group of American scientists wrote in 1938, 'Until more is known of the tolerance of the human foetus and of the newborn for sulphanilamide, the drug should be administered with the utmost caution during pregnancy and the period of lactation.'

In 1940 a German physician pointed out that a large number of pregnant women were treated with the sulpha drug Albucid, and consequently a large number of foetuses in every stage of development came into contact with the drug. He further reported cases of intoxication of the newborn by Albucid and argued that, because of well-known sensitivity of the foetus, especially during the first months of pregnancy, the sulpha drug might damage it.

Well before Kelsey's experiment with quinine in 1943, clearly, there was a good deal of literature available on the subject of the effect of drugs on the foetus. By the time thalidomide was introduced on the market in 1957 this experience had been broadened by clinical studies of the effects of drugs during pregnancy. On the basis of this experience it could be concluded that many drugs in use were harmless to the foetus. Furthermore, these conclusions were not theoretical but were based on animal experiments and clinical trials. A good example of how one of these trials was conducted is given in an article by Clay N. Wells in 1953 describing the treatment of nausea during early pregnancy with cortisone (*American Journal of Obstetrics and Gynecology*, Vol. 66, 1953). Wells offers statistics based on the study of twenty-nine cases. The condition of the child at birth was noted including any malformations. If thalidomide had been tested in this manner the terrible properties would have been revealed at an early stage and only a few cases of phocomelia might have occurred instead of the thousands of deformed babies. As early as 1946 a long-term epidemiologic study of the reproduction of man was begun at the Columbia Presbyterian Medical Centre in New York and given the name 'The Foetal Life Study'. The investigation's purpose was to study the frequency of foetal death and malformation among a sample of the population. All medications taken by the mothers were noted in their detailed records because of the potential teratogenic hazards associated with the use of drugs during pregnancy.

Many further examples may be easily found in the medical literature available before the thalidomide disaster, where physicians and experimental embryologists express their concern about the use of drugs during pregnancy because of the potential danger to the foetus.

In a few cases drugs such as aminopterin and quinine were shown to be teratogenic in man. As aminopterin was known to be an abortifacient in experimental animals, John B. Thiersch tried it in patients during pregnancy where abortion was indicated for medical reasons. In a few cases where it failed to induce abortion, malformations were produced. Professor John B. Thiersch, director of the Institute of Biological Research and Professor of Clinical Pharmacology in the University of Seattle, declared in a statement to the court of Södertälje :

In the ten years preceding the appearance of thalidomide, that is by 1959, not less than twenty-five compounds were shown by various investigators ranging from Japan to the United States, to England and France to effect the foetus *in utero*, either killing many foetuses or inducing malformations ... The findings by the various investigators were published in scientific journals and distributed internationally. The results of the experimental work were also presented at international conferences, conferences attended by thousands of scientific workers, and certainly by observers of drug houses. In the United States the investigation of the effect of compounds affecting the foetuses through the mothers were actively supported by a number of drug houses. All investigators were unanimous in their opinions that the compounds acted directly on the foetuses and that the effect either of death, malformations or stunting of the foetuses was direct evidence of intoxication of the foetuses and not an indirect effect of the mothers.

The investigators always considered that their findings in animal experiments were applicable to humans, because human tumour-carriers, treated with these compounds, showed the same response in their tissues that the experimental animals had shown. For this reason it was anticipated that the foetus of man would respond in the same way as had the foetus of the experimental animals. In his clinical papers published in 1952 Thiersch described a high percentage of malformations occurring in attempted foetal abortions in women treated with 4 amino PGA, and specifically warned that the compound should only be given if surgical evacuation of the uterus was assured, to avoid the induction of malformation in the foetus. Thiersch's experiments were later confirmed by Meltzer and Warkany. Professor Thiersch further writes:

In the case of thalidomide, the human experiments preceded animal investigations. The induction of malformation in the human foetus corresponds directly to those seen induced in experimental animals with any of the other twenty-five compounds listed. Thalidomide is similiar in its chemical structure to the folic acid antagonists and in some respects also to AZA and DON (teratogenic compounds). As such, the molecule was under suspicion for the effect it might have on the foetus.

Many responsible pharmaceutical industries like Merck, Burroughs Wellcome, and Smith, Kline and French, were well aware of the possible deleterious action of their drugs on the foetus and had this aspect fully investigated. Thiersch himself tested compounds for possible teratogenic effects for several pharmaceutical houses. For example, the drug Diamox for Lederle and Daraprim for Burroughs Wellcome. Several drug houses carried out a considerable amount of testing of this kind, especially in the USA. It was a different story when Richardson-Merrell Inc. undertook such trials with Triparanol in 1960 (MER/29), and purposely withheld from the FDA the fact that the drug had toxic effects on the foetuses of animals. In their brochures the company cautioned against the use of the drug during pregnancy 'purely on theoretical grounds', but in fact the real grounds were the results they had obtained in animal experiments.

Although some types of drug, anti-cancer drugs for example, were considered more likely to produce malformations than others, the potential risk of administration of *any type of drug* was seriously considered by many physicians, scientists and drug houses. Internal reports from Smith, Kline and French reveal that the tranquillizer Prochlorperazine, used for the treatment of nausea during pregnancy, was tested in animals for its effects on the foetus in 1956. The animal experiments showed no negative effects and they were followed by clinical trials during pregnancy. The effect in pregnancy of Doriden, produced by CIBA, was similarly checked in 1959.

By using the experimental methods which were already available in existence before the introduction of thalidomide it would have been possible to detect the teratogenic properties of thalidomide. The internationally known teratologist, Professor Walter Landauer, who has published more than 160 scientific publications in the field of experimental embryology and teratology since 1922, wrote in his statement to the court of Södertälje on 14 June 1967:

STATEMENT

I wish to make the following expert statement in answer to certain questions arising from the thalidomide trials in Sweden and other countries which have been put to me by Mr Sjöström through Dr Nilsson of the University of Stockholm :

(1) Were any methods available in 1959 by which the teratogenic properties of thalidomide could have been demonstrated?

The answer must emphatically be in the affirmative. All animals which are currently in use for testing the teratogenicity of thalidomide and other drugs have for long been commonly employed by pharmacologists, nutrition specialists, endocrinologists, general physiologists, developmental geneticists, and others. The tests were made then as they are now, by incorporating specific compounds of antagonists of metabolites either into experimental diets, or through direct oral application and by injecting the dissolved test compounds into pregnant animals or by exposing the embryos to them by various routes. In specific situations such tests were extended even to the possible consequence that exposure of the father might have on his progeny. This could be documented in great detail, but a few references of long standing should suffice ... Since it was then well known that the morphogenesis of embryos passes through stages of specific response to external agents, and since ordinary test animals were already available, it required only imagination and initiative to inquire into the teratogenic qualities of specific compounds.

From earlier experience it seems clear that the teratogenic properties of *any compound* can be, and could have been, tested satisfactorily, *provided* that the intact compound (or such decomposition products as may occur physiologically) reaches the embryo. It was also known, from earlier experience, that teratogenic responses can vary greatly between genera and even within a species and that it was therefore imperative to base tests on a broad basis. Actual events have shown (a) that in the hands of Tuchman-Duplessis and Giroud the teratogenicity of thalidomide, and even its organ-specific effects, could be demonstrated without any but the customary test methods, and (b) that negative results with thalidomide were in the majority of cases readily explained by the fact that the tests had been done with solutions of hydrophylic decomposition products, rather than with the complete compound, and that these decomposition products are much less likely to penetrate through cellular membranes than does the intact drug.

In a similar vein, Professor Thiersch also wrote:

DISCUSSION OF THE THALIDOMIDE DISASTER

Question One: Were there any methods available in 1959 by which the teratogenic properties of thalidomide could have been demonstrated?

The methods available to examine foetal abnormalities of foetuses did not differ in the years after 1959 from earlier methods. They consisted of obtaining the foetuses from the uterus of pregnant animals or newborns, inspecting them, measuring them, fixing them in various fixatives, cutting the foetuses in serial sections for microscopic studies, clearing and staining their skeletons with oil of wintergreen, alizarine and methylene blue. In other instances, X-ray photos were taken to study the malformation of the skeleton. In certain respects the rabbit blastocyst technique of Dr C. Mann represented some new features in the years from 1950 to 1959. However this technique was also well established by the time thalidomide came on the market. The entire field of teratology and the investigation of drugs affecting the foetus *in utero* received a new impetus after Thiersch and Phillips in 1949 (1) made their dramatic discovery at the Sloan Kettering Institute for Cancer Research in New York that three small doses of 4-amino-PGA (aminopterin) would destroy foetuses *in utero*. Unlike nutritional experiments carried out by M. Nelson and her group in Berkeley, California, or by Giroud and his group in Paris, or by Warkany in Cincinnatti, Ohio, (2) it was demonstrated for the first time that small doses not too toxic to the mother animal would seriously affect the foetus *in utero* within hours. This effect was considered to be directly on the foetus and not on the mother.

Thiersch then gives a detailed account of the experimental

techniques developed before thalidomide, and concludes: 'Summing up, one has to say that the methods used later in an attempt to define the action of thalidomide on the embryo were well established before 1959.'

At the beginning of 1965 Chemie Grünenthal stated in a television interview that it had still not been possible to obtain malformation in monkeys. A few weeks earlier representatives of Chemie Grünenthal had visited the laboratories of Chaz-Pfeizer in the USA. In the laboratories of Chaz-Pfeizer in the USA pregnant mothers of the monkey *Macaca irus philippinenis* had been given thalidomide. When the drug was given to the pregnant monkey between day 34 and 40 after the last menstruation *every single embryo of these animals became deformed!* The foetuses were damaged in exactly the same manner as had been observed in man. Ears and arms were lacking, or only rudiments of the arms were to be seen. The lower extremities were extensively malformed and in the middle of the face a red hemangioma was seen. Further internal malformations could also be found.

Surely many representatives of the medical profession were not sufficiently aware of these problems before thalidomide. However, the real roots of the problem lay with the many pharmaceutical companies where, as Senator Hubert Humphrey put it in the famous Hearings before the US Senate in 1962, 'there has been almost completely ignored certain longstanding evidence to the effect that chemical agents can cause injury to babies in their mothers' wombs'.

In his deposition to the Court, Professor Duow G. Steyn at the Ministry of Health in the Republic of South Africa, stated:

(1) For some thirty years or more I have been warning against the free and unwarranted use of drugs (any drug) during pregnancy, that is long before the tragic thalidomide disaster . . . For decades, I have been teaching my students (medical) to exercise

the utmost care in the prescribing of drugs to pregnant women because of the danger of teratism. I have given them long lists of known and potential teratogenic agents, and also referred to teratism in relation to disease and nutrition.

In the enclosed article you will notice that already in 1954 I sounded a warning note about the dangers of the administration of drugs to expectant mothers.

Before and since that time I have constantly impressed this danger on my medical students as well as on members of the medical profession *and pleaded that all drugs likely to be administered to pregnant women should be tested for their possible teratogenic effects.*

Professor Steyn further pointed out:

The fact that the greatest danger to the foetus exists during the first trimester of pregnancy has also been known for many years. This is the reason why I have, for so many years, warned especially against the administration of *any drug* to pregnant mothers during the earliest stages of pregnancy . . . It is quite obvious why the degree of damage done to the foetus is most marked during the earliest stages of its development – the processes of organogenesis are most active during these stages.

The worst degrees of anatomical abnormalities in the foetus are produced by teratogenic agents taken by the mother during *the first trimester of pregnancy* . . . Reliable methods of testing the possible teratogenic effects of any substance, including drugs, are known and could also have been applied in 1959 and before that time.

Steyn concluded:

Any firm manufacturing pharmaceutical preparations should for decades have been fully aware of the possible dangers of drugs to pregnant mothers and foetuses.

During the period preceding the thalidomide disaster there was an increasing awareness of the unsatisfactory state of affairs prevailing in the field of drug safety and pregnancy, and many scientists and physicians were seriously concerned about the slackness in checking the effect of many new drugs for possible deleterious effects on the foetus. In the October 1961 number of *Paediatrics* written eight months before the effects of thalidomide became known, the following statement can be found:

It is a BASIC PREMISE of paediatrics that physical size is not the most important difference between children and adults. There is increasing awareness that it is also necessary to make more than a quantitative distinction between infants and children. The foetus and the newborn infant often behave so differently as to warrant consideration as separate categories of the human species. This necessitates re-evaluation of the effects of drugs independently in each category of the human so that they may be used safely.

Existing drugs and agents that are developed in the future for use in the foetus and in infants must be subjected to more extensive preclinical investigation than is being carried out at the present time. The pharmacologic responses of the immature human may differ greatly both quantitatively and qualitatively from those of the adult. As a result, data obtained from tests in mature animals and human adults or older children cannot be accepted as a satisfactory basis for recommendations concerning the foetus and infant.

In order to pursue these principles, it is recommended that drug labels should specifically indicate the extent of existing information concerning the use of the agent in the foetus and the infant. When there have been no pharmacologic studies of a drug in immature subjects, an explicit statement of this fact should be indicated on the drug label or in a readily available package leaflet. Physicians who administer drugs to the foetus and the infant must be alert to unusual effects in this subdivision of the human species.

COMMITTEE ON FOETUS AND NEWBORN
William A. Silverman, M.D., Chairman
Fred H. Allen, Jr., M.D.

J. Edmund Bradley, M.D.
Eugene H. Crawley, M.D.
Paul A. Harper, M.D.
David Y. Hsia, M.D.
Benjamin M. Kagan, M.D.
Joseph A. Little, M.D.
Henry K. Silver, M.D.
Samuel Spector, M.D.
J. R. Fouts, Ph.D., Consultant
William H. Kessenich, M.D., Consultant
James M. Sutherland, M.D., Consultant
May 1961.

Dr Jerold F. Lucey wrote in the May 1961 issue of *Pediatric Clinics of North America*:

Unknown Harmful Agents

Clinicians are not sufficiently aware of the great gaps which exist in our knowledge of the pharmacology of drugs administered either directly to the newborn infant, or indirectly through administration to his mother. All too often we have assumed that if a drug is nontoxic for the mother it will also not harm the foetus. This has proved to be a dangerous assumption.

Currently many new drugs (diuretics, oral hypoglycemic agents, and tranquillizers) are being given during pregnancy, and there is no adequate evidence on which to judge that these are completely non-toxic to the foetus. Unnecessary human experiments can be prevented in the future only if the clinician is alert to the vulnerability of the foetus to transplacental [caused by substances penetrating the placenta] neonatal disease.

In the *Annals of the New York Academy of Sciences* in 1965, Professor Lenz wrote in his article 'Epidemiology of Congenital Malformations':

The possibility of manmade chemical malformations might have been envisaged since the early fifties. In 1955 Giroud, in a review on congenital malformations and their causes devoted 18

179

pages to the role of chemical substances. He gave a bibliography of 191 references to chemicals. The Austrian pharmacologist von Brücke wrote a paper in 1958 on 'Injuries to the Fetus Through Use of Drugs by the Mother' in which he sounded the following warning : 'It therefore appears very useful to point out as early as possible in the medical care of early pregnancy, that, in addition to a well adapted diet containing sufficient vitamins, any drug therapy should be avoided which is not absolutely necessary.' Early in 1959, Kühne submitted a far-sighted plan on epidemiological studies of malformations to the 'Deutsche Forschungsgemeinschaft' which is the chief institution in Western Germany giving financial support to scientific studies. Kühne rightly explained : 'Both in problems of radiation genetics and in pharmacological and toxicological evaluation, the actual incidence of human malformations is acutely important.' If this well founded proposal had not been turned down by the Deutsche Forschungsgemeinschaft, the existence of the thalidomide epidemic as well as its cause would probably have been found out at least one year earlier.

According to the propaganda sponsored by some pharmaceutical industries and the Swedish Health authorities, nobody thought to test drugs for their effects on the foetus before the thalidomide disaster.

An especially aggravating circumstance in the case of thalidomide is that in many countries the pharmaceutical companies concerned specifically claimed that thalidomide was safe for mother and child when given during pregnancy, in spite of the fact that this claim was not supported by appropriate clinical experience.

If the distributors of thalidomide and the responsible governmental agencies had taken proper notice of the existing medical literature and scientific knowledge and had listened to the warnings often expressed by many scientists, the thalidomide disaster might never have happened and this unnecessary experiment in human teratology and its attendant vast suffering for thousands of people would have been prevented.

In the same article (1965) in the annals of the New York Academy of Sciences, Professor Lenz concluded: 'Unfortunately most people have been slow in appreciating the reality of the danger. Dozens of valuable scientific papers as well as solitary warning voices passed unheeded. It took thousands of malformed babies finally to alarm the public.'

On 3 August 1962 the Medical Adviser, Dr Dennis Burley, of Distillers Co. in England wrote a letter to the Director of Scientific Relations of the William S. Merrell Co.:

I am going to be a nuisance to you, but a rather urgent matter has come up. In the *Guardian* today there is an article by Alistair Cooke which in the main is a pat on the back to the FDA in general and Dr Frances Kelsey in particular. I would be interested in your observations on it, but in particular about the sentence, 'In May, 1961, Dr Kelsey told the Company that she suspected it might have some ill effect on unborn babies.' Can you confirm or deny this? If she did suspect that thalidomide might have some ill effect on unborn babies what was the nature of her suspicions? You can readily appreciate that we are likely now to be faced with the question, 'If Dr Kelsey suspected ill effects on unborn babies on reasonable grounds why didn't the Distillers Co. similarly suspect?'

10

What Safety Tests Were
in Fact Made?

The various companies described thalidomide as 'completely non-toxic'. Now that we have seen the falseness of this claim, and the possibility of knowing in advance the drug's deleterious effect, it will be useful to see what tests were in fact made by these firms.

From a purely technical point of view one may point to a number of inadequacies and inaccuracies in the material available from pre-clinical testing. Even some of the fundamental chemical properties of the active compound had not been properly investigated. The scientists at Chemie Grünenthal claimed that thalidomide was chemically a very stable substance 'which is only attacked by alkali of a pH-value not encountered in the organism under physiological conditions'. In reality, thalidomide even at neutral pH and under physiological conditions is rapidly broken down into at least eight different decomposition products, as clarified later by a team of scientists from the CIBA pharmaceutical company in Basel. This peculiar behaviour is of importance from many points of view. Besides its sale in the form of tablets thalidomide was also marketed in the form of a suspension, 'the baby-sitter' version of thalidomide, especially intended for consumption by children. Because of the decomposition of thalidomide in water solutions, after some time these suspensions would not only contain thalidomide but also an undefined mixture of thalidomide and its eight decomposition products, the pharmacological and toxicological properties of some of which were completely unknown. This was a clear case of drug mislabelling. The instability of the drug later proved to be a pitfall to many research workers trying to study the effects of this compound. When testing on a large scale in laboratory practice one tends to have solutions or suspensions made up by the gallon and to use these not the same day, but over a period of time, unless one is aware of some instability in the drug. When unable to dissolve the drug in water some scientists added strong alkali, which immediately decomposed the drug. Obviously negative results were obtained in animal tests when decomposed solutions were used to induce malformation.

At the end of 1959 some rather disturbing reports came from the Distillers laboratory, the licensee in England. One of their scientists, Dr Somers, found that the presence of certain sugars increased the toxicity of finely ground (micronized) thalidomide when this was milled to a suspension. In a pharmacological report published in the *British Journal of Pharmacology* in 1960 Dr Somers suggested, 'It may well be that the absence of toxicity is due to limited absorption, for the compound has a low solubility in body fluids.' In an internal report Dr Somers wrote:

Hitherto thalidomide has shown no demonstrable toxicity and mice have survived oral doses as high as 5 g/kg. The safety of the drug has been confirmed clinically, and emphasis of this has been made in our advertising material.

The observations that our formulated suspension is toxic is disturbing for it means that if we market in this form our claims are no longer justified; and it is suggested that the formulation is amended to avoid this situation.

In a letter to Dr W. P. Kennedy on 2 January 1960 Dr Somers again pointed out, 'The safety margin is high, but the fact that it can be toxic is the worry. You will appreciate that our claim for non-toxicity would not be valid with this preparation.' A letter dated 30 December 1959 to Dr G. F. Somers, from J. J. H. Hastings of Distillers reads: 'I have of course been advised of the emergency action it was necessary to take to withdraw clinical samples of an experimental "Distaval" Elixir owing to the toxicity which was reported from your laboratory after the material had been forwarded.'

Chemie Grünenthal later informed Distillers that they had repeated Dr Somers' experiments and had arrived at the conclusion that the preparation was completely non-toxic to the mice used at Chemie Grünenthal, and that the British mice they had used must belong to some particularly sensitive strain.

Another unresolved question was whether the low acute toxicity of thalidomide was just illusory, and was due to the low solubility of the compound and/or to its poor absorption from the gastrointestinal tract. As was evident from the article written by Dr Somers which appeared in the *British Journal of Pharmacology* in 1960, this question was still not clarified three years after Grünenthal put the drug on the market. This is also noted by Dr Kelsey at the FDA who wrote in a memorandum of 16 December 1960:

The firm called to present additional data in support of their NDA [new drug application] for Kevadon [thalidomide] which had been classified as incomplete. The main parts of discussion included: (1) the question of absorption of the drug from the gastrointestinal tract: i.e. was its low toxicity due to poor absorption ...

The question of absorption and solubility is not an academic one, since there may be conditions in which absorption is increased, such as by changes in diet or in certain pathological conditions, at which point a latent toxicity of the compound could become apparent. This is clearly explained by Dr Kelsey on 9 February 1967, in her deposition before the United States District Court for the Eastern District of Pennsylvania:

Attorney Gary Leeds: What was known to you, if anything, as of September of 1960, as to how the drug was absorbed and distributed?

Dr Kelsey: Little or nothing was known of this aspect.

Gary Leeds: And to what extent did the New Drug Application add to your knowledge?

Dr Kelsey: It gave us insufficient information, so we couldn't draw any conclusions.

Gary Leeds: Can you tell us whether or not it is important that one who evaluates the safety of a drug knows how it is absorbed and distributed?

Dr Kelsey: Yes, this is quite important in regard to claims for non-toxicity. If this were due to the fact that it is ordinarily rather poorly absorbed, there might be conditions under which absorption might be greatly increased or elimination decreased, and these are all important factors for taking the toxicity of a drug.

In a statement to the District Court of Södertälje of 11 November 1965, the Astra Co., manufacturers of thalidomide in Sweden, described briefly how, in their opinion, a drug should be tested in animal experiments before it is introduced for human usage:

2 (b) *Toxicity upon long-term administration* gives information about effects produced by daily administration during a shorter or longer period of time. The animals are weighed every week to check their growth. At regular intervals blood samples are taken and at the same time kidney and liver function (among other things) are studied. By this procedure possibly deleterious effects may be discovered. The test is terminated by killing the

animals and subjecting them to a complete autopsy. At this stage samples from the majority of organs are taken. These are analysed microscopically.

According to Astra this was a part of the routine test procedure to be followed during the pre-clinical testing at the time in question.

A thorough check of the material on which Astra based their decision to introduce thalidomide in Scandinavia reveals quite another picture on this point. There was no data available to support the claim that, for example, thalidomide did not cause any change in the composition of the blood. The presentation of the effects of thalidomide on growth were inadequate. The autopsies of the individual animals did *not* include several of the most important organs, such as the central nervous system, bone marrow, adrenals, thyroid, parathyroid, stomach, sex organs, pancreas, lymph nodes, gall bladder, small intestine or large intestine. In contrast to what Astra claimed should be done, no investigation of kidney and liver function was performed.

This last negligence is particularly remarkable since a common side-effect of many types of drug is the capacity to damage the liver when given over a long period of time, and yet the manufacturers claimed that thalidomide was especially suited to patients suffering from liver damage.

It is true, of course, that in further extensive use thalidomide proved to lack any liver toxicity. Later investigation in animals has also failed to reveal any significant effect at many of the points where severe criticism could have been directed towards the original material presented before the drug was introduced. Legally this negligence does not have any *direct* bearing on the possibility of revealing harmful effects of thalidomide on the foetus. The totally inadequate material available before the introduction of thalidomide in various countries, the faults of which must have been quite obvious to Chemie Grünenthal and to its licensees, proves one point though. Thalidomide was introduced according to the method of Russian roulette. Practically nothing was known about several aspects of this new drug at the time of its marketing. Far-reaching claims were made about absence of toxicity and lines of usage which were not supported by available investigation and which lacked the support of clinical experience.

All the drugs in use until today may, under certain conditions, give rise to side-effects, a fact that is well recognized by pharmacologists and physicians. The frequency of incidence of the side-effects must of course be set in proper relation to the nature of the disease it is intended to cure. In the treatment of fatal diseases like cancer one is willing to accept side-effects which would be impermissible when using for example some antibiotic against a throat infection. In the case of a tranquillizer or a hypnotic like thalidomide, which is expected to be used without continuous medical supervision in a variety of conditions of anxiety and insomnia, for children as well as for adults, naturally, the requirements for safety must be very rigorous. Especially so, considering the way thalidomide was advertised as 'completely safe', 'completely non-toxic', etc.

In the routine of developing a new drug the pre-clinical testing should be done on animals as exhaustively as possible. However, these animal experiments leave some questions open concerning the effects to be expected in man, for the following reasons:

(1) The effect of a drug may vary in different species of animal.

(2) The effects evoked in an animal may differ from those it exerts in the human organism.

(3) Many diseases occurring in man cannot be induced in

experimental animals, and certain diseases develop quite differently in animals.

The reason for carrying out extensive animal trials is that the disadvantages are slight compared with the advantages. In general, the effect of a drug in animals is very similar to that exerted by it in man. When animal experiments are run on a large scale, it is possible to analyse the effects observed with a much greater accuracy than would ever be possible in human beings. The influence of disturbing external factors causing variations in response, such as differences in diet, temperature conditions, etc. may be eliminated in this type of testing. Even more important, the use of pure inbred animal strains may eliminate variation due to different hereditary factors within the group under study. Although an investigation of this type can never provide an absolute guarantee that a drug will be efficient for the treatment of a certain disease or will be innocuous to man, it can furnish clear-cut evidence that a beneficial effect is very likely and that the risk for unexpected side-effects is probably small. For these reasons animal testing is indispensible for pharmaceutical research.

Animal experiments with thalidomide demonstrated that no toxic reaction could be observed as a result of the administration of very high *single* doses. Reports from suicide attempts with thalidomide later confirmed these animal findings. However, in a few cases of accidental intoxication of young children by thalidomide severe damage has been noted. This demonstrates another basic toxicological principle, that a drug that is found to be innocuous to adults may cause severe damage in the young underdeveloped child.

More surprising to the prosecutor was the disclosure by Dr Mückter, the director of the scientific laboratory of Chemie Grünenthal, that all the original test protocols were destroyed before 1959 because 'it seemed unnecessary to keep the individual test protocols for the future'. This is quite contrary to the practice followed by other pharmaceutical industries, which keep such information on file for a considerable time. After Astra was confronted with this statement in the court of Södertälje, Dr Svedin of Astra made a telephone call to Dr Mückter to inquire about the fate of these records. The explanation Dr Mückter gave to Dr Svedin on that occasion was that 'the records had disappeared during moving of the files some time during 1959!'

With the exception of teratogenic effects no other harmful effects from thalidomide have been definitely demonstrated by animal experiments. We know for certain that Chemie Grünenthal did not carry out any trials to demonstrate teratogenic effects in animals before the introduction of this drug. In the first publication on the pharmacological and toxicological properties of thalidomide, published in *Arzneimittel Forschung* in 1965 by Kunz, Keller and Mückter, a study which can only be regarded as a summary of some preliminary tests, it is contended that thalidomide (K17) has sedative properties in mice. From internal reports made in 1956 by the laboratories of Smith, Kline and French it is evident that even when used in doses of 5,000 mg. to each kilogramme of body weight it is not possible to induce sleep in mice. This dose is 50 times as large as that claimed by Chemie Grünenthal to be 'sleep inducing'. The scientists at Smith, Kline and French failed to find any effect on the spontaneous activity of mice in doses up to 500 mg./kg. body weight. This was about 650 times the dose effective in man. Richardson-Merrell evidently obtained similar results, since Dr Kelsey wrote to a solicitor's firm, Kumber, Bull & Co., in 1962:

At first, the thalidomide application was turned down because it was felt that the evidence submitted with the application was not extensive enough to permit evaluation of the safety of the drug. For example, the drug appeared to have a definite hypnotic effect in humans but not in animals. We were concerned that it could elicit toxic effects in human beings that would not show up in animal studies.

In an internal report made by CIBA in 1962, called 'Pharmacological Data on Thalidomide', it similarly proved impossible to demonstrate any sedative effect in animal experiments. It cannot be doubted that an unbiased test in animals would lead to the same conclusion as found in the CIBA's report : 'Our results are essentially the same as those published in the literature. They give a very unpromising pharmacological picture and a very poor outlook for successful clinical use.'

The finding of Smith, Kline and French, Richardson-Merrell and CIBA that the results from animal studies did not parallel human experience is an important one, as was well pointed out by Dr Kelsey. Since man is more than fifty times as sensitive as animals to the sedative effect of thalidomide it would not be surprising if man similarly was much more sensitive to possible negative reactions from the drug, which may not even be possible to elicit in animal experiments. The safety factor could just be an apparent one. The fact that sleep could not be induced in the experimental animals used demonstrated that in this case, for some reason, the animals reacted quite differently from man, and the apparent safety observed in animals would be absolutely no guarantee that this was valid for man, as was indeed proved later. No attention was paid to this special circumstance by the manufacturers of thalidomide and the low acute toxicity in animals was used over and over again as an argument to prove its safety in clinical use.

Dr Somers of Distillers in England was evidently quite aware of this weak point, since in connection with the increased toxicity observed for suspensions of thalidomide, he wrote in his memorandum: 'Admittedly the toxic dose in mice (3·15 g./kg.) is high, but it should be realized that mice are approximately sixty times more resistant than man to the sedative effect of this drug and the safety factor may not therefore be so wide as appears.'

In the case of thalidomide the pre-clinical testing done by Chemie Grünenthal before the clinical trials was indeed very superficial and incomplete, as shown by the available documentation. This weakness was realized by the potential business partner Smith, Kline and French in the US who carried out extensive animal testing on their own.

In view of the incomplete pre-clinical testing done by Chemie Grünenthal the hasty clinical trials appear the more questionable. The lack of proper government control of the drug industry in the Federal Republic may offer an explanation, though not an excuse. The reports of trials in man are acutely lacking in detailed observation, they merely convey general impressions about the effect of thalidomide. Side-effects of obscure origin were not followed up, and thorough clinical investigation of the status of the patients was either not properly done or not adequately recorded.

One of the physicians employed for pre-clinical testing, Dr Jung, tried thalidomide on over a hundred patients. Fifty of these were followed up for a period exceeding six months. However, most of the patients were suffering from tuberculosis. Dr Jung recorded side-effects such as constipation, temperature depression, blocked ears, and tremor of the extremities and even a few cases of inability to work, but it is difficult to draw any conclusions from his report about the severity and incidence of these side-effects. Attention should be paid to the mention of tremor of the extremities especially since at about the *same time*, the medical director of the Kurort-Heilstille hospital at Wasach near Oberstdorf, Dr Piacenza, reported that he was not satisfied with the new drug and had to interrupt all use due to '*absolutes Unver-träglichkeit*'. He reported several side-effects including one case of light paraesthesia. Both the tremor of the extremities observed by Dr Jung as well as the paraesthesia observed by Dr Piacenza point to some effect on the nervous system and certainly called for clarification: were these effects induced by the drug and, if so, under what conditions? No such follow-up was done by Chemie Grünenthal and the warnings were completely ignored. Dr Mückter suggested in a letter of 3 April 1956 that 'overdosage over a long period' may have caused interference of the nervous system. This did not prevent Chemie Grünenthal from claiming in its 1956 *Basisprospekt* that 'Extreme overdosage does not provoke any toxic reaction.'

On 10 November 1960, *three years after* the drug had been introduced on the market in West Germany, the material available concerning clinical trials was still so inadequate that Dr Frances O. Kelsey wrote of it in a letter to William S. Merrell Co:

It fails to report the clinical studies in full detail.

The reports should include detailed information relating to each individual treated, including age, sex, conditions treated, dosage, frequence of administration of the drug, results of clinical and laboratory examinations, and a full statement of any adverse effects and therapeutic results observed.

Many of the cases reported in the application are in summary form without the necessary details included. In addition, the application is inadequate under section 505 (b) (1) of the act in that insufficient cases have been studied. Many of the 3,156 cited cases are in foreign literature reports and in many instances the reports do not represent detailed studies to determine the safety of the drug. The application should contain more cases in which detailed studies have been done.

The application is further inadequate and incomplete under section 506 (b) (1) of the act in that the chronic toxicity data are incomplete and therefore, no evaluation can be made of the safety of the drug when used for a prolonged period of time.

It should be realized that a considerable amount of new clinical material had appeared during the four years since Chemie Grünenthal introduced the drug.

Again, it is a known fact that a combination of drugs may give very unfortunate results. One of the drugs may activate the toxicity of the other (synergism) so that the toxicity of a combination of two drugs may not simply be the effects of one drug by itself added to the effects of the other. Such synergistic effects are not restricted to a combination of drugs. It is a well-known fact that you can get quite a 'kick' from combining alcohol with certain drugs. Even certain types of foods may give untoward reactions in combination with some drugs, as shown by the serious side reactions observed when the anti-depressive drug tranylcypromine is given in association with the eating of cheese. In some instances medical science is taking advantage of synergistic effects as in the case of the opium alkaloids which activate each other.

In the case of thalidomide no proper systematic evaluation of synergistic effects was made for a long time even for such a likely combination as alcohol and thalidomide. This is the more alarming since the use of the drug was recommended in the treatment of alcoholism! Actually in 1960 Somers obtained experimental evidence for a clear synergistic effect between alcohol and thalidomide in that thalidomide increased the toxicity of alcohol. This was evidently the first time this combination had been tested.

This brings us to one of the most serious aspects of the marketing of thalidomide. Claims were made for the beneficial effect of thalidomide in conditions, or for types of patients, where experience was either fragmentary or completely lacking. Sometimes general or diffuse terms were used in order to suggest that the clinical experience was larger than in fact it was. Astra of Sweden wrote in a pamphlet to physicians in 1960 about experience in gynaecology and obstetrics and stated: 'Blasiu (9), who reports good results from trials with gynaecological-obstetrical patients ...' The impression is conveyed that rather a wide spectrum of different types of patient within the field of obstetrics and gynaecology had been treated by Blasiu. The only type of patient in these fields mentioned in Blasiu's original article in 1958 are nursing mothers and operation cases. When the general practitioner reads such a pamphlet he will have neither the time nor the facilities to dig out the original article published in a German medical journal (*Medizinische Klinik*) with a small circulation; he has to assume that the information given in the brochures does not misrepresent the fact. How the basic information in this specific case was distorted by Chemie Grünenthal may be demonstrated by a covering letter sent to 40,000 doctors in 1958:

In pregnancy and during the lactation period, the female organism is under great strain. Sleeplessness, unrest and tension are constant complaints. The administration of a sedative and a hypnotic that will hurt neither mother nor child is often necessary. Blasiu has given Contergan and Contergan Forte to many patients in his gynaecological department and his obstetrical practice.

Before the prosecutor in Aachen on 5 June 1964, Blasiu gave the following testimony concerning his clinical trials, on which Grünenthal and other distributors of thalidomide had based their advertisements:

'I want to emphasize that the patients took Contergan for at the most eight to ten days. This drug was never prescribed for pregnant women. It is my absolute principle never to give sleeping pills or tranquillizers to a mother-to-be. It is an old rule in medicine that, basically, no barbiturates, opiates, sedatives or hypnotics should be given to mothers-to-be because these drugs can effect the foetus ... In my publication of 2 May 1958 I only said that I gave Contergan to nursing mothers and operation cases. There is no word of my giving this medicament to pregnant women.'

Chemie Grünenthal was by no means the only distributor of thalidomide specifically recommending their product for use during pregnancy. In October 1961 Distillers of England issued an advertisement which included the remark: 'Distaval can be given with complete safety to pregnant women and nursing mothers without adverse effect on mother or child.' Unfortunately, in the event doctors relied upon these assurances given by the company.

I I

The Fight for Justice: Sweden

In Sweden an association for the parents of malformed children was founded on 10 February 1962, on the initiative of Bengt and Hannie Örne, and was at first composed of only a few parents. Since the Swedish Medical Board kept silent their first task was to spread information to the public about the dangers associated with thalidomide. Most Swedish women, of whom some still had supplies of thalidomide in their homes, were completely unaware that thalidomide had been withdrawn from the market on the horrible suspicion that it caused foetal malformation. The association finally succeeded in engaging a small daily newspaper, *Dagen*, which was the first to give information about the withdrawal of the drug on 21 February 1962. *Svenska Dagbladet*, the large daily newspaper, related in an article on 29 January 1963 that the paper suggested on its own initiative that effective publicity measures should be taken to ensure that the potential risks of thalidomide were generally known. This suggestion was turned down by the responsible authorities. '*Svenska Dagbladet* then abstained, which was an error of judgement,' the journal commented. The Medical Association of Gothenberg, observing the insufficient information being given to the public, prepared a letter to the Medical Board at the beginning of March, urging the authorities to inform the public that they should destroy all supplies of thalidomide still being

kept in their homes. The letter was never delivered, since at
the meeting of the Association on 14 March 1962, it was
stated that 'the question arising today has been treated in the
press and on the radio and more is to be expected tomorrow'.
In a television interview on 14 March with Dr Åke Liljestrand
of the Medical Board and Professor Hans Hellberg of the State
Pharmaceutical laboratory, neither of the two responsible
officials issued *any kind of warning* to the public that all
supplies should be destroyed to prevent further consumption
of the drug. The violent reaction of public opinion forced the
Medical Board to investigate the question thoroughly. At the
request of the Medical Board, Dr Jan Winberg, a Gothenburg
paediatrician, on 1 April 1962 began a thorough survey of
thalidomide-damaged children in Sweden.

The Swedish Association for the Parents of Thalidomide-
damaged Children was outraged by the slackness of the
authorities. Five children had been born unnecessarily
crippled because their mothers had taken thalidomide after
the drug had been withdrawn from the market. A complaint
containing serious charges against the Medical Board was
submitted to the Ombudsman supervising the activities of
governmental agencies.

How could such a dangerous drug have been cleared by
the controlling authorities? How did it come about that the
drug had been stopped in the USA? Why were no effective
warnings issued as soon as the suspicion became known that
thalidomide could cause malformations?

According to Swedish law the Swedish Medical Board does
not take over any kind of legal responsibility in accepting a
new drug application. If drug-induced damage appears later,
complete responsibility still rests with the distributor of the
drug. However, moral responsibility for what had occurred
lay heavily on the shoulders of the responsible officials and
the authorities were pushed into a defensive attitude. How

could one explain the embarrassing fact that the drug was not considered safe for consumption during pregnancy in the USA and had been stopped by an alert official at the FDA? Dr Liljestrand later admitted: 'The thalidomide catastrophe demonstrated in a horrible way that until then our measures had been inadequate in preventing serious side-effects from drugs.' (*Farmaceutisk Revy*, 11, 15 April 1967).

The answer received by the Ombudsman from the Medical Board on 15 October 1964 turned out to be a one-sided and emphatic defence both of the manufacturers of thalidomide and of the Medical Board itself. It is regrettable that so many relevant facts were completely distorted.

The material submitted to the Medical Board, on which it based its decision to allow thalidomide to be sold in Sweden, was said to have been well founded. (The same material, although extensively complemented by new investigation, was found completely inadequate by the American authorities even before Dr Kelsey knew of the polyneuritis.) The Medical Board further said that towards the end of 1960 cases of nerve damage thought to be associated with thalidomide became known in West Germany and during the spring of 1961 'information about this damage was published in German technical journals which had only a small circulation in Sweden. The articles were not found in the literature supervised by the Swedish Medical Board and its associated control agencies.' Arthur Engel, the director of the Medical Board, and Åke Liljestrand, the manager of the section on drug questions, failed to mention in their statement that the first report of nerve damage was already published in the *British Medical Journal* in December 1960, and this had immediately attracted Dr Kelsey's attention. The *British Medical Journal* is one of the most widely circulated international medical journals in existence and copies could be found at that time in every medical library of the major medical and pharmaceutical institutes in Sweden. The truth seems to be that in this respect no proper check was made of all of the current international medical literature either by the Medical Board or by its associated control agencies. If officials at the section for drug questions had undertaken any literature studies to spot drug-induced side-effects, they would also have learned from the 14 January 1961 issue of the same journal that since August 1960 the British licensee, Distillers, had included a warning about nerve damage in their sales promotion material. The Swedish Medical Board did not finally advise the Astra Co. to include a warning for polyneuritis in their brochures until 8 November 1961. This was made effective on 5 December 1961, i.e. two weeks after Chemie Grünenthal had totally withdrawn the drug from the German market! Still more remarkable is the fact that when mention was finally made of nerve damage, this was done in a manner which obviously conflicted with the results published in numerous articles which had already appeared in medical literature.

In face of the extensive literature which existed before Lenz proved the contrary to be true, the Medical Board further claimed that the influence of thalidomide on the human foetus constituted 'a completely new type of side-effect'.

The reasons given by responsible officials for the inadequate information passed on to the public after the drug had been withdrawn from the market reveals the cynicism hidden in the guise of humanity: 'No direct warning to the public was considered warranted ... a warning could have caused increased psychic stress in those mothers who were already pregnant at the time in question and might not have remembered the names of various drugs taken earlier in their pregnancy.'

When on 23 November 1962 a warning was issued that another drug, Postafen, was suspected of having similar effects on the foetus, the hollow motivation of the Medical Board was revealed. No special consideration was given for any 'increased psychic stress' to mothers already pregnant. The warning was distributed through all available mass media and effectively directed to the public. On this occasion Dr Liljestrand of the Medical Board declared to *Dagens Nyheter* that the reason for taking such drastic measures was 'that those women who have Postafen in their medical chests might use it in a possible future pregnancy'.

In an interview with the evening newspaper *Expressen* on 15 March 1962 Astra declared that no law suit was to be expected. All medicines were being exhaustively tested. And, after all, the Swedish Medical Board had cleared the drug for sale on the Swedish market. On 12 March 1963 the Astra Co. donated 1 million Swedish crowns (about $200,000) to the parents of thalidomide-damaged children. Although it was a substantial help the sum was naturally far too small to meet the needs of these families. One of the members of the board of the parents' association commented aggressively in an interview to the press: 'Our silence cannot be purchased for a million.' It would be unfair to Astra to attribute their donation purely to good tactics.

Among members of the Swedish medical profession the idea of Astra as a reputable and conscientious firm was deeply rooted for quite good reasons. The company was marketing the local anaesthetic Xylocain, widely used all over the world. It was the largest pharmaceutical company in Scandinavia and possessed a well-qualified research department. It was taken for granted that thalidomide had been properly tested before its introduction. Nothing was known about Chemie Grünenthal.

It must have been a shock even to Astra that the German company had concealed the existence of thousands of cases of nerve damage.

Lawyers writing about the legal consequences of the thalidomide catastrophe, before the opening of the Swedish trial, took it for granted that there was no negligence in the development of thalidomide. Without any negligence it seemed doubtful that Astra could be forced to give compensation through a civil law suit on the basis of existing law.

The children's prospects for a civil law suit in Sweden seemed rather unpromising. The Swedish Medical Board, the highest medical authority in the country, had already openly declared that the catastrophe was unavoidable and that nobody could be blamed for what had happened. The Board's official declaration was written in such a way that Astra could later use the arguments almost word for word in their defence before the city court of Södertälje. Having no other information the medical profession did not protest against the version of events presented by Astra and the Medical Board. Even today few doctors in Sweden know the real reasons why thalidomide was stopped in the USA. And finally, most lawyers considered the chances very small of a successful outcome for the children in a civil law suit.

Despite this, the Association for the Parents of Thalidomide-damaged Children was quite determined to have their question tried before a court. They finally succeeded in interesting Henning Sjöström who did not consider the case completely hopeless. Even if negligence was difficult to prove, the questions of sales guarantee and strict liability could also be used as possible legal grounds. Was it reasonable that an enterprise should take only the profits from its product but pass on to society the responsibility for any damage its product might cause? On 17 September 1965, a writ of summons was given in to the city court of Södertälje. The first session in the preliminary hearings of the first thalidomide trial in the world was held on 15 December 1965. Choice of legal representative for Astra had fallen on Per-Axel Weslien, the president of the Swedish Law Association. Professor Lars Werkö, the chairman of the Swedish Medical Association, was a member of Astra's board. It is evident from Astra's answer to the writ of the plaintiffs that the defendants, backed up by the Medical Board, counted on an easy victory. Astra was satisfied in the main to repeat the principal contents of the statement given by the Medical Board to the Ombudsman. Instead of an easy victory the trial was the beginning of a long-drawn-out exchange of written statements containing bitter accusations and counter-accusations. The atmosphere was often at boiling point during some of the preliminary hearings before the court. During this period Dr Robert Nilsson of the Royal University of Stockholm acted as a technical adviser to Henning Sjöström. Dr Nilsson was the target for many personal attacks during these difficult years and his activities were viewed with suspicion by some prominent members of the University Faculty.

On one occasion the plaintiff's lawyer, Leif Silbersky, made contact with the director of the Swedish branch of the Belgian Pharmaceutical Co. UCB, Mr Lenstrup. The kind of information wanted was not of a nature to cause the company any damage. Mr Lenstrup, however, regretted that he had been given strict instructions from Brussels not to give any kind of information to the plaintiffs in the thalidomide law suit. All the pharmaceutical companies within their branch organization had agreed to support the interests of the Astra Co. to a man. If the outcome of the trial went against Astra this would have far-reaching implications for the whole sector.

During the late spring and summer of 1966, the Astra Co. was quite content, for the plaintiffs were in a very isolated position in Sweden. No important interests were backing them up. Faced with these initial difficulties in obtaining expert witnesses they realized that the only solution was to look for technical support outside Sweden. In view of the situation in West Germany, where many scientists and physicians were very upset by the behaviour of Chemie Grünenthal, the plaintiffs made their initial approach to German scientists engaged with these problems.

Professor Widukind Lenz in Münster ranked of course as number-one specialist in this field and he gave invaluable support in various matters throughout the trial. Professor Weicker in Bonn also gave assistance in building up the plaintiffs' position. The problem with most of the German experts was that they were already engaged in preparing testimonies for the prosecutor's office in Aachen. Quite understandably the prosecutor did not want these experts to appear as witnesses in Södertälje and be cross-examined there before their work was finished on the German trial. This made the position awkward, since it was expected that the Swedish trial would be finished much more quickly than the corresponding trial in Germany. Through Professor Richter, director of the Board for Public Health of the DDR, Dr Nilsson got in touch with Professor Jung, chairman of the Control Advisory Committee for Drug Commerce (*Zentraler Gutachtes Ausschuss für den Arzneimittel Vorkehr*). Jung also held the position of Professor of Pharmacology and Toxicology at Humbolt University in Berlin and was a prominent member of the Academy of Sciences. He had previously assisted in the Nuremberg trials, and was experienced in questions of a medical-legal nature. Seferin, the Minister of Public Health, declared that DDR would be prepared to give such support as was within their scope. From then on Professor Jung supplied much valuable information and sound advice on tactics.

The Swedish Foreign Office was of great assistance in obtaining information about the thalidomide situation in other countries. In this way questions could be directed through Swedish embassies all over the world, which greatly simplified the task.

One of the plaintiffs' greatest successes was an offer obtained from Professor Walter Landauer, the well-known embryologist and teratologist, to prepare depositions for the court trials in Södertälje. Landauer had come originally from Heidelburg and he became associated with the University of Connecticut from 1927 to 1964; he then became active as Honorary Research Associate at University College, London, and as guest scientist at the Nuffield Institute of Comparative Medicine of the Zoological Society in London.

Landauer has published more than 170 works on experimental embryology and teratology and is surely 'the grand old man' of experimental embryology, well known in his field throughout the world. Another expert who gave valuable help to the plaintiffs was Professor John B. Thiersch, the director of the Institute of Biological Research and Professor in Clinical Pharmacology at the University of Washington, in Seattle. Thiersch was the first scientist in the world to observe the teratogenic effect in man as a result of drug treatment. He has also a vast experience in experimental teratology. Both these scientists gave well-formulated support to most of the plaintiffs' standpoints which until then had only met with ridicule from the defendants.

When the final statement of proof, comprising about 1,000 pages of technical material, was submitted to the court of Södertälje in the spring of 1969, Astra seemed to finally realize that it could no longer be certain that the outcome of the trial would be in favour of the defendants. The administrative costs of the trial were no doubt also becoming a serious obstacle to Astra. Many qualified members of their scientific and medical staff had to devote most of their time to the trial instead of doing productive work on the company's pharmaceutical problems. The situation was not clear and since the personal relationships between the two contestants had considerably improved, there seemed to be good reasons for seeking a settlement out of court.

Meanwhile several civil law suits in other countries against the producers of thalidomide had been settled out of court. In England the Distillers Company agreed to pay 40 per cent of the maximum amount which could possibly be obtained for the children by legal procedures according to existing practice. Initially the Distillers' lawyers had counted on all cases, except for some sixty children, coming under the Statute of Limitations. However, in some twenty cases of this kind the Supreme Court decided that no such restrictions were applicable, and the settlement was followed by a series of trials to obtain a verdict on the applicability of the Statute of Limitations in individual cases and to set the maximum sum for compensation for damages.

In Sweden the terms accepted for settlement on 4 October 1969, by the Association for the Parents of Thalidomide Children, were far more advantageous. The agreement included 100 children of whom twenty to thirty cases were 'questionable', in that for some children it seems doubtful if it would have been legally possible to prove, for example, that intake of thalidomide had in fact occurred. In other cases the types of abnormality were more or less atypical. Taking into account that it would not have been possible to prove causality in more than twenty cases, a prolonged trial, if it was won, would have given total compensation of about 49,000,000 Swedish crowns (about $10,000,000). In the settlement, however, the compensation was based on an inflation-proof annuity. With the index-clause taken into account, the settlement agreed upon amounted to 68,000,000 Swedish crowns. For the children the settlement was thus more favourable than the positive outcome of a court decision would have been. A few cases from Denmark were also included in the 100 cases.

In Norway a separate agreement was reached which was modelled in all essential details on the Swedish settlement.

Finally, similar settlements have been reached for several cases in Canada and for the few which occurred in the USA mainly as a result of clinical testing.

12

The Fight for Justice: Germany

On 15 March 1961, Karl Schulte-Hillen, a young Hamburg lawyer, went to see his sister who had recently had a baby. Since his own wife was in the last month of pregnancy and did not want to undertake a long journey he went alone. The visit proved to be a shocking experience, as his sister's baby did not look like any other normal child. Her arms stopped above the elbow and her hands carried only three fingers. Six weeks later his own wife gave birth to a child having almost exactly the same malformations. Was there some hereditary disease in the family? Schulte-Hillen could not believe this because there was nothing in the past history of the family to suggest it. Was there some external factor in common which could be responsible? Mrs Schulte-Hillen was exceptionally healthy and the pregnancy had been completely normal, all medical treatment being unnecessary. Schulte-Hillen consulted the paediatrician, Dr Lenz. These particular kinds of malformation were not unknown to the Hamburg physician. He had seen several such cases in the Hamburg area and was conducting retrospective inquiries to find out the cause. Was Mrs Schulte-Hillen sure she had not taken any kind of medicament during her pregnancy? She then recalled an incident which had previously seemed of little relevance. In August 1960 her father had died suddenly and 'I needed something to quieten my nerves.' The local pharmacy provided a mild sedative. She took two tablets of Contergan. That alone proved sufficient to wreak such fearful damage on her unborn child. Schulte-Hillen joined with Lenz in the struggle to force Chemie-Grünenthal to withdraw thalidomide. His family had been heavily struck. The behaviour of the Grünenthal representatives tended only to increase his bitterness. He made contact with other families in the same situation. The children needed the medical care of orthopaedic surgeons and expensive artificial limbs of special construction. Many parents despaired. In most cases the necessary financial means were lacking.

In 1962 Schulte-Hillen was active in organizing an association among the parents of thalidomide-damaged children to give strength to their justifiable demands. The question of the legal responsibility of Chemie Grünenthal needed to be tested before a court. Preparations for a civil law suit were begun. However, the German association was soon shattered by internal dissension. Prominent members were accused of making questionable transactions and a heavy beaurocratic machinery led to open conflict.

The association was split into two sections, one radical and one moderate. The parents who advocated a tough policy against Chemie Grünenthal became centred around the solicitor Schulte-Hillen. This group demanded an admission of guilt and insisted on a continuing legal action against the Company. The more moderate group was formed around the businessman Helmut Hering. These parents were willing to come to terms with Chemie Grünenthal out of court. Meanwhile the German Federal Authorities remained strikingly inactive and only minor sums were occasionally diverted to the parents' association. This contrasts with Switzerland where the obligatory health organization took over all costs of therapy, prostheses, etc. In Sweden, similarly, where obligatory health insurance covers the whole population, the State made major contributions to solving the special problems of therapy and adaptation encountered in the lives of these children.

The public prosecutor's office in Aachen had already started its independent investigations on the thalidomide catastrophe by the beginning of December 1961. There seemed to be sufficient grounds to justify a criminal law suit against the responsible businessmen and scientists of the Stolberg Company. The procedure was slow and tedious because of the enormous amount of material at hand and the complicated technical questions involved.

Nevertheless, the work continued steadily, and on 2 September 1965, the prosecutor's office concluded its investigations. The inquiry had been concentrated around eleven people associated with Chemie Grünenthal. Two of them were not called on to stand trial. Dr von Veltheim, represented by Josef Neuberger of Dusseldorf, the SPD deputy in the *Landtag*, was thus acquitted. The preliminary bill of indictment was directed against the remaining nine Grünenthal associates. Very little of the material from Grünenthal's internal files, which was to play such an important role in the trial, was handed over voluntarily. Most of the documents were seized in police raids.

According to the rules of the West German judicial procedure the defendants were allowed to have full access to all the documents and records compiled by the prosecutor. After the inquiry was over the defendants were initially given three months to decide if they wished to make use of their right to institute a final hearing (*Schlussgehör*); if they did so the case had to be opened one month after the defendants had made their decision. The 'final hearing' was introduced in German law in April 1965. This hearing is the last opportunity for the accused to avoid an act of indictment by producing substantial evidence against the various points of accusation. The defendants protested about the shortness of time available because of the immense amount of material that had to be analysed. On 3 March the Federal Constitutional Court (*Bundesverfassungsgericht*) rejected the defendants' objections, but because of the exceptional nature of the case the Ministry of Justice allowed them a further six months. In August 1966 the final hearings were begun. During this period Grünenthal mobilized all its resources and produced an immense amount of material to support the defence.

Professor Irle took up the cudgels for Chemie Grünenthal in the first number of the *Kölner Zeitschrift fur Soziologie und Sozialpsychologie* for 1966. He claimed the relationship between deformities and thalidomide were not proven. The interviewers had not been objective. We must therefore assume that the interviewers did not simply record in a neutral way, but argued with the subjects and tried to change their opinions and views on certain points ...

In August 1966 Professor Dahs from Bonn, the legal representative and defendant of Hermann Wirtz, demanded that the law suit should be withdrawn immediately. In an interview with *Stuttgarter Zeitung* on 15 August 1966, Dahs described the inquiry carried out by the prosecution as 'partial, incomplete and non-objective'. The prosecution promptly announced that such an open polemic to the press by the legal representative of Grünenthal would not influence the decision by the prosecutor, who had only to consider facts and objective considerations. Such methods were not fit to use in a search for truth.

On 24 February 1967, Baron von Münchausen, the new state secretary to the Minister of Justice, declared that a decision about the trial could be expected in two weeks' time. Finally on 14 March 1967, long overdue, Dr Gierlich, the chief prosecutor, announced that a decision had been reached to bring action against nine persons at Chemie Grünenthal.

Gierlich could not specify when the main proceedings would be opened but he did not expect a delay longer than one year up to 1 October 1968. The defence were now given an opportunity to present objections against the opening of the main trial proceedings or to protest about specific evidence brought forward by the prosecution. The defence were also entitled to apply for a preliminary inquiry. A decision on such requests was to be first obtained from the first criminal chamber of the *Land* court in Aachen, and then from the appeal court in Cologne. Only when no new aspects could be presented and all the stipulated formalities had been fulfilled could a decision be made about institution of the main court hearings.

Dr Gierlich asked the press, radio and TV to understand why the public had not been kept well informed about what had been going on. The case was without precedent, and if the strife concerned with the decision whether to take up the trial had been allowed publicity, it might have caused the accused unnecessary suffering. Finally Gierlich said, 'I would very much like to repudiate the assumption that the whole pharmaceutical industry is being put in the dock. Contergan is an exceptional case, unprecedented in the history of law, as regards its nature, scope and proportion.' On 12 April, the 972 page indictment was officially handed over to the defence. Of the 5,000 cases of damage investigated, fifty representative cases of foetal malformation had been selected and sixty cases of nerve damage.

On 19 December 1967 the president of the district court of Aachen and the press information service of the Ministry of Justice (*Justizpressestelle*) decided that the trial should be postponed because of certain phrases in the bill of indictment which, it was feared, might cause misunderstanding. The indictment was therefore sent back to the prosecutor's office for revision. The association for the parents of thalidomide children protested in vain. Already the investigation had been going on for six years! Why this new delay? In January 1968 the prosecutor again made a request to open the main court proceedings.

Late in the autumn the trial seemed to be stuck again.

The parents of the affected children were getting desperate; the children were already between six and ten years old and very little help had been obtained for them. The pending civil law suits were dependent on the outcome of the criminal law suit. The claims amounted to DM 170 million for the 470 most severely crippled children alone, to cover expenses for their medical aid, treatment and compensation.

On 26 February 1968 the Ministry of Justice of Nordrhein-Westfalen decided that the main hearings could be opened.

The rooms in the classical-style court house were found to be far too small and the Ministry of Justice decided that the trials were to be held in the Casino of the mine 'Anna', belonging to the Eschweiler mining association in the small town of Alsdorf, situated 10 kilometres from Aachen, with 32,000 inhabitants. This building had sufficient space for 600-700 persons. The prosecution alone proposed to call twenty-nine technical experts and 351 witnesses. 400 co-plaintiffs had been registered for the main trials and several hundred press reporters were expected from all over the world. In the side rooms of the main hall of the Casino, space had to be arranged for the judges, members of the jury, secretaries, stenographers and the prosecution and defence staff. A press centre had to be organized, as well as the necessary connections for TV broadcasting. For the court proceedings a complete secondary set-up, consisting of three judges and six jurymen, was to take part in the proceedings and they were ready to replace any of the regular members of the court who might be unable to attend. If the trial had to be postponed for more than ten days, because of the lack of a deputy, there was a danger that the whole trial would be stopped and the complete procedure started again from the beginning.

The arrangements were planned in minute detail for the largest trial in Europe since the war. Contact was made with lawyers in Frankfurt who had had similar experience at the large Auschwitz trial. Even the traffic problems in Alsdorf which were expected to result from the proceedings were considered. The German Red Cross provided two assistants to be present during the trial. Chemie Grünenthal organized a News Agency of its own, which skilfully prepared special press releases. All pharmacies throughout the Federal Republic were regularly furnished with the Grünenthal version of what was happening at the Alsdorf trial.

The PR section consisted of the News Agency with four permanent experts, two reporters and twelve staff engaged on deformity and nerve damage, four staff engaged in the legal section and sometimes as many as eight stenographers and six typists working continuously to give full records of the hearings.

In order not to delay the trial further the *Land* court of Aachen decided on 21 May to grant the request that one of the accused, Hermann Wirtz, the director of Chemie Grünenthal, should be withdrawn from the trial because of illness which made him unable to attend the proceedings.

On 27 May 1968, the Minister of Justice, attended by press, radio and TV reporters from all over the world, opened the main proceedings of the trial in the large hall of the Casino, its gilded pillars and tapestries dimly reflected in the indirect lighting.

The accused followed the proceedings from behind a team of competent and efficient lawyers from all over the Federal Republic. By the second day the prosecution, represented by Dr Havertz, Dr Knipfer and Dr Günther, had already run into difficulties.

After concluding the formalities of the criminal law procedure, the court announced that Dr Kelling, one of the remaining eight accused, was to be withdrawn from the trial for health reasons.

Prosecutor Havertz on his side demanded that Dr von Veltheim should be dismissed from his position as counsel for Dr Sievers since von Veltheim was heavily involved in the Contergan story and until the final hearings he had been included amongst the accused. Dr Weber, the chairman of the court, saw no evidence for a conflict of interests in the case of von Veltheim, and the prosecution's request was rejected.

On the second day of the proceedings the prosecution requested that 200 or so registered co-plaintiffs should be included in the proceedings, including cases from several countries outside West Germany. In most of these non-German cases, Contergan had been obtained during visits to the Federal Republic. The defence protested violently. There was not sufficient documentary material present to cover these additional cases. Only those cases specifically included in the primary indictment could be treated. The prosecution had deliberately excluded damage cases. Schmidt-Leichner, solicitor for Dr Mückter, considered the prosecution's methods were a threat to legal security. Dr Havertz was prepared for this attack. The fundamental question was not how many cases should be included in the indictment; the important point for the court was to try to establish the question of the general causality between foetal damage and the taking of thalidomide. That is, if thalidomide is a teratogenic drug, does it cause nerve damage and did the company bear responsibility for the birth of thousands of deformed children throughout the Federal Republic? There was no use in taking up individual cases until this question had been decided. Havertz further contended that the defence had not made use of all the possibilities offered to them to use the complete material to which they had had unrestricted access. Schulte-Hillen, legal representative of the co-plaintiffs, protested against the distribution of Schmidt-Leichner's duplicated declaration of the defence to journalists in the court room and asked the court to prohibit such propaganda during the trial. The chairman declined : 'Let us finally come to the point.' Ares Damassiotis, Dr Siever's counsel, argued that the indictment was a composite question consisting of many individual cases which had to be examined separately. Until more evidence had been presented by the prosecution, the court proceedings should be suspended. Dr Havertz demanded that Damassiotis's request should be rejected. On the following day the chairman of the court, Dr Weber, announced the court's decision to reject the defence request. When Dr Weber called the accused, Dr Mückter replied, 'I would first like to say that I still regard the charge as a gross injustice against me personally, but I have nothing to say at the moment about the specific issue.'

It was not until the fourth day of proceedings that all the objections raised by the prosecution and defence were eliminated, and matters of a more concrete nature could be considered. Not unexpectedly, the prosecution was allowed to take up the question of nerve damage before the more complex one of deformity. Technical experts and witnesses were now endlessly giving testimony and being cross-examined. Many of the witnesses giving evidence about nerve damage, mostly elderly persons, were obviously confused by the running fire of questions from the defence. The defence tactic with these witnesses was to try to make them disclose the intake of additional medicines which could be suspected of causing the neurological damage, and also to try to reveal over-dosage of Contergan and previous health disturbances. The argument of the defence was that in no single rigorously controlled case could it be *proved* that Contergan had ever caused polyneuritis. The most embarrassing fact for the prosecution was that some witnesses who had claimed initially that they had not consumed any drugs other than Contergan, when cross-examined admitted that other medicaments had indeed been taken. In view of the age of most of the patients this was not surprising, but it considerably weakened the position of the prosecution in some individual cases.

Many witnesses summoned before the court failed to appear. A few had died during the seven years of preparation of this mammoth trial. Some prominent representatives of industry and the military declared that they could not afford to have their reputations damaged by an indiscreet court inquiry, and gave bad health as their reasons for absence. As more and more witnesses on both sides failed to appear, Dr Weber, the chairman, warned: 'Some of the excuses being given are not acceptable.' One physician could not find a locum, another was on duty, a third was on vacation abroad. Of the first nine witnesses claiming to have contracted polyneuritis from Contergan who were summoned to give evidence, two had died, three were ill and the remaining four could not be questioned satisfactorily since they claimed they were unable to be present, or simply did not appear.

Continual objections, requests, explanations, discussion and the defence's passion for repeatedly citing long passages from cross-examination transcripts made the proceedings exceedingly difficult to handle. The chairman had to use all his authority to calm down the participants when they engaged in the exchange of bitter accusations. The court members participating were put under tremendous stress. On 10 June, the sixth day of the proceedings, the prosecutor's office declared that one of the deputy jurymen had had to resign his commission because of a threatened heart attack. The prosecution also protested about unqualified and tendentious reports in certain newspapers where witnesses' names, descent, and intimate details about them were being revealed. The witnesses had been 'pilloried' by the gutter press and their testimony pre-judged before specialists and the court had commented on them. Such irresponsible journalistic methods increased the strain on witnesses quite unnecessarily and influenced the attitude of those witnesses waiting to be questioned. Dr Günter related one case where a vicar had made use of his right to refuse to give evidence because of his fears of being treated by the press in a similar way. In the gutter press certain testimonies were described as 'a mixture of whopping lies, and fraud attempts derived from distorted news items and citations'. Some witnesses had been described as possessed by 'compensation craziness'. The trial's tremendous publicity greatly added to the strain. No wonder that witnesses, most of them quite unused to any kind of publicity, were thoroughly nervous during the hearings, and sometimes fell an easy prey to the aggressive, well-oiled machinery of the defence. In the name of the entire defence, Professor Bruns said he was against all undue influence by the press on public opinion. However, in the defence's view the press had attacked with unerring instinct one aspect of the proceedings, namely the evaluation of the presented evidence. The press should have every right to assess what happened in the courtroom.

On the ninth day of the proceedings (18 June 1968) Dr Havertz announced: 'The experts who will appear during the coming week are without exception, suggested or even directly summoned by the defence. Some of these experts – we know this and have evidence to prove it – on account of their close relations with the firm of Chemie Grünenthal or personal friendship with one of the accused, are open to suspicion of partiality, even on a cautious assessment. Those concerned are indeed academics of distinction. But whether in this trial of these defendants they can be independent assistants of an independent court is another question. It is the intention of the law that an expert should not represent any interest but be an independent assistant of an independent court. Nevertheless the prosecution does not intend, for the time being at least, to exercise its right under section 74 of the rules of criminal court procedure to reject experts on the grounds of suspected partiality. We believe that it is quite possible and feasible in this trial to give proper weight to our reservations about experts within the framework of the right of cross-examination possessed by every participant in the trial and the later opportunity to assess the evidence.'

Defendant Dr Schmidt-Leichner was upset. If a few scientific experts were acquainted with Chemie Grünenthal or with some of the accused he thought it was of no relevance, and there was no cause for alarm.

The first expert to give testimony was Professor Otto Rudolf Klimmer from the Institute of Pharmacology of the University of Bonn. On the basis of 'unpublished' experiments, reports in the literature and numerous animal experiments carried out by scientists associated with Chemie Grünenthal, Professor Klimmer concluded that 'a strict and scientifically unchallengeable proof – which is what I have been asked for – of thalidomide neuropathy among animals used in the tests cannot be found in the literature so far available to me.' When questioned by Dr Weber, Klimmer had to admit that it was not possible to produce polyneuritis in animal experiments, caused by such agents as barbiturates and phenuron, even though their nerve-damaging properties were a medically established, undisputed fact.

If animal experiments fail to reveal polyneuritis for compounds which are known by medical science to produce polyneuritis in man, then clearly the experiments are not suited at all to a study of such toxic reactions. A negative finding in such an experiment can be used even less as proof that such and such a compound is *not* apt to cause neurological damage in man. As Professor Schimert of Munich had pointed out to Chemie Grünenthal in the late spring of 1961, it is extremely difficult to simulate this disease in animal experiments because of the subjective nature of the symptoms. Although more distinguished than most people seem to think, the mental abilities of the rat are not quite sufficient to enable him to tell a scientist that since Contergan was included in his diet he has felt an increasing sensation of numbness in his tail and paws.

On the following day Professor Felix Sagher of the Hadassah University Clinic in Jerusalem testified that he had not seen any kind of neurological disturbances resembling those described for thalidomide neuritis in the treatment of twenty-four patients suffering from lepra (leprosy) with very high doses of thalidomide. According to Chemie Grünenthal this was the final proof that thalidomide would not cause any neurological damage when given under strict clinical conditions and supervised in a hospital ward to ensure that no alcohol or other drugs were taken. However in lepra patients the nervous system is often already damaged and the victims are already suffering from polyneuritis. Obviously, this makes them completely unsuitable for use in such a study. A negative result says very little. Excluding the specific circumstances alluded to by Dr Havertz, there are innumerable reasons why such an experiment would fail to give a positive result. The diagnostic facilities may not be sufficiently refined, the clinical trial may not be adequately planned, and the number of patients studied may be too small, etc.

The first medical expert called by the prosecution was Werner Scheid, Professor of Neurology and Psychiatry at the University of Cologne. Scheid had had experience of a large number of cases of thalidomide polyneuritis, and he gave a thorough description of the clinical picture of this type of nerve damage. For the defence, Schmidt-Leichner protested that Scheid was reading his prepared statement word for word. Dr Weber rejected the protest and announced that in view of the extremely complicated nature of the material, Professor Scheid would be given permission to continue his reading. Scheid concluded:

(1) Thalidomide is capable of producing polyneuritis. This conclusion is based on the following considerations:

(a) This polyneuritis shows a thoroughly typical clinical picture, together with an unusual development. The clinical picture corresponds to that of a predominantly sensory polyneuritis, often with striking and severe paraesthesia. The development of the condition is characterized by the fact that the symptoms, particularly as regards sensations, do not abate, or only slightly, even after several years. This combination of clinical picture and development of the disease is not familiar from other forms of polyneuritis.

(b) In the case of all patients with this particular form of polyneuritis it is admitted that they have taken thalidomide.

(c) This particular form of polyneuritis first appeared after Contergan had come on to the market.

(d) No new cases of the condition were observed after Contergan had been removed from the list of available drugs.

(2) Thalidomide polyneuritis can be shown to have occurred only among a certain number of those who took the tested sleeping-drug regularly. From this it follows that other factors are involved in the case of thalidomide polyneuritis. These other factors, that is to say the whole question of pathogenesis, are not relevant here. Even if such factors can today be presumed with certainty, even regularly, thalidomide remains the cause of the thalidomide polyneuritis inasmuch as it is the first link in the chain of causality.

(3) Theoretical considerations from other branches of medicine cannot decide whether thalidomide polyneuritis as such exists or not.

(4) Similarly, negative results in animal experiments cannot

exclude the possibility of thalidomide polyneuritis in man or even cast doubt on it.

(5) Systematic experiments on human subjects designed to show the side-effects of thalidomide under standardized conditions cannot be undertaken responsibly. Anyone who carried out such experiments would, in view of the volume of clinical experience already available, contravene both the ethical norms which apply to doctors and the criminal law.

(6) Clinical neurology has for a long time been able, with its own specialized methods, to give accurate descriptions of many other toxic polyneurites without error. In spite of all the advances in medicine and medical methods in the past year, clinical neurology has both the right and the duty to give valid and independent evidence on the question of thalidomide polyneuritis.

In the testimony which followed, Dr Ellen Gibbels of the University Clinic of Cologne drew similar conclusions. Dr Dörr, one of von Schrader-Beielstein's counsel, asked Gibbels to reveal the names and addresses of the individual patients she had examined. When Gibbels refused, Schmidt-Leichner requested that the court should reject her deposition, since she had denied the defence an opportunity of checking the accuracy of important details of her investigation. The following day the court announced that the defence request was rejected.

On 1 July Eberhard Bay, Professor of Neurology from the University of Dusseldorf, told the court:

'Frequently – not once but many times – I found that when patients described the typical symptoms without mentioning thalidomide it was already clear that the damage was caused by thalidomide, and I was able to ask the patients directly "And how long have you been taking thalidomide?" Naturally this astounded the patients, and they would ask, "But how did you know?"'

'I had the impression at the time that Chemie Grünenthal had no doubts whatever about the polyneuritis caused by

Contergan,' Professor Bay said. The conclusion that Contergan causes polyneuritis was fully supported by the other two experts who gave testimony on the same day, Jörg Zütt, Professor of Psychiatry and Neurology at the University of Frankfurt, and Paul Vogel, Professor of Neurology at the University of Heidelberg. Professor Vogel stated that it was recognized throughout the world's medical literature that Contergan causes polyneuritis.

Professor Hans Heinrich Wieck, giving evidence before the Alsdorf trial as the twentieth medical expert, referred to the thalidomide polyneuritis as 'a scientifically proven fact' and described a method developed at his clinic to diagnose doubtful cases. Wieck's speech induced defence counsel Schmidt-Leichner to interrupt the neurologist and ask 'Who is "we"?' Wieck referred to the rules of the court and asked not to be interrupted during his lecture. 'I will interupt you whenever I wish to. Make sure of that!' Schmidt-Leichner retorted.

Professor Wieck's testimony was severely criticized by eighty-one-year-old Professor Löffler from Zürich. When cross-examined by the co-prosecutor, Günter, the Swiss professor confessed that he had never seen a single one of the twelve cases referred to in his criticism. His deposition was founded wholly on the material given to him by the defence. This upset the solicitor, Schulte-Hillen, the legal representative of many of the co-plaintiffs. 'I really must protest. To think that a distinguished scientist and his reputation have been exploited in this way in this case!' Defence counsel jumped up and there was an uproar. Once again the chairman of the court announced a pause to give the two sides time to cool down. 'Even the good nature of Dr Weber, the chairman of the district court, is useless against the stubbornness of the defence,' was the *Frankfurter Allgemeine*'s comment on the day's events.

On 17 July Dr Weber declared that no proceedings could be held as one of the judges had been operated on the night before. When the proceedings were resumed, the tough cross-examination of Dr Gibbels, which had already taken up the whole of 16 July, was continued for almost another two days.

On 12 August 1968, the twenty-seventh day of the proceedings, the court held hearings concerning the causality of the malformations. Professor Widukind Lenz was the first medical expert to be heard. During twelve days of continuous cross-examination Lenz never faltered, despite the combined attempts of the eighteen defence lawyers to make him contradict himself. Although the defence methods and behaviour certainly impressed many press reporters, others were clearly more critical as is seen from an article in *Die Zeit* of 22 August 1968. The reporter wrote,

Hardly a single day passes without Schmidt-Leichner accusing the court of violating the rules of procedure.

Schmidt-Leichner and his colleagues are using every conceivable rhetorical and dramatic device. When they mention the injured their voices are choked with emotion, when doubt is cast on the irreproachability of a defence expert, the defence counsel leap to their feet in indignation, when a prosecution expert comes forward his credibility and competence are constantly challenged. Nevertheless, the course of the proceedings so far has shown more than once that the court is well able to distinguish between verbal fireworks and facts. Who are all the sound effects meant to impress? It can only be experts without experience of courts, and, of course, the co-plaintiffs.

And not least, the style of the Grünenthal trial is making an impact on public opinion. Doubts are assiduously raised about the objects of the trial and the difficulty of holding a medical trial are widely emphasized ...

'In the interests of the discovery of truth the Grünenthal press office even spreads the latest scandals about the Association of Parents of Injured Children,' *Die Zeit* commented bitterly.

During the questioning of Professor Lenz, the main difficulty was that the defence lawyers did not understand – or pretended not to understand – the type of scientific method used in biological research. The defence would not accept that in an empirical science it is impossible to give the sort of proof afforded by a mathematical theorem. They also failed to appreciate that conclusions offered by disciplines such as biology are founded basically on probabilities. Day after day Lenz tried patiently to explain these facts without ever losing his temper or being provoked by the defence accusations that he was 'incompetent, untrustworthy', etc.; the whole hearing was sometimes completely lost in the realms of the theory of scientific method. In his anxiety to analyse the problems objectively from all possible points of view, Lenz even pointed out certain weaknesses of details in his own investigation. He probably soon realized that such an attitude was a rather thankless one. The defence's aggressiveness sometimes produced an extremely explosive atmosphere. The prosecution demanded that remarks such as 'Experts and prosecution are the same thing,' should be denounced by the chairman. Weber, the chairman, took little notice. He did not consider that he had allowed any improper behaviour during court proceedings.

When Havertz requested that further well-known medical experts from Japan, the Netherlands, England, Switzerland and Sweden should be called to give evidence, Schmidt-Leichner declared that this would mean that the prosecution declared Lenz incompetent as an expert. The request could only be granted and other experts heard if the court had any doubts of the competence of Professor Lenz. Against this grotesque attack, Havertz said, 'The prosecution has not the slightest doubt that Professor Lenz possesses expert knowledge and wide experience to a quite unusual degree, such, in fact, as has been very rarely seen in court.' The witnesses called would merely demonstrate 'that there is not a scientist of repute in the whole world who doubts the connection between Contergan and deformities'. A bitter clash arose between the defence and the prosecution when Schmidt-Leichner asked venomously, 'Do you have different rules for court trials here in Alsdorf?'

'I feel that you should perhaps look a little more at the rules of procedure, as you keep asking others to,' retorted prosecution counsel Knipfer. 'So far it is your points of order that have been rejected, not the prosecution's.'

When Lenz was asked whether he considered it possible that some unknown virus could have caused the epidemic of malformations, he replied, 'A virus would not stop at the frontier.' It is hard to imagine that the Berlin Wall could halt such a virus. When Lenz added, 'The burden of proof for such an absurd claim rests on those who make it,' the chairman reprimanded him.

When on one occasion the defence tried to ensnare Lenz with questions of a more legal nature he commented: 'I am not interested in the results of trials but in scientific accuracy.'

The great calm Lenz showed during cross-examination made a deep impression on those present. 'The only one who retains his self-control in Alsdorf and refuses to be shaken out of his stoical calm by hostile questions, increasing insinuations about his knowledge and the claim that his methods are "useless" is Professor Lenz. He answers every question that is put to him in great detail,' wrote *Westfälische Nachrichten* on 31 August.

Outside the courtroom three children with crippled arms and legs were playing, not knowing that inside that room the question why they and thousands of other children had not been born healthy and normal was being debated. The participants in the court had to pass the deformed children playing, several times a day, three silent accusers cared for by Red Cross sisters, while their mothers were inside following the proceedings.

Lenz was by no means alone in his fight. The overwhelming majority of the medical experts giving testimony before the court supported him on the question of causality. Professor Johannes Thomas from Mulheim-Ruhr described four cases of mothers who gave birth to deformed children where he had known before delivery that the mothers had taken thalidomide during the sensitive stage of pregnancy:

In the course of my studies in teratology I regarded these cases as involuntary human experiments and assessed them in the normal way. On the basis of these observations I now have empirical and scientific proof that thalidomide causes malformations in man.

That three children, whose mothers had admitted before delivery to having taken thalidomide, should one after the other all exhibit the Wiedemann syndrome, was a chance of around one in a billion, Thomas continued, and he went on to say that thalidomide embryopathies, together with the embryopathies caused by X-rays and rubella (german measles) were included in the world literature of his scientific field as classic examples of deformity caused by external influences.

Professor Otto Hövels, director of the University Paediatric Clinic in Frankfurt, then gave a critical review and evaluation of all the facts known about the epidemiologic increase of specific deformity described by Lenz and others as occurring after the appearance of thalidomide on the market, and then suddenly disappearing about nine months after the drug had been withdrawn. Hövels concluded: 'There is such a high degree of probability for the conclusion that thalidomide is the *conditio sine qua non* for the epidemic proliferation of the Wiedemann syndrome that I cannot imagine scientifically based grounds for excluding a causal connection.'

While Professor Hövels was being questioned, Dr Sievers, one of the accused, produced a graph which appeared to demonstrate that the number of peromelia cases (a type of malformation different from the 'thalidomide-type') was as much as half that of the so called thalidomide syndrome. Hövels reacted immediately : 'You have chosen a logarithmic scale of representation, and I must comment on this in case anyone in the court does not understand the implication of this.' He then made it clear that the relationship between the curve representing peromelia and the curve showing the beginning of thalidomide deformities was more like one to twenty-five when judged on a normal (non-logarithmic) scale.

To everyone's surprise, Chemie Grünenthal was able to produce certain medical experts who claimed that the hypothesis that thalidomide caused abnormalities was unproven. At a time when the impact of the thalidomide disaster had caused the medical authorities of most civilized countries to tighten their legislation for drug control considerably; when the teratogenic action of thalidomide was included in elementary textbooks for medical students as a horrifying example of the teratogenicity of a drug in man; when the intake of thalidomide during the sensitive period of pregnancy was considered sufficient reason for legal abortion in Sweden; when scientists all over the world were working jointly in cooperation with the controlling authorities and pharmaceutical industries to prevent a repetition of what had happened; when at international meetings on medical science no single voice had ever been raised against Lenz's interpretation; when drug companies all over the world in the West and the East had included the testing of drugs for teratogenicity as a standard procedure for testing drug toxicity; when the Astra Co. who manufactured the drug in Sweden under licence for Grünenthal had admitted in the trial in Sweden that thalidomide was to be regarded in principle as teratogenic in man; and when, finally, the English manufacturers, Distillers, had agreed to pay compensation to the parents of malformed children in an out-of-court settlement, nobody would have expected a professor of anatomy from the University of Göttingen (Erich Blechschmidt), a professor in pathology (Karl Ferdinand Kloos), a professor of orthopaedics from the Medical Faculty of Aachen (Anton Hopf), and a professor in forensic law (Gerhard Rommeney) from Berlin, to stand up in the Casino in the small town of Alsdorf in Nordrhein-Westfalen and claim that it had never been shown that thalidomide caused foetal damage. To confuse the medical experts who were giving evidence in favour of the prosecution on the question of causality between thalidomide and deformity, the defence lawyers repeatedly resorted to the claim that in countries such as Czechoslovakia, Hungary and Poland, where thalidomide was not sold, a remarkable increase of thalidomide malformations had occurred. The defence never gave material support for this contention, which in fact was quite false.

The trial continued. Miles and miles of tape were used for the recordings, innumerable pages of stenographed papers piled up. The trial had become an autonomous machine which carried on a laborious life of its own.

In contrast with Sweden and many other countries, the press of West Germany from the beginning became markedly polarized. As the proceedings advanced a group of right-wing newspapers emerged which more or less one-sidedly supported the producers of thalidomide and assisted in spreading the Grünenthal version of the 'Thalidomide Story'. On the other hand papers like *Der Spiegel, Westfälische Nachrichten, Die Zeit,* and especially the *Frankfurter Allgemeine Zeitung* consistently attempted to give a more objective account of the trial proceedings.

Professor Heinz Weicker, like Lenz, had made a thorough and detailed study of the causes of the deformities induced by thalidomide. When the defence realized that no cross-examination could destroy the case built up by Lenz and Weicker, they resorted to a new tactic. These uncomfortable medical experts had to be eliminated from the trial. On 11 September the defence demanded that Professor Weicker, who had been called as a prosecution witness, should be rejected by the court on the grounds that he was prejudiced against Chemie Grünenthal. To the consternation of all, on 30 September the court gave in to the defence and denied this internationally known expert his right to present evidence for the prosecution.

When Friedrich Coulston, Professor of Toxicology and Pathology at the Union University of Albany, New York, was called by the defence and was being heard on 23 October, Schulte-Hillen, the co-prosecutor, insinuated that his testimony was tendentiously written to suit the Grünenthal position. There were violent protests from the defence and when Schulte-Hillen asked: 'Did you receive any offer of financial help?' Damassiotis, counsel for the defence, was enraged: 'We are not prepared to tolerate the use of such guerilla tactics against scientists.' Schulte-Hillen defended himself: 'All of us present in this room would be interested to know if this expert testimony is being given according to the rules of American justice, which allows the witness to take sides, or according to the rules of German justice.' At the request of the co-prosecutor the expert was put on oath.

A short pause served only to cool the resentment on both sides temporarily. Prosecutor Günter then requested that an expert recently called by the defence, Professor George Gott-schewski, director of the Max Planck Institute of Immuno-biology, should be heard only after some weeks, so that the prosecution could first be given an opportunity to go through the evidence offered by him. When the court rejected this request, Havertz asked Gottschewski about his personal relations with Chemie Grünenthal. The professor retorted angrily that he was only present to discuss matters of science. But Havertz insisted. 'In view of the special relations of this special scientist in this special trial against these special defendants, is he an independent expert?' Gottschewski said he could not burden his ordinary budget with expenses for investigations he made for private companies.

Schulte-Hillen pointed out that this type of questioning was completely legal and it was even his duty to carry it out, even if the defence takes the view that these are guerrilla tactics'.

The prosecution supported Schulte-Hillen's request. After a long drawn-out fight between the prosecution and the defence, on 18 November the chairman declared that the prosecution's request was justified and Gottschewski was rejected as an expert.

During the next round of court proceedings, scientists engaged in the development of thalidomide were questioned. Professor Keller, who was carrying out the animal tests, told the court that originally they had thought thalidomide to be an anti-histamine compound, but later its sedative properties had been discovered during animal experiments. All the records of his experiments had been handed over to the company when he left his post. Keller had also made trials on himself and on one occasion he had taken as much as 10 grammes of thalidomide. When asked about a symposium on thalidomide which Grünenthal had organized in 1955, the prosecutor, Knipfer, asked what was 'the conclusion of the symposium as regards the preparation and testing of thalidomide'.

Professor Keller replied, 'As far as I remember the testers were not particularly enthusiastic. It was said, "Well, yes, it works. But there are quite enough other sleeping pills on the market. It isn't all that clear what real advantages K17 has, apart from its remarkable lack of toxicity."'

Keller also said that he had been sceptical about the possible future of thalidomide, especially when compared to other sedatives marketed by competitors. When Weber was asked by the chairman whether he had had any other special doubts about the substance Keller answered: 'Since 1961 I have racked my brains to try and remember if mistakes were made in the testing of preparation K17, whether something important was overlooked or left out. Please let me assure you that no one can have been less happy than I about the discovery and the subsequent history of this substance. But to foresee the consequences in store for us would have needed prophetic gifts.'

During a discussion about the teratogenicity of thalidomide Keller stated, 'I should like to say that at that time a teratogenic effect simply never occurred to me. And not just not to me – it never occurred to anyone at Chemie Grünenthal or anyone in the whole pharmaceutical industry.'

Keller also claimed that his results had been verified by detailed animal experiments done by Smith, Kline, and French. This was altogether not true. In contrast to the results published by Kunz, Keller and Mückter, the animal experiments done by this company did not demonstrate any sedative or sleep-inducing effects whatever, even when very high doses of thalidomide were given to the animals. When Dr Gerhard Osterloh, another pharmacologist, who had done some pharmacological testing on thalidomide, was asked whether he had kept and still had any records of his tests, he replied,

'Yes, of course. I have the records still.'

So Osterloh still had some of these records but they had already disappeared from the company's files in 1959. To shed some light on the curious question of what actually happened to the original records first possessed by Chemie Grünenthal, Dr Hilmar von Veltheim, the company's legal representative, was questioned by the prosecution on 6 November 1968. Von Veltheim stated that Dr Mückter had told him that the records were no longer of any use since the results of the investigations were to be published in a separate article. When the research department was moved into the new building in 1959, the individual records 'had been lost'. Quite a number of files had been left in the old building. Chairman Weber remarked, 'Then they must still be there!'

Von Veltheim replied, 'What was left has somehow been moved away.'

Chairman Weber: 'Then destroyed all the same?'

Von Veltheim: 'It is possible that they ended up in the cellar where all the records are kept.'

The prosecution and the chairman showed this interest in clarifying the fate of the records because the final publication by Kunz, Keller and Mückter concerning the results of their tests contains hardly any data to justify the paper's conclusions. As regarding toxicological tests the publication merely contained statements in summary form lacking all specific details necessary to evaluate the worth of the investigation.

Some of the physicians who had first tested thalidomide clinically had very different recollections when questioned about which tests had actually been carried out during the trials. Usually records of the tests no longer existed. No proper test plans had been made. Dr Esser, who with Dr

Heinzler had published one of the first articles on clinical experiments with thalidomide, admitted that no testing was done of liver and kidney function, and he could not remember if the compound had shown any effects on the central nervous system or on blood pressure. Esser admitted that he had little experience in testing new drugs.

Chemie Grünenthal resorted to propaganda methods outside court, which were often debatable. Articles started to appear in newspapers in which famous scientists were said to have doubts about the outbreak of deformation being caused by thalidomide. 'What is the effect of Contergan? Scientific defenders for sleeping pill.' (*Christ und Welt*, 9, 4 March 1966). 'Experts denounce the Contergan theory' (*Hannoversche Allgemeine Zeitung*, 27 May 1966). 'New doubts about the Contergan theory' (*Sonnabend*, 26 February 1966). 'The deformities were due not to thalidomide but to radioactive fall-out,' Cecil Frank Powell, the 1950 British Nobel prize-winner in physics, was supposed to have said. Other well-known pharmacologists and medical embryologists, such as Professor Degenhardt of the University of Frankfurt, and Professor Tuchmann-Duplessis of the Sorbonne, were said to have expressed doubts about whether thalidomide had caused any malformations.

Many of these articles could be traced to a certain Alfred Püllmann. Lenz himself wrote to the scientists quoted by Püllmann. In their replies all of them denied categorically that they had ever made such statements. They were all absolutely convinced that thalidomide was the cause of the outbreaks of phocomelia! Lenz repeatedly requested a personal interview with Püllmann, but this was stubbornly refused.

On one occasion, when accusing Grünenthal of manipulating the press, Schulte-Hillen cited an interview which had appeared in *Düsseldorfer Handelsblatt* on 13 September 1968.

In this interview the defence counsel, Dahrendorf, said, 'Manipulation? We would call it "influencing". Certainly we try to influence the press through our handouts. In our opinion this is not only not dishonourable, it is our duty.' On 26 May 1970 prosecutor Knipfer said that at least five journalists had contacted the prosecution during the trial and complained that they had been threatened with 'reprisals' by representatives of Chemie Grünenthal because the firm had not cared for their journalistic activities.

Another clinical investigator, Dr Jung, who had obtained a regular monthly payment for testing Grünenthal drugs, stated that Contergan had proved to be an excellent sedative. When questioned about a report in which Jung had written that he had 'stopped administration' of the drug in three cases because of side-effects, Jung declared that the expression, 'stopped administration (*abgesetzt*)', was badly chosen. In fact he had merely reduced the dose! During an hour-long interrogation in which the prosecution tried to clarify the relationship between Jung's publication and the original test reports Jung declared : 'I think you are under the impression that medicine is an exact science. You are quite wrong. A doctor has to take many decisions on the basis of experience and intuition. I am not very happy about the way you put so much stress on figures.'

When Günter wanted to know why information about the duration of treatment was not included in his publication, Jung replied : 'That was overlooked.'

A Professor Kloos had taken part in the symposium arranged by Chemie Grünenthal in 1955. Three physicians had reported unsatisfactory experiences with thalidomide. The professor could not remember clearly. The prosecution tried to refresh his memory by citing his own testimony given to the police some years before. 'How is it that in the courtroom you can only describe positive results?' Prosecutor Günter asked. 'Maybe the memory gives an idealized picture, in the same way that one always sees one's youth in a rosy light.'

In the University Clinic at Bonn, thalidomide had been tested on 140 children, seven of whom were less than a year old. Forty children, most of whom had brain damage, had been given the drug for up to nine weeks under the supervision of Dr Konrad Lang. The parents were not asked for their permission nor were they informed that their children were being treated with an entirely new sedative on clinical trial. Chairman Weber did not conceal his surprise at the high doses employed: they were 11 to 20 times higher than the recommended dose for adults. Lang replied that half the children were mentally disturbed or had brain damage. He admitted that there were also other children who had received thalidomide in the same high dosage. Lang had not observed any side-effects. One child had a circulatory collapse, one child died from a congenital heart defect, a three-month-old baby died from heart failure, a twenty-one-month-old baby with convulsive disorders temporarily lost her vision. Lang considered it very questionable if any of these reactions were connected with the medication. After he had heard from colleagues during 1960 of less satisfactory experiences with thalidomide, he stopped using the drug.

Havertz asked him, 'I would like to take up another point. Your written report, on which the chairman has already made a number of points – I would like to take up the last sentence from volume 18, page 233. The report ends as follows: "In general terms Contergan could be described as a rapid-acting sedative particularly suited for use with children." My question is: When you wrote that last sentence, did you base your opinion on the fact that the material under test and the children in the tests were such as to allow such a statement essentially on the basis of the effect and the suitability with children? You have told us, you remember, that for the most part the children were mentally defective.'

Dr Lang replied, 'The material isn't really compiled so exactly as to give a firm answer of that kind. You see it wasn't a systematic clinical trial.' Lang admitted that he had never before tested a drug before it came on the market.

Dr Augustin Blasiu's deposition during the prosecution's investigation before the trial opened has already been cited and undoubtedly carried great weight. It must have been very embarrassing for the accused. Blasiu said that he had never given thalidomide to pregnant women. On that occasion he had also stated that he had had no knowledge of the manner in which Chemie Grünenthal had misused his publication in their sales promotion material, by suggesting thalidomide as a suitable drug during pregnancy. He would have protested energetically against the distribution of such propaganda, which he found 'unfair, misrepresentative and irresponsible'. When Blasiu was being questioned before the court on 25 November 1968, the defence made the startling and serious accusation that Blasiu had been intimidated by police officers during questioning, and that they had tried to influence him. According to the defence the police officer was supposed to have said, 'You've got a nice practice – Grünenthal paid for it all for you,' and 'Are you responsibile for the deformities?' Blasiu then recounted his investigations with thalidomide to the court. He also mentioned that he had never given the drug during pregnancy. Chairman Weber asked for Blasiu's comments on the defence's accusations against the police officers. As against the defence accusation Blasiu said that he had never been accused of being responsible for deformities. Had Blasiu been in any way threatened or bullied, Weber asked.

'Yes, at the end, they just asked me one question: Why hadn't I given the drug to pregnant women?' To this question

236

he had replied, 'We learnt as students never to give any drugs during pregnancy.'

In answer to questions from the prosecution Blasiu declared: 'I don't know if the investigating officers asked me whether Grünenthal had paid for the setting up of the practice. They asked me if I had made trips abroad at Chemie Grünenthal's expense, to America and England.'

Had any kind of undue pressure really been exerted on him, the prosecution wanted to know. Blasiu told them, 'The first time you come into contact with the police you feel a bit anxious.' Although there seemed nothing to substantiate the defence accusations, in view of their seriousness the police officers were questioned. Both officers assured the court that no kind of pressure had been exerted on Blasiu. The investigation took place in a very good atmosphere. Dr Blasiu had himself dictated most of the transcript, which had been gone through sentence by sentence. On finishing the inquiry he had called for Mrs Blasiu, each of them had obtained a copy and the transcript had been gone through again sentence by sentence.

Hans von Kress, the Professor of Internal Medicine, was asked whether a completely new type of sedative, such as thalidomide, with its possible risks of harmful effects on the embryo, should have been given at all during pregnancy. He replied, 'It was a new substance. If you ask for my own opinion, I would not have allowed it to be given to a pregnant woman in the field for which I am responsible. But other people may have felt they could take that responsibility ...'

On the same day that Blasiu appeared before the court, the defence made another surprising request: that Professor Widukind Lenz should be rejected by the court as a medical expert on grounds that he was suspected of partiality. The next day the whole defence jointly presented a seventy-four-page justification for their request.

The defence described Lenz as being 'An expert obsessed with his position, with an almost religious conviction of his mission he has made it his duty to bring to light the causes of the recent deformities by proving the sole responsibility of the sedative Contergan and the responsibility of its manufacturer.' Lenz was guilty of 'polemics against the associates of the Grünenthal Company, slander and treachery against the defendants,' and had 'even before the main trial gone on record with disparaging remarks, implicit and explicit criticism, not to mention other offensive behaviour'. He had also 'personally attacked his scientific opponents with arrogant lectures and insulting insinuations and criticisms'.

Other accusations were that he had been engaged as a private expert for foreign, adverse interests, in as far as he had certified causality in the case of at least twenty cases of malformed children, and this had been used against Chemie Grünenthal in civil law suits. (The truth behind this accusation is that Lenz, in cooperation with Dr Jan Winberg, appointed by the Swedish Medical Board as official investigator for thalidomide damage, had made statements about the causality of thalidomide in a survey of suspected drug-induced deformities. Lenz and Winberg had gone through these cases to separate questionable cases from typical thalidomide deformities. Their statements were to form the basis of negotiations for settlement with Astra.)

Lenz was further supposed to have actively supported civil law suits against Chemie Grünenthal and to have acted as a medical and legal adviser to the parents of the damaged children. He had also maintained a close contact with the prosecution and had given technical advice of a non-objective nature. He had also been active in collecting funds for thalidomide-damaged children.

In their rejection request the defence concluded: 'For the purposes of these proceedings Professor Lenz has no special value, but rather, judged by the requirements of objectivity, he is the most unsuitable expert imaginable.'

Co-prosecutor Schulte-Hillen became agitated: 'In 1961 there was one man who single-handed checked this huge catastrophe. This man gave new hope to thousands of parents all over the world and probably saved thousands of children. It was this man who on 24 November 1961 had to hear, at a discussion in the Ministry of the Interior, that the Grünenthal Company was reluctant on financial grounds to withdraw the drug from sale. Professor Lenz has fought for years to prevent the truth being suppressed by financial power. I regard the defence's statement in support of its challenge as a public scandal.'

Prosecutor Havertz declared in a detailed answer on 20 December that he found the defence request completely unjustified; he considered the tactics of the defence were directed against the reputation of Lenz personally. He concluded: 'Uneasiness at the behaviour of the defence is steadily increasing. Walter Dirks, without question one of the leading journalists writing in German, wrote about the trial which is taking place here in Alsdorf in *Frankfurter Hefte* for November 1968:

'We are currently witnessing a moral scandal. It has already been going on for some time. The scandal consists in the way in which the defence plays around with experts, the public prosecutor, the co-plaintiffs and the court. The approach and attitude of the defence cannot have been settled without the agreement of the defendants and their company. Doesn't the company realize that it has lost face by its behaviour during this period? Doesn't it realize that the methods of its defence are bringing it into contempt? We are witnessing a moral scandal.'

Defence Counsel Schmitz countered: 'Mr Chairman, if the First State Prosecutor, Dr Havertz, is associating himself with the remarks of Mr Dirks and takes the view that the defence is bringing itself into contempt, I shall leave the court until this is explained. I ask for a statement.'

Co-prosecutor Schreiber: 'Why does defence counsel interrupt? Please allow the prosecutor to finish. We allowed you to make your challenge, a full three hours of complaints, without interrupting.'

Defence Counsel Dörr: 'In our challenge we didn't quote any publication such as the one Prosecutor Havertz has just quoted. Will Prosecutor Havertz please say whether he identifies himself with this publication. If he will not say, we will take it that he does.'

Co-prosecutor Schreiber: 'If he doesn't then I do.'

Defence Counsel Dörr: 'Under these circumstances the defence can take no further part in the proceedings.'

Prosecutor Havertz: 'In order that these events can be recorded, may I request that the whole submission be included as an appendix to the record of today's proceedings?'

Chairman Weber: 'I cannot prevent the defence from leaving the court.'

Defence Counsel Dahrendorf: 'Perhaps, Mr Chairman, if you told the First State Prosecutor that there are limits which should be respected.'

Chairman Weber: 'Mr Dahrendorf, I am not here to correct every remark that is made, like a schoolmaster. I will not do so. If the defence wishes to leave the court then it must do so. If this means that the trial cannot continue, the consequences will have to be accepted.'

Dörr then left the court room. Schreiber declared, on 30 December 1968: 'I submit that the defence's challenge of the expert witness, Dr Lenz, on the grounds of suspected partiality should be rejected. The defence submission does not rest on suspicion of partiality, it is an attack on Dr Lenz, whose expert knowledge and courage have prevented Chemie Grünenthal from making further profits from a drug which has brought indescribable suffering to thousands of people. We do not know how many doctors and medical scientists have had suspicions that Contergan might be the cause of the wave of deformities but have not made them public. We do not know how many doctors and medical scientists on account of their position did not wish to admit that Contergan could be the cause. We do not know how much knowledge about the cause of the deformities was disregarded in other cases by sympathetic superiors or colleagues. We do not know the extent of the opposition among the medical press to such admissions out of regard for their advertisers. We do not know what disadvantages lay in store for all those who dared to oppose the greed of certain firms. But we do know that Professor Lenz was the first one who dared to mention it, and say that Contergan might be the cause. We know that Professor Lenz incurred bitter hostility for protecting us from the further spread of the disaster. We know that Professor Lenz was threatened with legal action if he did not keep silent. And we know that even today this expert is under attack from opportunists in the medical profession. If in spite of all that a man still says what he believes to be the truth, no allegation of partiality can be substantiated against him.

'Furthermore, the court can see from the evidence itself that there is no suspicion of partiality. The expert has not – as some other experts have – brought forward obscure opinions, but has explained, in a week of careful work, the primary sources from which the evidence was prepared and the methods by which the results and primary sources were obtained. Everyone was able to follow the growth of the evidence from the very beginning. There was no opinion of this expert witness which he was unable to support, under examination, with evidence. The defence's challenge against Dr Lenz as an expert witness is a further step towards punishing the courage and devotion to truth of a scientist who did not subordinate himself to a firm's lust for profit. A court which fell in with this greed would carry out the punishment. By such a decision a court would encourage opportunism and further discourage honesty in our social life. After all that we have seen and heard in this court the challenging of Dr Lenz seems outrageous to anyone who has the slightest feeling for fair play. The challenge will also seem outrageous to the court; only a court directed by undue influences and capable of accommodation to expected favours would allow such a submission. We know that the defendants and the defence place their hopes on such favours.'

During the discussion which followed, signs of friction between the prosecution and Weber, the chairman, became evident.

Chairman Weber: 'First State Prosecutor, I did not ask you to approve of my conduct of this case. It is your business whether you approve or not.'

Havertz: 'Of course, Mr Chairman, but ...'

Weber: 'And I will continue to conduct the case as I see fit.'

Havertz: 'Quite so, Mr Chairman and I do not require your approval to make a statement. I have the procedural right, when I think it necessary, to make statements, and I will make statements when I think it necessary and appropriate. And may I say, with great respect, quite plainly that the prosecutor's office is not subordinate to the court. The public prosecutor's office has comparable status in its own right and has its own tasks to perform. It will perform them in these proceedings, even if it is sometimes not easy.'

When Dr Ralph Voss was heard as witness he explained the background of his letter to Chemie Grünenthal of 2 October 1959 in which he related his first observations of nerve damage and inquired whether Chemie Grünenthal had knowledge of any such side-effects caused by Contergan.

When asked by prosecutor Knipfer if he had ever received the impression during his contacts with Dr Mückter that Chemie Grünenthal had any doubts about the existence of nerve damage induced by Contergan, Voss replied : 'I cannot remember a single conversation in which any attempt was made to refute me on the matter. And in this connection I should like to make another point. If the doctors of the Chemie Grünenthal company felt that my observations were incorrect, if they felt that there was no such connection, they had an opportunity to make their views known at the advanced course in neurology in 1960. They had an opportunity to express their views at the conference in February 1961. On neither occasion was the opportunity taken. I was left with the strong impression that the Grünenthal doctors did not doubt the validity of my observations but were merely anxious to prevent as far as possible their being made public.'

In some cases when witnesses made statements during the main hearing which obviously contradicted their previous testimonies, the prosecution could not let it pass.

On 1 January 1969, Havertz said, 'I should like to announce to the court that the State Prosecutor's Office has initiated preliminary proceedings (reference No 7 Js 36/39) against Professor Kloos from Göttingen, who gave evidence here yesterday, on suspicion of making a false statement to the court while under oath in the course of his examination yesterday in these proceedings.'

The defence described this declaration as injurious to the principles of legality and a threat by the prosecution to institute legal action against witnesses who made declarations which did not suit them. 'This statement is so outrageous that I must consider bringing it to the notice of the Minister of Justice,' was Havertz's reply. During a pause in the proceedings he carried out his intention.

Professor Kloos later announced that he would sue prosecutor Havertz for false accusation, slander, defamation and misuse of office. In his letter to the Minister of Justice of Nordrhein-Westfalen, Professor Kloos wrote:

While the chairman conducted my examination with exemplary calm, skill and politeness, the attitude of the First State Prosecutor, Dr Havertz, from the first, when his turn came to speak and ask questions, was hostile, aggressive and bitterly ironical towards me . . . I am sorry to disappoint Dr Havertz, for whom this is the 'trial of his life' (and may well bring him promotion to the rank of Senior State Prosecutor) . . . I request that the information I have laid against the prosecutor should be transferred to the Prosecutor General of another state of the Federal Republic, as – with an old psychiatrist's professional suspicion – I cannot feel certain that in the state of Nordrhein-Westfalen under the masters of the said prosecutor it will be handled with the necessary competence and absence of prejudice.

To ensure himself against 'fictitious legal reprisals', Kloos sent a copy of his penal report to the judicial committee of the Diet of Nordrhein-Westfalen.

A macabre jubilee was celebrated on 12 March 1969. The trial had now been going on for an effective 100 days. More than 150,000 yards of tape had been recorded. Next day the first thalidomide trial in the USA, Diamond vs the William S. Merrell Co., which had been going for only about a week, ended with an out-of-court settlement, the form of which was not disclosed. The plaintiffs had demanded 2.5 million dollar compensation in a civil law suit in Philadelphia.

The trial in Alsdorf went on. Again and again requests for the hearing of new witnesses and experts were raised on both sides. The trial had indeed become a 'monster'. Meanwhile the reading of internal reports continued. Often the defendants were in great difficulty when trying to give evasive explanations of compromising documents. In an internal memo written in May 1960 Dr Wolfgang Kelling wrote, 'The most serious side-effects which have been confirmed from various sources are: (1) polyneuritis, (2) influence on the circulatory system involving depression of the blood pressure and a tendency to collapse (with children too), anxiety, sweating attacks, shivering' – evidently serious warnings clearly expressed a year and a half before the drug was withdrawn went unheeded. The defence protested vehemently. There had been absolutely no question of minimizing the seriousness of the reports of side-effects. Defendant Dahrendorf declared that Dr Kelling's statement should be regarded purely as a 'dramatized exaggeration' intended to 'provoke' his colleagues in the public relations department to intensify their inquiries into the nature of the side-effects. The prosecution then announced their intention to call Dr Kelling, the previous director of the public relations department, as a witness about the management's actual policy on this issue. Dr Kelling would be able to certify that because his news reports had attracted 'deprecatory criticism' from the management, he had been 'muzzled'. The defence then admitted that the word 'muzzle' had been used in this connection.

Meanwhile great activity was going on behind the scenes. During a press conference held in Stolberg at the end of April, Counsel for the defence, Dörr, revealed that serious discussions were being held between Chemie Grünenthal and the representatives of the parents of damaged children in order to investigate the possibilities of a settlement out of court. Counsel for the defence Dahrendorf did not wish to comment on a sum of 150 million marks mentioned in *Der Spiegel*. The lawyers partly blamed the criminal law suit for the fact that nothing had as yet been paid out to the children. If compensation were paid it would be tantamount to a confession of guilt. The prosecution had announced before the opening of the main trial that this trial would reach a conclusion whatever happened. Representatives of the company declared: 'If we wait to see where the trial gets us, we shall still be sitting here in ten years' time and the children will have nothing. If we are forced to, we shall fight to the end – and that will of course diminish the resources available for any payment by the company.'

By this Chemie Grünenthal evidently wished to put the prosecutors and the associations for parents of damaged children under pressure in order to put an end to the Alsdorf trial. However, according to the rules of German law in such a case, a criminal trial may only be suspended under conditions found in Sections 153, II and III of the West German Code for criminal procedure:

II. Where in the case of an offence the guilt of the agent is slight and there is no public interest in the prosecution, the public prosecutor may, with the agreement of the court competent to decide on the opening of the principal trial, abandon the proceedings.

III. Where a charge has already been laid, the court may nevertheless, with the agreement of the public prosecutor and after hearing the accused, abandon the proceedings in any event; the decision to do so cannot be contested.

It should be pointed out that the question of *guilt* has first to be decided on. In principle, a court decision must first exist according to which Chemie Grünenthal was in fact guilty, but that the *guilt of each accused individual is relatively small*. Secondly, the public interest would not be served by the trial being continued, and, finally, the prosecution must consent. In this case this would probably in practice imply that Chemie Grünenthal would have above all to dig sufficiently deeply into their resources to ensure substantial compensation and thus satisfy the condition that the public interest would not be served by continuing the proceedings.

On the other hand one important question would remain. Would it not be in society's interest to create a precedent and remain in the future as a leading case for the protection of the consumer of drugs? If the present German law could be judged to contain insufficient basis for convicting Chemie Grünenthal then a reform of the law might be thought justified.

In a TV interview on 21 April, defence counsel Dahrendorf declared that since 1962 Chemie Grünenthal had endeavoured to come to terms with the parents of deformed children in an out-of-court settlement. During the court proceedings held on 23 April, the prosecution denounced this statement as untrue. Since the prosecution began investigations Chemie Grünenthal had never been willing to do anything to compensate for the damage caused by thalidomide. The very existence of such damage was consistently denied.

On the contrary, since October 1961 Chemie Grünenthal had suspended all such negotiations, even those concerned with the sporadic and low compensation claims already raised by damaged patients.

On almost every other day of the trial the defence, and sometimes the accused, made provocative charges against the prosecution, which resulted in prompt and temperamental repudiation; over and over again the defence threatened to leave the proceedings. Often the atmosphere was so explosive that further negotiations were made impossible.

On 1 July the most serious charge made against the prosecution so far was raised by the defence. According to Schmidt-Leichner, prosecutor Günter tried to influence a civil law suit opened in Duisburg by Chemie Grünenthal against one of the witnesses who appeared at the Alsdorf trial. Dr Obertür, the judge of the court, was alleged to have informed Chemie Grünenthal on 24 June that the prosecution in Aachen had not only made non-obligatory requests, but had produced large-scale declarations that the trial in Duisburg would result in unnecessary expenditure and that the opening of such proceedings would be irresponsible. The defence considered this an attempt to manipulate the trial and to put a stop to it. 'A public prosecutor who acts in this way loses the confidence of citizens and the public as an independent official,' Schmidt-Leicher expostulated.

Dr Günter was enraged and rejected the accusations. In fact this was the first time he had ever heard the name of the judge in question. He had never made a single telephone call to Dr Obertür. He had talked, it is true, with representatives of the Duisburg court in connection with handing over court records. On that occasion it had been mentioned that the prosecution in Aachen had instituted an investigation of the witness in question. He had then expressed some hesitation about leaving the results of this investigation to be used in the Duisburg trial before they had been dealt with in the Alsdorf proceedings. Prosecutor Havertz said Schmidt-Leichner had 'accepted factually incorrect information without adequate checking, put it forward in a public session and based conclusions upon it'. His statements were 'a conglomeration of half-truths, misinterpretations and slanderous assessments aimed at creating confusion and diverting attention from the evidence of the last few months which goes totally against the defendants'.

The next day Günter declared that he had telephoned Obertür, the Chief Judge, and also Gerichsrat Hahn, who had declared that any attempts to influence the court proceedings in Duisburg had certainly not been exerted by the prosecution in Aachen, and that no such statements had been made to the legal representative of Chemie Grünenthal.

The higher prosecution authorities interfered for the first time during the proceedings. Heinz Gierlich, chief prosecutor of the District Court of Aachen, demanded that Dr Mantell, the Chemie Grünenthal legal representative in the Duisburg trial, should be sentenced for defamation. In a press release Gierlich stated: 'The defence in the Contergan trial has for a considerable time been making serious professional and personal attacks against the public prosecutor's conduct of the case which for the most part have no connection with the proceedings.'

The requests made by defence counsel Ares Damassiotis and the witness Professor Kloos to institute legal action against prosecutor Havertz were firmly rejected.

During the proceedings on 3 September the question was raised why Chemie Grünenthal had stated that neurological side-effects would disappear after medication was stopped, despite the fact that some physicians had claimed that the damage was irreversible. Why had Grünenthal waited until May 1961 to request that the drug be put on prescription in Nordrhein-Westfalen when, in fact, a decision to do so had already been made on 28 February. Dahrendorf explained that the defence would later make a statement about these issues. 'I would very much like to hear an explanation from the accused and not from the defence,' chairman Weber announced. Dahrendorf's reply was, 'The explanations of the defence are the explanations of the accused.' From the start of the trials the accused had chosen to remain completely silent with very few exceptions, and Weber remarked, 'The accused have a right to refuse to say anything but I would have liked very much to have heard something from them.'

On grounds of ill health Peter Weber resigned from his office on 9 September 1969, after 155 tough days as chairman of the Alsdorf trial. Dr Benno Dietz was chosen as his successor for this difficult task. From the start Dietz made it clear that he would keep a much firmer grip on the proceedings than had his often too-lenient predecessor. He certainly had a difficult job. After a long-drawn-out debate on judicial sophistry between the defence and the prosecution, Dietz once complained : 'Lawyers are certainly difficult people'.

The hearing planned for 15 September of Dr Günther Nowel, manager of Grünenthal's department for commercial policy, had to be cancelled. According to prosecutor Knipfer, Dr Nowel was nowhere to be found. The prosecution assured the court that it would institute appropriate measures to search for the witness. A few days later the witness himself got in touch with the prosecution. He had been ill and had been treated in the home of some friends.*

'The most aggressive claimants, or those who made the highest claims, were taken care of quickly', said Dr Hans Sippel, previously working in the Grünenthal public relations department. He spoke on 23 September about his work in negotiating compensation claims brought by damaged patients. Sippel's task was to look up such patients and make a preliminary investigation of the situation. The final terms

---

*Dr Nowel was a key figure in the evidence collected by the prosecution. As director of the commercial policy department he had made numerous detailed notes concerning the internal affairs of Chemie Grünenthal which later fell into the hands of the prosecution. Following his first absence he was again summoned to the court on 8 December, and once again did not appear. On this occasion the court decided that the witness had no valid excuse for not being present and imposed a disciplinary penalty. Cross-examination in court now seemed unavoidable and Dr Nowel finally appeared in Alsdorf on 20 April 1970. Damassiotis, the defence attorney, promptly made the accusation that together with other employees of the firm Dr Nowel had been promised immunity from the prosecution if he proved cooperative during the preliminary hearings. This hardly improved the atmosphere in the courtroom and the prosecution was enraged. However, the charges had to be investigated and thus a further delay in the questioning of Dr Nowel was achieved. Investigation showed that the accusation was unjustified and the cross-examination began on the 255th day of the trial, 7 September 1970.

of the settlement, on the other hand, were recommended by a representative of the Gerling concern.

Chairman Dietz: 'Who took part in these discussions? Who expressed what opinions – was that clear?'

Dr Sippel: 'Mr Chairman, naturally a company which produces a drug and is overwhelmed by such an avalanche of alleged side-effects racks its brains night and day to find out whether there is a genuine connection or not. In my opinion these genuine connections could not be discovered at that time.'

No satisfactory answer could be given to the question of why Chemie Grünenthal had paid out compensation on claims if they were not convinced that the nerve damage in question had been caused by thalidomide. Naturally the court was extremely interested in this aspect and several employees of the Gerling insurance company were called for cross-examination. When the representative of Gerling concerned, Josef Wilhelf Mertin, was questioned about the compensation claims paid to individual damaged patients on 26 October 1969, the witness refused to answer on the ground of his company's obligation to professional secrecy in favour of the insured. The court, however, rejected this argument and declared that the witness, under the present law, had no right to refuse to give testimony. Still Mertin refused to accept the court's verdict. Prosecutor Havertz demanded a prison sentence for contempt – but the court imposed a fine of DM 250.

The Superior State Court in Cologne (*Oberlandesgericht*) subsequently upheld the decision of the Aachen court and emphatically declared that Mertin had no constitutional right to refuse to appear as a witness. However he persisted in his refusal and during 1970 two other employees similarly refused to answer any questions relating to their activities as employees of the Gerling concern for the same reason. Nominal fines were imposed on them both.

On 10 October 1969 Chairman Dietz declared that the court had rejected Professor Lenz as an expert on the grounds of non-objectivity. Dietz underlined, however, that the decision was not to be taken as in any way depreciating his great scientific achievements, and the court had *not* decided whether *in reality* Professor Lenz was prejudiced. The verdict was based solely on consideration of whether the defence had reasonable grounds, from their point of view, to assume that possibly Lenz was not as unbiased towards the accused as he was required to be. To a non-German lawyer this decision seems very questionable.

As time passed, it became more and more obvious that although the proceedings were threatening to swell uncontrollably, Dietz, the chairman, intended to keep their scope within certain limits. A number of defence and prosecution requests to question new witnesses and experts were turned down.

In connection with the rejection of further requests to hear new experts on 10 November the court announced an important decision. 'As has been convincingly shown by expert witnesses, Professor Hövels and Professor Schönenberg, in their evidence for the existence of a causal connection between thalidomide and deformity, the case for the existence of this causal connection is not disproved by the fact that individual mothers under consideration did not take thalidomide during the critical period or that in the case of individual mothers the taking of thalidomide during the critical period cannot be proved. As the evidence of expert witnesses has convincingly shown, the existence of a causal connection between thalidomide and deformities cannot be refuted on the ground that not all mothers who took thalidomide in the critical period gave birth to deformed children. On the contrary, it corresponds to the experience of biologists – as these experts explained – that not all individuals react in the same way to the same toxins. Teratogenous effects need not therefore always occur.'

Dr Eckert, scientific adviser to Grünenthal's export department, assured the court that business policy was never in conflict with medical interests. In a declaration in the final hearing Dr Werner had said, 'It was Mr Leufgens's instructions alone that were decisive. He met medical considerations with the interests of the sales campaign and claimed the last word, but took care not to sign statements and public declarations of a medical character himself, as I had suggested. When I referred to my responsibility as a doctor I was told that I wasn't in a clinic or a medical practice but in an industrial concern. I did not take the responsibility, he did. In other words, company interests were placed before medical interests.'

On 12 January 1970 the defence declared, evidently in desperation, that physicians, especially clinical physicians, were in general incompetent to judge a causal relation between intake of drugs and observed side-effects. This tactic may be explained by the fact that whereas most clinical physicians were quite convinced that thalidomide could cause damage to the nervous system, some theoreticians, especially those who had never been confronted with a single case of polyneuritis, found the evidence insufficient to prove a causal relationship. To support this contention, on 16 December 1969 the defence had requested that Chain, the Nobel Prize winner, should be called as an expert.

The defence further claimed that damage to the embryo from a strictly judicial point of view could only be considered in connection with criminal abortion. According to the defence the foetus lacked legal protection, and, according to the present laws of West Germany, unless abortion was intended, the administration of a drug causing malformation of children was not to be considered as a criminal offence.

On 26 January 1970, the 199th day of the proceedings, Chemie Grünenthal declared that the company was prepared to pay DM 100 million as compensation to the deformed children.

In the present state of the proceedings we feel able to accept such a settlement without prejudice, now that the trial has satisfied the public's natural desire for information. The Company is concerned to avoid the legal wrangles which may possibly follow and which in the light of the experiences during this trial may prove interminable, so that it and its employees may once again devote themselves without distraction to their proper tasks. This sum was fixed after mature reflection and is the highest figure the finances of the Company will allow.

The court and the prosecution did not wish to comment on this move by Chemie Grünenthal. The next day Dörr declared that the negotiations were of a strictly civil nature 'and had nothing to do with the criminal trial'. In *Frankfurter Allgemeine Zeitung* the headline ran 'Justice for sale?' On the other hand, the consequences of a continued trial were clear to everybody: continued criminal procedures to the highest court of appeal, taking another three years. Following this, civil law suits on three levels, taking at least five more years. Evidently parents would have to wait another seven to ten years to obtain compensation, if any at all would result.

The most outrageous feature of the whole situation was that, irrespective of the outcome of the trials, the government of one of the richest industrial nations in the world had not until then shown enough initiative, compassion or responsibility for its citizens to give substantial and meaningful aid to the parents of these unfortunate children. After the change in government, the West German Social Democratic Party, who in 1962 as the opposition party had demanded State aid for these victims, did little more than its predecessors. Here surely lies the greatest 'moral scandal' in this whole miserable affair. The parents of 2,000 crippled children were now faced with a choice: to take the 100 millions, or to wait another ten years and perhaps receive nothing. The prosecution was also in a difficult position. Could it, by continuing the proceedings, take responsibility for sabotaging the compensation settlement? Should justice be bought?

On 21 April Chemie Grünenthal declared that the compensation would be paid out irrespective of the outcome of the criminal trial, provided that the parents abstained from civil proceedings against the enterprise. Costs of administration, medical examinations, etc, were to be taken over by Grünenthal so that the whole sum would be of use to the children. Surprisingly, Professor Weicker and Professor Lenz were chosen to give medical certification of which cases were to be considered as caused by thalidomide and which were of other types. A few days later the organization of the parents for thalidomide children accepted the Grünenthal offer. Simultaneously the Bonn government at last seemed willing to contribute another 50 to 100 million marks.

On 3 February 1970 Chain, the Nobel Prize winner, was questioned. The sixty-three-year-old biochemist, who had been rewarded with the Prize as co-discoverer of penicillin, declared that the existence of pharmaceutical science itself was threatened by the general atmosphere of suspicion which the thalidomide case had caused on an international scale. He declared: 'The action against the Grünenthal Company is one of the results of this reaction, which naturally and understandably demands a scapegoat for what has happened. Nevertheless, the case contains elements which could easily be used, in the hands of irresponsible political opportunists eager for short-term victories, in a direct attack on the whole international pharmaceutical industry.'

According to Chain clinical trials had clearly and indisputably *proved* that thalidomide did not cause any nerve damage, which was more than even the defence had ever claimed. The defendants' position had been, not that thalidomide was *excluded* as the cause of nerve damage, but that sufficient judicial proof was lacking. When questioned by the chairman he admitted to having never done a single experiment with thalidomide nor had he any clinical experience of toxic polyneuritis. Even more amazing was Chain's attitude to other kinds of nerve damage caused by other toxic substances.

Did the expert consider that diabetes polyneuritis existed?

Chain: 'No, a causal relationship in a strict sense does not yet exist.' When pressed by Chairman Dietz, Chain admitted that there were certain 'indications' that diabetes might cause polyneuritis. He was asked if the polyneuritis which occurs after diphtheria and, or, on taking thallium had been proved clinically?

Chain: 'No.'

According to Chain conclusive evidence may only be based on stringently controlled experiments. He also considered that there was no proof that thalidomide had caused any malformations. Had he not stated as a fact that malformations had been caused by thalidomide in a lecture before the Royal Society of Arts in 1963? This question was asked by prosecutor Knipfer and Chain replied: 'This lecture was held in 1963. It was never intended that this lecture should be used as evidence of proof in court.' On the occasion in question he was 'influenced by the press' and it only showed 'how even a scientist, critical scientists [like himself], could fall under the influence of the press, the technical as well as the lay press. It was of no consequence for a scientist. Today I would not write it.'

Prosecutor Knipfer: 'You wrote it then.'

Chain: 'Under the impression, that I did not properly

investigate – I am thoroughly convinced – I would like to stress this once more, that we owe 90 per cent of our drugs to the pharmaceutical industry and that in general the investigations are carried out with the utmost precision. This I can tell from my own experience. This is my opinion. I do not like the atmosphere which is spreading: it is all humbug.'

Professor Chain said that he had known Dr Mückter of Grünenthal for more than a decade. The firm possessed a number of highly qualified scientists, the laboratories were excellent and the testing of thalidomide had been carried out with all possible care. Knipfer wanted to know on which sources he based these opinions.

Chain: 'This knowledge? I suppose I have talked with various people, who very accurately ...'

Knipfer: 'With which people, Professor?'

Chain: 'I do not want to name these people here. They are anyway reputed colleagues within my field, but I do not want to drag them into the thalidomide trial. It would certainly not please them, it does not please me either.'

During the time thalidomide was on the market, how much or how little information was usually contained in the package inserts of drugs? Professor Walter Kreienberg, recommended by the German Drug Commission of the German Medical Association, gave the answer: 'There were then and there are now a wide range of leaflets with the packets, from nothing to full information.'

Prosecutor Knipfer: 'Well, was there any "norm" at all?'

Kreienberg: 'That's a very good question.'

On 3 April 1970 the court announced a second important decision. A proof of causality 'which presupposed mathematical certainty excluding any possibility of contradiction' is not required for clarification of the relationship between thalidomide and nerve damage. This was the kind of proof Chain demanded and in consequence he was forced to declare that polyneuritis caused by thallium and diphtheria was not proved although nerve damage as a consequence of diphtheria and thallium is considered a medically established fact throughout the world.

By the autumn of 1970 the proceedings seemed virtually to have reached a deadlock. A serious set-back for the prosecution was the refusal of the American Food and Drug Administration to allow Dr Francis O. Kelsey to testify in the Alsdorf trial. The settlements had been made out of court both with the organizations representing the parents of damaged children and with individuals suffering from thalidomide nerve damage, and strong pressure was put on the prosecution to drop the case. On 18 December 1970, with the explicit consent of the prosecution, the court announced that a decision had been reached to suspend the trial. Gross misrepresentation by many newspapers, and other mass media, of the reasons underlying this decision have given some of the public the impression that the court completely acquitted Grünenthal on questions of guilt. This was far from being the case.

The relevant background for this decision may be found in two documents: the prosecution's declaration of 11 December 1970 and the court's declaration of 18 December 1970, presented by chairman Dietz. The court's reasoning is based essentially on the prosecution's declaration and the two documents must be treated together.

By referring to paragraph 260, section III, and to article six of the Declaration of Human Rights, at the end of the year the defence requested that the trial be suspended. It had been prolonged to such an extent that no real basis any longer existed for the accused to obtain a fair trial. This line of argument was emphatically rejected both by the court and by the prosecution. The fact that legal proceedings against Chemie Grünenthal had been so lengthy – six years of preliminary investigations and hearings and two and a half years of main court proceedings – did not violate any basic principles either of German criminal law or of any fundamental principles expressed in the Declaration of Human Rights. The prosecution pointed out that 'The extraordinary, unprecedented quantity of material before the court and the unusual difficulties involved in hearing the evidence, which for the most part only became apparent during the court proceedings, made a speedy completion of the proceedings impossible.'

Chairman Dietz replied, 'Neither article six of the Convention of Human Rights nor any other statute requires the abandonment of the proceedings in the present case. It is not simply a point of law, disregarding people and their rights, if the permissible length of a criminal trial is considered in the light of the practical and legal difficulties of the situation under examination and of the significance of the issue.'

In the opinion of the court a legal procedure of this kind, directed against commercially powerful interests, necessitated such considerations, especially in view of the forceful manner in which the accused had been defended. 'Equality before the law would otherwise evidently be endangered,' Dietz said. To an observer it seems obvious that the inherent difficulties of this complicated trial are not alone to blame for the long duration of the proceedings. Chemie Grünenthal and its legal representatives gave little, if any, assistance in clarifying the many obscure aspects of the company's dealings. Nor, at times, was the behaviour of the defence and some of the accused likely to promote a peaceful and constructive atmosphere during the main proceedings.

The prosecution and the court stressed that, in considering the suspension of the trial, the only rules applicable to this particular case are contained in paragraph 153 section III of the West German criminal law. *The court specifically underlined that a suspension of the trial due to an expected aquittal was excluded in this partcular case.* Consequently the declarations of the court and the prosecution presented a detailed evaluation of each of the more important charges originally brought against the company.

To begin with, the court and the prosecution stated that it must be considered a proven fact that thalidomide had caused both malformations in the human foetus and nerve damage in adults, and that there is no sensible reason to doubt this causal relationship. 'In view of the evidence so far a causal relationship has been proved between the taking of thalidomide over a long period and nerve damage,' the court stated. In individual cases such a causal relationship may be legally proven both for nerve damage and for malformation. 'The court is convinced, finally, that, in view of the typical symptoms and the extreme rarity of a comparable syndrome, a causal connection between the taking of thalidomide and malformations is proved also for individual cases where the mother has taken thalidomide during the critical period.'

In connection with nerve damage the prosecution noted that the accused themselves were clearly convinced that thalidomide caused such toxic reactions. This was stated as a fact in Grünenthal documents from 1961, written by von Schrader-Beielstein, Wirtz, Michael, Sievers and Werner. The reasons behind the court's conclusions were based essentially on the arguments already presented in this book. The defence objections, and those raised by experts called by Grünenthal, were also subjected to detailed analysis. With regard to the teratogenic properties of thalidomide 'the testimonies of experts, Professors Blechschmidt, Coulsten, Hopf, Kloos and of Dr Puschel, are not sufficient to shake the conviction of the court'. The prosecution stated: 'Everything shows that there can be no doubt about the teratogenic properties of thalidomide in man, which were discovered by Professor Lenz and scientifically established by both him and Professor Weicker. As a result of their work thalidomide embryopathy has achieved an assured place in medical literature as the classical example of damage to a foetus caused by an external toxic.'

On the question of nerve damage the court pointed out that even experts called by the defence 'have by no means denied the existence of such a causal relationship'. An exception was made for Professor Chain from Britain : 'The court is unable to accept the evidence of Professor Chain,' it said.

In a separate section the prosecution treated eight separate charges where negligent and unlawful conduct on the part of Chemie Grünenthal was considered to have been proved: '(1) The testing of the drug before it was placed on the market itself gives cause for serious concern, to put it no more strongly.' As regards the clinical trials it was claimed that these trials 'could hardly be described as a really systematic observation of the people under test from all the relevant medical aspects, with a precise evaluation of the results obtained'. The prosecution also found 'that the testing of thalidomide partly without the knowledge of the patients concerned or of their legal representatives appears highly questionable'. Even though immediate responsibility remains with the physicians in charge of these investigations, the drug company must make certain that only physicians who are fully able to carry out 'independent' and 'technically sound' scientific research are employed on such tasks. On this question it was finally noted that the responsible officials at Chemie Grünenthal 'used a different, and much less exact, standard of proof in the clinical trials from that which they demanded in connection with the proof of side-effects during this trial.'

Under section (2) the prosecution stated that 'To declare the drug as "completely non-toxic, atoxic and harmless" in marketing terms was both negligent and legally relevant'. Such claims were not justified by previous tests. The court described the usage of such terms as 'highly questionable'.

Section (3) stated that Chemie Grünenthal had been guilty of negligent conduct by failing to warn physicians against the potential nerve-damaging properties of thalidomide. Such warnings ought to have been issued at least during the early autumn of 1960 after several well-known neurologists, independently of each other, had informed the company of their well-founded suspicions, based on their own observations. 'At this stage frank and complete information to physicians was called for,' the prosecution said. The court, laying heavy stress on this point, stated that after Ralph Voss, the neurologist in Dusseldorf, had taken up the issue of possible nerve-damaging effects of thalidomide in a letter to Grünenthal in October 1959, an increasing number of reports of polyneuritis were received by the company during the summer and autumn of 1960. Many of these reports were of a serious nature and could not be overlooked, such as those from the University Clinic in Cologne (Professor Scheid and Professor Wieck), from the Medical Academy of Dusseldorf (Professor Bay), from the city hospital in Essen (Professor Laubenthal) and from the private clinic of Professor Amelung in Königsstein Taunus. 'It was quite evident that this was not a case of a vague, improbable or erroneous suspicion, especially as the company was unable to exclude the possibility that thalidomide could cause polyneuritis. To this must be added that fact that with polyneuritis we are dealing with a serious disease and, as there had been several warnings (Dr Voss, for example, had pointed out definite therapy resistance to this damage), the company should have acted with particular speed to avoid further damage ... After November 1960, when the company finally recognized the need to warn consumers against possible damage by changing the package inserts, physicians should at least have been simultaneously informed. This was not done. The attention of physicians was first called to the problem in a letter of February 1961. This action came too late. The change in the *Basisprospekt*, which was not made until May 1961, was also not carried out soon enough, and it should be noted that the *Basisprospekt* is of primary importance in informing physicians about the drug.'

The court also severely denounced the manner in which physicians were later informed as well as the wording of these warnings. 'These letters of information should have been quite distinct from sales promotion material. Otherwise there is always a danger that they are thrown away unread.' As regards the wording, 'the letters were insufficient both in form and in content. It is especially aggravating that the warning did not recognize the extent of the risk connected with the administration of Contergan. No single warning letter contained reference to the fact that a failure to discontinue medication could, under certain circumstances, lead to severe, therapy-resistant and even irreversible polyneuritis. In addition, the so-called warning syndrome was not, as was proven later, an absolutely certain way of preventing the development of serious damage in all cases.'

As the court pointed out, one sure way of preventing such serious damage would have been to restrict the duration of consumption of the drug. Recommendations for such a measure should have been prompted by Dr Voss's lecture on 15 February 1961 in Dusseldorf, by Dr Bresser's lecture of 11 March of the same year in Cologne, and also by the remarks made in discussion by Professor Scheid, who had pointed out the need to restrict the duration of administration of the drug. (These conferences had been attended by representatives from Chemie Grünenthal.) The court further found it proved beyond doubt that the company had tried to underplay the seriousness of side-effects by 'minimizing explanations'.

Under section (4) the wording of the package inserts was described by the prosecution as misleading and negligent. Package inserts for drugs sold without prescription should without exception be formulated in a style readily understood by the layman, especially when connected with contra-indications and warnings of side-effects. The use of all technical terms should naturally be avoided. 'That a package insert should be honestly phrased – i.e. no minimizing of risks – does not require any further comment.' The court added that when the original package insert was changed, a clear reference to this should have been made in a conspicuous place on the package and not hidden in such a way that in all probability the consumer would never read it.

In section (5) it is stated as inexcusable that polyneuritis was described as an 'allergy', although the company was well aware of the fact that this damage was generally considered by neurologists to be of a toxic nature.

6) It was also inadmissible to exert pressure on the editorial boards of medical journals to prevent, or delay, the publishing of articles which were hostile to thalidomide.

7) The failure to inform the authorities about the side-effects of thalidomide was negligent, as was the obstructive policy adopted by the company to prevent thalidomide from being placed on prescription.

8) In summary the prosecution concluded 'that the accused had not paid proper attention or given due consideration to the warnings and hints which the company had received from clinical physicians, or treated such warnings with the seriousness that was to be expected of them'. According to the prosecution the actions of the accused were, until the first part of 1961, based on the expectation that clinical physicians and physicians in free practice, because their opportunities of surveying the situation were limited, would not be able to prove a causal connection between thalidomide and nerve damage. 'For this reason – this was the opinion of the accused – no definite action was called for with regard to consumers and prescribing physicians. This behaviour was negligent.'

The court judged that the company had no right to postpone action until it was technically proven beyond doubt that thalidomide caused nerve damage. The manufacturer is not only responsible for his product during the initial development and testing, he is also obliged to follow up all aspects of the subsequent use of the drug. This point is of great general importance. Far too often it has been shown that individual scientists or physicians have to prove conclusively that such and such a product causes damage before the producer even considers taking any sort of action. The burden of proof that his products are not harmful should clearly rest with the producer, especially when well-founded suspicions have been raised. We consider that this principle not only has relevance to the pharmaceutical field but should also be applicable to all forms of industrial and commercial activity. The Aachen court, and the prosecution, argued that failure to take adequate measures after due warnings must be considered equivalent to the taking of a deliberate risk, and if such suspicions are later found to be justified, this should result in legal responsibility, since it is the producer who creates the dangerous situation at the expense of the consumer's security. 'The over-all behaviour publicly shown by the company, Chemie Grünenthal, did not correspond with the standards required of a serious and conscientious producer of pharmaceuticals . . . In the matter of nerve damage deviations from what is prescribed by law and justice were considerable,' the court concluded, and added : 'The nerve damage would have been easy to foresee'.

When considering foetal malformation and the question of guilt the court and prosecution statements were less explicit. The situation was different from that concerned with nerve damage, in as far as the drug was withdrawn more promptly from the market after the first suspicions had become public knowledge. It was stated that responsibility in this matter must centre around the question of the possibility of foreseeing such damage. The prosecution pointed out, however, that the proceedings were never completed on this issue. Many specialists called by the court (Professor Thiersch of Seattle amongst others), who were originally scheduled to be heard during 1971, have never been given an opportunity to give evidence. Consequently, the prosecution left this important question completely open. The court did not consider that the evidence so far obtained during the proceedings gave support to the idea that this damage could probably have been foreseen. However, the court made a strong reservation on this point, since the matter had not been fully investigated. 'The court considers it possible that if the hearing of evidence was completed the possibility of foreseeing the malformations would be established.' It is pointed out that it was a well-known fact, before the introduction of thalidomide, that a great number of chemical substances were suspected of being harmful to the foetus, and a few had been proven to be teratogenic for man. Although, so far, no sedative had been proved to have such effects, there was basically no reason to believe that one day such a drug would not be shown to cause injuries to the foetus. This aspect of the trial was treated with great caution by the court.

'Taken as a whole, the sum of the unlawful actions of the accused cannot be considered as slight in the sense of paragraph 153 section III of the criminal law,' the prosecution summed up. 'The evidence presented so far – excluding the question of causality – has dealt exclusively with the matter of whether unlawful acts have been committed within the circle of the accused.' The prosecutor noted that 'the question of individual responsibility for each act is still open'. Guilt in connection with West German criminal law is concerned, fundamentally, not with the unlawful behaviour of a group, but refers to unlawful acts committed by individuals. The prosecution described the accused as belonging to a group 'which as a collectivity of persons is open to the charge of accepting an improper division of risks between the justified interests of the consumers and the commercial interests of the company. The individuals accused as members of the said collectivity were victims of the existing group pressure.' This main trial demonstrated that the actions and negligence of the accused were centred on one aim : 'To fight to the bitter end' for the market position of Contergan, which, as time passed, became more and more the subject of attack. In an evaluation of guilt, consideration should not only be given to the unlawful actions for which the trial was originally instituted, but account should also be taken of developments which have occurred after this relevant time. 'Certain methods of conduct revealed by the accused after 1961, i.e. towards people who had previously uttered warnings and towards scientists who did not share their opinions, have been as unsuited to the creation of a favourable situation for Chemie Grünenthal as has been the behaviour, at times, of some of the accused during the main trial.' The prosecution added that one could possibly ascribe this, in part, to the nervous tension to which the accused had been subjected since the opening of the criminal investigations back in 1962. The prosecution considered that, in view of the personal sufferings of the accused during this long period, they had partly expiated their guilt. It was also pointed out that the accused had voluntarily made considerable contributions from their private fortunes for the benefit of destitute victims damaged by thalidomide. In a criminal trial like this, such facts must be taken into account when appraising the guilt of the accused at the time of judgement. Each of the accused had been under pressure from the group centred around the company and they were 'impeded by the social structure characteristic of modern industrial society'. The prosecution went on to say that this general situation, extending far beyond the boundaries of Chemie Grünenthal, continues to this day to be a threat to the justifiable individual interests of patients and physicians. 'But the individual who belongs to a group is also in danger, since it is difficult for him to exempt himself from the rules of its particular game, which are not always compatible with the requirements of the law. The individual often stands alone against the interests of the group, which are partly explicit and partly carefully hidden in small print. He is in many cases left to his own resources when the economically stronger party – individual or group – can also rely on the support of influential figures or institutions, for whom our social order makes it quite possible not merely to conceal mistakes from the public but even, in extreme cases, to declare them legitimate practice.'

The support for the accused which had been shown by certain influential persons in the fields of science, industry and the mass media may have persuaded them that their activities had, on the whole, been in accordance with prevailing practice. Another mitigating factor was the fact that federal control over the pharmaceutical industry in West Germany was in practice non-existent. Other enterprises had evidently been guilty of similar unethical marketing of their products, though with less disastrous consequences. The prosecution noted with resignation that one of the expert witnesses, Professor Kreienberg, the representative of the Drug Commission of the German Physicians, was unable, even in 1970, seriously to consider the reasonable interests of West German consumers.

In its reasons for the suspension of the trial the court laid heavy stress, as did the prosecution, on the mental sufferings which the accused had already endured, as well as the prevailing conditions of the commercialized society of post-war Germany. 'It was inherently dangerous in these conditions that a producer of pharmaceuticals would give priority to commercial interests as being of the most immediate importance . . . The temptation was great to place the supposed interests of the company above the objections voiced mainly by subordinate colleagues with a completely different and much broader training. For their part the medical profession and the chemists found themselves involved with a company whose organization and aims gave a secondary role to scientific workers and general medical opinion. The struggle for a reasonable market position demanded the emphatic promotion of commercial goals.'

According to court and prosecution, it was not in the general interest to pursue the trial. Although a verdict from the Supreme Court would undoubtedly be of great value in obtaining clear guidelines for solving matters of major interest, this factor in itself was not considered sufficient justification for the continuation of the trial. Final responsibility for tackling the serious problems involved in the control of drugs lay with the legislators in Bonn. And further, for obscure reasons, the court was in serious doubt that a verdict would have any generally preventive effect.

As to the interests of the victims, the court and the prosecution considered that Chemie Grünenthal had already fulfilled their obligations, so far as this had been economically possible for them, by paying out 114 million marks in a settlement out of court.

The court's final position leaves no doubt that most of the charges originally brought against Chemie Grünenthal by the prosecution were considered to have been legally substantiated. The strong net of evidence and proof, carefully woven around Chemie Grünenthal with German thoroughness, remained unbroken until the end. The reasons given for the suspension of the trial are open to evaluations of a necessarily more subjective kind. The reference to the mental stress to which the accused must have been subjected during this un-usually prolonged trial seems completely justified. The fact that the company had, in an out-of-court settlement, made considerable financial compensation to the victims constitutes a further extenuating circumstance which must be taken into account.

Other reasons are less attractive to a member of the modern consumer society – for example, the negligent and unlawful action revealed by the Alsdorf trial, which the court took to be regrettably widespread and gave as an extenuating circum-stance. The unsatisfactory conditions prevailing in general in this sector of industry were commented on at great length. Unethical practices have existed for a long time and still flourish. This was ascribed to a lack of federal control and the absence of adequate legislation. Surely another important point has been left out? The Alsdorf trial revealed that negligence and unlawful conduct can also be technically proven according to existing, possibly inadequate, German law. Respect for the law is not strengthened if the courts do not carry out their duty to curb such practices for the general good, by enforcing existing law however incomplete this may be. The court and prosecution may also have shared this view, but judged the final outcome of such a law suit, before the Supreme Court, as exceedingly uncertain for as long as legis-lators and politicians in the Federal German Republic show such general indifference to the justified interests of the public. On its own the city court of Aachen could not carry such a load.

13

Conclusion: General Remarks on Drug Safety and the Control of Drug Production

In matters of drug safety the principal evils, apart from pure fraud, lie in the problems of inadequate testing and the inefficiency of responsible controlling governmental agencies. These two last factors seem to show a very good correlation. Where governmental control is poor the chemical industry tends to be less scrupulous in marketing inferior and hazardous substances. The general conditions which existed in West Germany and Japan, and which, surprisingly, still partly exist today, were surely responsible for the extensive damage caused by thalidomide in these countries. Another example of this correlation between slack governmental control and a lack of restraint on the part of the pharmaceutical industry is given by Astra's behaviour in Argentina as compared with its activities in Scandinavia. Whereas the sales promotion distributed to doctors in Sweden, Denmark and Norway was rather carefully formulated, avoiding far-reaching claims such as 'completely harmless', 'atoxic,' etc, the daughter company's promotion material in Argentina was quite unrestrained. Whereas Astra withdrew thalidomide from Scandinavian markets at the beginning of December 1961, decisions about similar measures in Argentina had to wait until March of the following year.

Although a large measure of responsibility naturally lies with the manufacturer of pharmaceutical products in proving the utility and security of his products, at least an equal share of responsibility lies with the controlling authorities. It is naïve to believe that everything will be achieved along voluntary lines. The costs of testing drugs are high and tend to rise. Unless specific guidelines are laid down by the state, it is rather unrealistic to expect that an individual pharmaceutical company will take up some new expensive routine procedure for toxicity testing which may put the firm at a disadvantage with its competitors.

Strongly impressed by the recent experience of thalidomide, the World Health Organization took up the problems of classifying drugs in May 1962. On that occasion the Director of the Swedish Medical Board, Dr Engel, representing Sweden, raised the question of the growth of the pharmaceutical industry and the increasing number of new drugs appearing on the market. While medical science should be grateful to industry for its contributions to pharmacological therapy, the high therapeutic activity of many of the new drugs rendered them dangerous in use and liable to produce undesirable side-effects. Recent experience had revealed shortcomings in the existing measures for control, and a need for better laboratory testing. He had thalidomide particularly in mind and some of the psychopharmaceuticals, such as the ataractic (tranquillizing) drugs.

Dr Engel gave his opinion that international cooperation was essential both in methods of testing and in communicating results; he suggested that WHO's activities towards international cooperation in chemical and pharmaceutical drug control should be extended to include laboratory testing. Drug control was a matter of serious concern to health authorities in all countries, and what the medical profession needed to know was a drug's therapeutic qualities and potential dangers before prescribing it for patients.

On 24 May 1962 the Fifteenth World Health Assembly approved the following resolution:

The Fifteenth World Health Assembly.
Considering

i) that new pharmaceutical preparations appear in a steadily increasing number on the market;

ii) that in many of these preparations great therapeutic activity may be combined with serious side-effects demanding particular care in administration;

iii) that recent experience has shown certain defects in existing safety control measures;

iv) that these defects are especially related to insufficient clinical trials;

v) that clinical evaluation represents the final assessment of pharmaceutical preparations and is the principal means of detecting harmful side-effects following long-term use;

vi) that clinical trials are highly time-consuming, need very large numbers of patients to be observed according to generally accepted principles, and would often be facilitated by international co-operation;

vii) that it should be the responsibility of national health authorities to ensure that the pharmaceutical preparations available to the medical profession are therapeutically efficient and that their potential dangers are fully recognized:

(1) Requests the director-general to pursue with the assistance of the Advisory Committee on Medical Research, the study of the scientific aspects of the clinical and pharmacological evaluation of pharmaceutical preparations;

(2) Requests the executive board and the director-general to study the feasibility or otherwise, on the part of WHO,

(a) of establishing minimum basic requirements and recommending standard methods for the clinical and pharmacological evaluation of pharmaceutical preparations;

(b) of securing a regular exchange of information on the safety and efficacy of pharmaceutical preparations, and, in particular,

(c) of securing prompt transmissions to national health authorities of new information on serious side-effects of pharmaceutical preparations, and to report to the Sixteenth World Health Assembly on the progress of this study.

Efforts directed towards the use of generic names have recently shown results:

In 1968 Senators R. Long and J. Montoya introduced bills in the American Senate to base on generic name the federal payment of pharmaceuticals on prescription in certain health service programmes. In the same year a similar bill was introduced by delegate W. Orlinsky in the Maryland legislature. The Senate rejected the Long-Montoya bills and the Maryland bill was vetoed by Governor Agnew. However, in 1969, a revised version of the Orlinsky bill was made law.

To remedy some of the more obvious evils caused by the existing jungle of trade-names, all companies selling pharmaceuticals in Sweden have jointly prepared an extensive catalogue (FASS) where, among other things, the various prescription drugs are grouped according to their generic names and areas of intended usage. Medical counter-indications, side-effects, chemical constituents, prices, etc., are included to facilitate the comparison and choice between similar drugs produced by different companies. The catalogue is distributed to every physician in the country and constitutes a welcome and positive improvement on previous practice.

As has been seen, when thalidomide was introduced the situation in West Germany was in general much worse than, for example, in the USA, because of the absence of any proper control over the pharmaceutical industry. The thalidomide disaster has, surely, made the pharmaceutical industry much more cautious and less inclined to be tempted by prospects of quick and temporary success. Drug regulations in most countries have also been considerably tightened.

Although the price of drugs was the primary concern of Senator Keafauver's famous investigation, his bill would probably never have been passed if public opinion had not been focused on the thalidomide story.

It is very doubtful whether any form of governmental control can alone offer absolute safety against the marketing of poorly tested drugs. Nor can any state-controlled agency take over complete responsibility for drugs approved by the authorities. To do so, such an agency would have to obtain facilities to carry out extensive testing of its own, which would undoubtedly both delay the introduction of valuable drugs and greatly increase the total cost of marketed drugs. Any form of official regulation pertaining to drug development and drug testing will not alone guarantee the consumer's reasonable interests. In a collection of specified rules for drug testing it is impossible to foresee all possibilities. Each new drug may present new specific situations which are not covered by any officially published guidelines. The chief responsibility must remain with the producer, since nobody else knows, or at least should know, as much about the product as the producer himself.

In such a situation there will always be the danger that less scrupulous firms will take the chance of marketing an insufficiently tested product. Major tragedies, as in the case of thalidomide, are fortunately rare. On the other hand, the regulating authority cannot be expected to issue strict regulations, and take over entire responsibility for the safety of pharmaceuticals. Strict governmental control must be supplemented by other legislative measures. One such approach would be to introduce strict legal responsibility for this sector of industry, i.e. the producers would be liable for any damage (in disproportion to the desired effect) caused by their products whether or not the company in question had taken all possible precautions.

It seems, in principle, self evident that no free enterprise can expect only to share the profits of their products without also taking responsibility for any damage caused by them. It was very surprising to hear Astra's argument during the thalidomide trials, that society, i.e. the Swedish state, should pay compensation for the damage caused by Astra's products, Neurosedyn and Noxodyn. It is preposterous to assume that the drug industry can be allowed to prosper when their results are positive, but refrain from paying damages and pass the burden of responsibility on to society when something goes wrong with their products.

One argument put forward by the pharmaceutical industry against any application of strict liability is that the drug industry is working for the benefit of mankind in a unique way and cannot be compared with other types of industrial enterprise. It seems that the pharmaceutical industry does not wish to recognize the fact that the main impetus for the running of the pharmaceutical industry, like any other type of industry in the West, is profit.

In a testimony before the Senate subcommittee one of the expert witnesses, Dr Console, formerly chief medical director of E. R. Squibb & Sons, described the pharmaceutical industry as 'unique, in that it can make exploitation appear a noble purpose . . . If an automobile does not have a motor, no amount of advertising can make it appear to have one,' Dr Console said. 'On the other hand, with a little luck, proper timing and a good promotion programme, a bag of asafoetida with a unique chemical side chain can be made to look like a wonder drug. The illusion may not last but it frequently lasts long enough. By the time the doctor learns what the company knew at the beginning, it has two new products to take the place of the old one.'

It should be mentioned that other branches of commercial activity, such as passenger airlines, which also operate for the public interest, are subjected to strict liability in the case of an accident which can in no way be blamed on the company concerned.

Socialization in itself does not seem to afford any clear solution. There is no guarantee that a state-owned company will only produce faultless drugs. Past experience of the bureaucratic inefficiency of monopoly enterprises in the governmental sector of most societies does not encourage the belief that governmental monopoly would guarantee the production of either safer or better drugs. The diffuse distribution of responsibility within state agencies will probably make it more difficult for an individual to obtain compensation from the state than it would have been from free enterprise, which is usually much more sensitive to pressure from public opinion, at least when strongly expressed through the news media.

This is not to say that the existence of a state-owned drug industry is unjustified. On the contrary, provided state involvement does not lead to monopoly, such an industry may fulfil a complementary need within the sector and also break up an unsound non-competitive situation within certain types of product produced by privately owned industry.

To reduce the price of drugs in Sweden, the State has become actively engaged in the pharmaceutical industry by forming a large state-owned enterprise to compete on equal terms with the private sector.

Another serious difficulty in securing the efficiency and safety of drugs and other chemical substances may be ascribed to a certain conservatism amongst the medical profession. Basically it is related to difficulties in the exchange of information between the various rapidly expanding fields of modern science. In spite of the obvious advantages of an integration and fusion in certain aspects of research and teaching between faculties of natural sciences and medical institutions, every intrusion into what has always been regarded as the realm of medicine is viewed with suspicion by certain conservative elements in the medical profession. The rigidness of the old guild system of the medical profession has often been a serious obstacle to the application of the latest scientific findings. Conservative physicians employed by the controlling agencies have no doubt been responsible for many unnecessary failures in medical practice. At the beginning of this century it was found that X-rays could cause malformations in experimental animals. It took decades before the practice of not unnecessarily exposing pregnant women to X-rays became generally accepted. In 1927 Muller found that X-rays and ionizing radiation caused changes in the hereditary characteristics of the banana fly. It took a Nobel Prize in medicine to Muller and two atomic bombs before the genetic hazards to man of ionizing radiations became generally recognized by the majority of the medical profession.

At the beginning of this century experimental embryologists were able to induce malformations in lower animals by chemical treatment. At the beginning of the fifties methods were developed for routine screening of the teratogenic activity of drugs and the methods available before, let us say, 1959 were in general no different from those used today. It took a terrible disaster to make the responsible authorities enforce their general usage. During the years 1936 to 1938 the Soviet scientist Sakharov demonstrated that certain chemical agents could induce mutations in lower organisms. Since then the ability of a great number of compounds to induce mutations in lower and in higher organisms has been demonstrated. Yet the results of modern science in this field failed to convince controlling governmental agencies of the relevance of these results in man. One reason for this general sluggishness seems to be that certain physicians in responsible positions cling to pre-Darwinian concepts about the uniqueness of man as an animal species. Many of these administrators, who have long ago lost contact with science, have failed to understand that, for example, the underlying mechanism for inducing mutations by external agents on the molecular level is the same in the vast majority of cases, irrespective of the type of organism. This is a natural consequence of the fact that the basic chemical and physical properties of hereditary material (nucleic acids) are identical in all living organisms, from bacteria to man. What happens in lower animals with respect to effects on genetic material will also happen in man, provided that the active agent reaches the structures in which the genetic material is organized (the chromosomes) inside the cells. In spite of all warnings we shall evidently have to wait for a 'genetic' disaster to occur before the authorities and the chemical industry wake up. When this occurs owing to the failure to control the properties of some widely used chemical to induce hereditary change, we shall certainly hear from the authorities and from industry that 'nobody ever thought of such a possibility', that 'this catastrophe was unavoidable'. Our society cannot afford to retain any narrow-minded barriers between the different fields of modern science.

The thalidomide disaster can also be seen partly as a result of a lack of adequate exchange of information. The knowledge required for large-scale screening of drugs for teratogenic activity *was* available within the field of experimental embryology but, with some exceptions in the USA, no use was made of these methods within the pharmaceutical industry.

The staff of governmental agencies responsible for controlling the production of drugs and other chemicals must incorporate scientists from different fields on a much broader basis than is now the case in most countries. A state agency composed of staff with a purely medical background cannot be expected to cope with the many ecological, biological, biochemical, genetic and sociological problems associated with the use and abuse of industrial chemicals. Officials in such agencies are also likely to be isolated from recent scientific developments by excessive administrative burdens, and their scientific knowledge becomes rapidly out of date unless there is continuous contact with the latest developments.

It has to be realized that the pharmaceutical industry is only a small, though important, part of the huge industrial sector producing chemicals. As such it can now, on the whole, be considered much better controlled, by comparative standards, than other branches of industry producing chemicals for general use.

There is no reason whatever why the same rigorous controls used in appraising drug safety should not be applied to many other industrial chemicals. This is especially so since much larger sections of the population are affected by these substances in a completely uncontrolled manner. This dark side of industrialization has been amply illustrated in this book.

The final step in achieving his patients' safety is to ensure that the physician correctly balances the risks against the benefits when administering drugs. If a patient suffers a drug-induced injury through negligence either in administration or in prescription of the drug, then legal proceedings should follow. The only Western country which enforces this principle with stringency seems to be the USA, as is amply demonstrated by a number of American court decisions.

The USA also seems to be the only country in which we know with certainty that a drug company can be indicted for marketing drugs for which misleading claims are made, and can be required to pay compensation for physical damage resulting from treatment by such drugs.

Led by the indefatigable Dr Havertz, the admirable work

done by the prosecution of the City court of Aachen has shed light into some dark corners of modern society, and revealed astonishing weaknesses in the system for controlling the pharmaceutical industry. However, some of the reasons given for the suspension of the gigantic trial in Alsdorf are symptomatic of the conditions still prevailing in many countries. Although certain improvements have been made, the time does not yet seem ripe, despite the thalidomide disaster, for putting a strong fence around one sacred cow of our society – the powerful chemical industry.

The situation encountered in the use of modern pharmaceuticals has been described by Lasagna as a miniature version of our problems with atomic power:

The mind of man has removed the stopper from the medicine jar. The chemical genie, formerly imprisoned within, now stands before us. He is a spirit known to work miracles, but also to wreak havoc – to improve life or destroy it. It is not clear that we are yet sufficiently wise to control the genie adequately. It is quite clear that we can never wish him back into the jar.

The question voiced by Senator Paul H. Douglas, commenting on the passing of the Keafauver Bill in the USA, might return to our minds: 'Mr President, can we learn from this lesson, or can mankind educate itself only by disaster and tragedy?' Sometimes man does not seem to learn even from disaster.

More about Penguins

Penguinews, which appears every month, contains details of all the new books issued by Penguins as they are published. From time to time it is supplemented by *Penguins in Print*, which is a complete list of all available books published by Penguins. (There are well over three thousand of these.)

A specimen copy of *Penguinews* will be sent to you free on request, and you can become a subscriber for the price of the postage. For a year's issue (including the complete lists) please send 30p if you live in the United Kingdom, or 60p if you live elsewhere. Just write to Dept EP, Penguin Books Ltd, Harmondsworth, Middlesex, enclosing a cheque or postal order, and your name will be added to the mailing list.

Note : *Penguinews* and *Penguins in Print* are not available in the U.S.A. or Canada

Drugs

Peter Laurie

What are the known facts about the 'dangerous' drugs?
What actual harm, mental or physical, do they cause?
Which of them are addictive, and how many addicts
are there?

Peter Laurie has talked with doctors, policemen, addicts,
and others intimately involved with this problem. He
has tried some of the drugs for himself and closely
studied the medical literature (including little-known
reports of American research). The result of his
inquiries into the pharmacological uses and social effects
of drugs today appears in this book.

Originally published as a Penguin Special which went
through five prints, *Drugs* was the first objective study
to offer all the major medical, psychological and social
facts about the subject to a public which is too
often fed with alarmist and sensational reports. For
this second edition in Pelicans Peter Laurie has added
fresh information and statistics concerning English
users of drugs and noted changes in the law.

A *Pelican* Book

British Capitalism, Workers and the Profits Squeeze

Andrew Glyn and Bob Sutcliffe

According to the authors of this provocative Penguin Special, British capitalism has in the last few years given the lie to the basic assumption of the great majority of Western economists that the work-force's share of the economic cake, like that of Profit, remains more or less constant. They see the implications to be revolutionary, in a literal sense.

They analyse the situation as follows. Because of increasing international competition, firms have been unable to pass on as higher prices the increased wages they have been forced to concede. Profit margins have been narrowed. The evidence is clear and plentiful. But without profit to finance dividends and reinvestment, capitalism cannot survive. So which will be sacrificed – the System itself or the prosperity of ninety per cent of the population? Either way the political consequences will be formidable.

A Penguin Special